Women of Color in Tech

Women of Color in Tech

A Blueprint for Inspiring and Mentoring the Next Generation of Technology Innovators

Susanne Tedrick

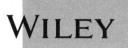

To my mother, Susan, who was my first true role model in strength and perseverance.

To my father, Ken, who lit the spark in me that would ultimately lead me to tech.

To my husband, Paul, who has always been my #1 fan.

Thank you all for your support, your sacrifices, and your unyielding and unconditional love. I love you more than words can express.

About the Author

 **Susanne Tedrick** is a technical specialist for a leading Fortune 50 technology company. In her work, Susanne helps organizations understand the benefits of creating cloud-native software applications and modernizing their existing IT infrastructure through cloud computing and tackling the complexities that come with the process. Prior to her transition into the tech field, Susanne worked in many administrative and operational roles with various companies in the financial services industry.

Fiercely committed to community service and increasing participation of women and people of color in STEM educational and professional opportunities, she performs volunteer work for P-TECH and Black Girls Code.

Susanne was the winner of CompTIA Association of Information Technology Professional's 2018 Rising Star of the Year Award and a 2019 nominee for CompTIA Advancing Women in Technology Mentorship Guide Spotlight Award for her dedication in advancing her tech career and that of future technologists. Susanne graduated with a degree in communication systems from Northwestern University and currently resides in New York City with her husband, Paul.

Acknowledgments

One of the themes of this book is that no one becomes successful on their own. While I had to put in the work and effort to get here, my successes—and frankly, still having my limbs and sanity—are largely a result of having people who cared enough to help me along the way.

Creating this book was no different. Writing this book has truly been an honor and incredible learning experience for me, but it is now on my top five list of challenging things I've had to do in my life! No joke—this is hard stuff! But what made it far easier is having the love, encouragement, and support of those around me to get me through. I could not have done this without them. I am truly blessed and privileged to have these people in my life.

First, my deepest gratitude to Wiley, and the wonderful team there, for bringing this book to life: Kenyon Brown, Kathryn Duggan, Pete Gaughan, Katie Gomez, Amy Laudicano, Michelle O'Connor, Michelle Pope, Barath Kumar Rajasekaran, Brent Savage, Michael Trent, and Kathleen Wisor. Thank you for recognizing that I had a story to tell.

A huge thank-you to my developmental editor, Adaobi Obi Tulton, for your wisdom, kindness, and patience during my writing "process." I'm deeply indebted to you!

Another huge thank-you to Dawn Michelle Hardy of Dream Relations PR, for your tireless marketing and PR efforts on behalf of this book and for giving me a crash course on the publishing industry. Thank you for listening, being my advocate, and keeping me together.

I'm eternally grateful to my interviewees for sharing their insights and knowledge: Teneika Askew, Dr. Tiffani Bright, Kailei Carr, Marc Bulandr, Ariana Davis, Angela Dogan, Hereford Johnson III, Juliet Okafor, Kimberly Paulissant, Micheal Lane, Eden Porsangi, Tameika Reed, Victoria Scott, Catt Small, Amanda Spann, Titilayo Robinson, and Joanna Vahlsing.

Thank you to my wonderful and supportive work colleagues. Not only am I fortunate to work at one of the best technology companies in the world, but I get to work with some of the best people in the world too. I've learned so much from all of you, and I treasure my relationship with each of you:

Hamza Ali, Ben Amaba, Conner Armstrong, Stephanie Ash, Lisa Behr, Janeen Blige, Sonja Bell, Taesha Callaghan, Patrick Carlin, Jocelyn Cheng, Sharon Coleman, Michael Corvette, Rich Counts, Carol Creter, Sam Demezieux, Mitsuko Ihaza, Stacie Johnson, Chris Knauff, Richard Lopez, Jennifer Lucia, Brian Mangan, Russell Marriott, Peter Menaker, Justyna Nowak, Chigozie Okorie, Francis Poeta, Gabriel Rosa, Natasha Rotella, Victoria Scott, Alpesh Shah, John Sheehan, John Son, Margaret Strauss, Sheila Thorne, Diane Vail, Amadi White, Kate Webster, and Kirk Yamatani.

To my mentees—thank you for allowing me to be part of your career journeys. I've learned so much from each of you, and I'm a better leader (and person) because of the time we've spent together. I'm proud of all your accomplishments and know that your lives will be filled with no shortage of success. I'm excited for what the future holds for all of you.

I'm incredibly appreciative to my IEEE mentor, Liang Downey. Thank you for encouraging me and pushing me to do my best. Thank you for believing that I was ready to take on new challenges, even when I didn't see it myself.

Thank you to my wonderful professors and faculty at Northwestern University, whose guidance and support helped me in my transition to tech. Special thanks to Dr. Daniel Moser for challenging me to seriously step up my public speaking game and for being one of the warmest and nurturing professors who I have had the pleasure of working with; and to my advisor, Howie Kantoff, for your incredible kindness and patience.

Special thanks to the Chicago chapters of IIBA, PMI, IEEE, CompTIA, and Northwestern Career Advancement for providing professional opportunities that refined skills I learned in the classroom and rounded out my professional skill set.

Many, many, many thanks to my friends, for letting me be myself and still hanging out with me anyway: Kriti Amar, Jessica Colon, Gwen Daniels, Ayana Field-Ridley, Annie Flora, Sharon Johnson, MariaCriselda Loleng, Siquan (Mavis) Meng, Kofi Mitchell, Ray Paltooram, Blondine Raphael, and Brianne Wilson. You guys and gals are the best!

To my family—King, Speights, Holodnak, and Tedrick—thank you for always loving me and helping me in the times when I needed you most. I love you all very much, and I'm extremely grateful for all of you: Alyssa, Anne, Arielle, Belinda, Bridgette, Chris, Dave, Debra, Denny, Denny Jr., Diane, Derian, Esther, Greg, Gwen, Hank, Ivan, James Jr., Jason, Jay, Jessica, John, John Jr., Jackie, Jim, Kathryn, Lilah, Lrma, Marti, Michael, Nanette, Nicole, Renee, Robin, Sally, Samantha, Sheldon, Sheron, Stephanie, and Stephon.

Very special thanks to my husband, Paul, for being the best, most supportive husband I could've hoped for. I can't thank you enough for your patience, kindness, and unwavering support as I went through both the career transition journey and now the book-writing journey. I'm not sure what I did to have a husband as awesome as you, but I'm grateful for you every day. Thank you.

Dad, thank you for caring for me under what were incredibly challenging circumstances. Even with the weight of the world on you, you still somehow kept things going, and always love. It is largely you who led me to tech (you buying all manner of electronics for the house; me deciding that they needed to be taken apart and examined); I'm glad that you continued to cultivate that in me as I grew up. My favorite memory of us is when you and I thought we could repair a TV set, and instead, we accidently set it on fire. Good times!

Mom, although you're not here, there's barely a moment you're not thought of; I wish you were here to share this moment with me. In our time together, you taught me true strength and resilience. I hope to make you proud. I love and miss you very much.

Contents at a Glance

Contents

Foreword

It all starts with a decision.

The willful choice to prioritize your interests in the face of the unknown, the uncharted, and what could be a long road of isolation.

It is met with an affirmation.

A belief that you belong here. That your ideas are worthwhile, your thoughts serve a purpose, and your perspective is a value add.

And accompanied by a notion.

A declaration that science, technology, engineering, and math don't have a color. They don't have a face. They belong to no one and everyone, for the whole and the betterment of all.

Your presence in STEM is an act of courage.

As if your choice to pursue your passions wasn't radical enough, here you are, prepared to beat the odds, defy the disparaging stats, and stare down adversity while carving a path, exploring new territory and laying our future.

Thank you for being a catalyst for innovation and the personification of endless possibility.

The work that you have done, and will do, is admirable, relevant, and necessary. You are just the right person to perform it.

Amanda Spann
Innovation Consultant & App Entrepreneur
AmandaSpann.com

Introduction

One of the important duties in my job is helping customers figure out "why": with all of the options that are available to them for their needs, and their limited time and resources, why is my product the one that they should choose?

Considering a career in tech prompts the same question. Of the career fields and options available, why should you, as a woman of color, pursue a career in technology? More specifically, why should you pursue this career field considering the well-known, heavily researched, and persistent challenges we continue to face in the field?

To be honest, I struggled with how to effectively answer that question every day while I wrote this book. I deal with many of the issues raised in this book, and more, such as the following:

- Keeping up with dynamic and complex technology areas, while balancing what's demanded of me daily at work and home.

- Dealing with the occasional insensitive comment made by the ignorant and the unpleasant, rooted in misconceptions about my race and gender, and then wrestling with whether to respond and be dubbed as "sensitive" or let the comment stand but let it slowly eat away at my spirit.

- Seeing many people willing to give easy praise and "advice," but few willing to publicly advocate on my behalf professionally. There are people who say they are allies but whose words, actions, and motivations reveal anything but.

- Being the only one like me in the room and sometimes feeling tokenized.

- For the women of color peers I do have, sadly watching them leave for other industries because they've simply had enough.

- Feeling like I had to work 10 times harder to be taken seriously, let alone advance in my career, and feeling pressure to always exude perfection rather than vulnerability.

Some days, it was tough to get excited about what I do, and I kept thinking, *if I can't excited about why I'm in tech and why I stay, then how can I inspire someone else to take this path?*

My "why"—what inspired me to come to tech and to stay—is that it is one of the few career fields that fully utilized my interests, skills, and passions. While I face challenges, and not always of the good, constructive kind, I am fully engaged. I love getting lost in my work, learning new things, and never having two days that are the same. I love what I do, and that love and the benefits I've received far outweigh any challenges that have come my way.

Tech is a field full of creativity, research, and discovery, where innovations can be used to solve the world's most pressing problems. Essential and purposeful work is being done all throughout the tech sector, and I love being part of the solution.

More importantly to me, I want to make the path easier for the future generations of female tech leaders. When they see other women of color out there and making it happen, despite the difficulties, then they know that there are not limited to opportunities that there have been historically. They know that these opportunities are out there, and they know that they truly are not alone, because we will always be there and have their backs.

It is not an easy path, but it can be a richly rewarding one—for your mind, your heart, and, hopefully, your wallet! I hope that you'll bring your talents and energies to the field, because you belong here, and you are very much needed.

Switching gears a bit . . . studying architecture is one of my favorite pastimes. What I love about architecture is that it can transform a building from being functional but ordinary into one that is memorable and iconic. It's what separates the Empire State Building or the Willis Tower from other tall office buildings. It can help a building become the standard that all other future buildings will measure themselves against.

Good architects require a strong understanding of what makes a building safe for people to enter and use on a regular basis and how to make it follow safety rules put in place by local agencies. Good architects also need to know how to take a client's requirements and translate them into a design that meets those basic needs *and* is pleasing to the mind and eyes. Considering that the average worker spends about a third of their life in an office, being in an office or building that is safe and pleasant is always ideal.

All great buildings start (and require) a blueprint before any major work is done. At a high level, a blueprint is a detailed technical drawing. Given the costs, resources, and time it takes to get a building from concept to reality, architects can't just approach the process haphazardly or without a solid plan. A blueprint details exactly what tasks or work needs to be done, what materials are to be used, and an estimate of the time and costs (tangible and intangible) that the project will take. Additionally, blueprints are constantly reviewed and revised, as needs (and challenges) arise.

To me, becoming a good tech professional is not much different. Tech professionals, at minimum, need to have solid technical skills. Depending on where you land in tech, this may mean knowing how and when to use various programming languages, knowing how to analyze massive amounts of data, or knowing how to keep computers and computer networks secure. In my job, I need to be able to effectively demonstrate complex technical concepts about cloud-native software development. If I'm unable to do that, I can end up losing credibility with clients and people within my organization.

Being an in-demand and respected tech professional, however, takes much more than technical skill. Tech professionals need to be able to communicate effectively in both oral and written forms. They need to be adept problem-solvers who treat challenges as opportunities and who know how to move forward even when things get tough. They need to have a continuous growth mind-set, understanding that skill and knowledge attainment is a lifelong process instead of having an "I went to school, so I'm done" attitude. To be successful, they need to be "renaissance women"—talented and knowledgeable in many different areas.

Great tech professionals also know that a huge attributor to success is a plan. They know that a great career will not materialize on its own and requires a plan. When there are changes along the way, they know that they should consult their "blueprint" as a guide and revise it as necessary.

This book will help you design your own personal blueprint for starting your tech career. Whether you are mapping out your first career or you're someone who is figuring out what your next career will look like, the tips, tools, and strategies discussed in this book are designed to help you figure out how to get the skills to be successful in the role and how to stand out among the crowd. What is in here reflects my own hard-fought and rewarding journey into tech—including my successes, failures, and lessons learned.

This book is also written with the challenges of women of color in mind. It's no secret—in fact, it's been *repeatedly* documented, analyzed, and studied for many years now—that women of color face unique challenges in general, let alone getting into and being successful in general in tech. This book will discuss some, unfortunate challenges that some women of color tend to encounter at home, at work, and at school in achieving their career goals, and try to provide strategies for how to navigate these challenges head on.

First, before going further, I should stress that as well-meaning as my advice and stories may be, they should not be taken as gospel, or as the only way to have a successful tech career. There are many ways to get into and be successful in tech; there is no one path. The approaches I discuss in the book have been the most helpful to me. I hope you find value in them as well! But I'm a firm believer in thinking for yourself, as you know who you are and what you want better than anyone else. Do your homework and do what makes sense for you, not because an authority figure, expert, or even me, says so.

Second, although I touch on matters related to personal finances and mental health, I am not a licensed professional in those areas, and what I talk about in the book should not be a substitute for getting personalized advice and help. *Please, please, please* seek licensed professional guidance where appropriate and needed.

Third, the thoughts, ideas, and opinions expressed here are my own. The views that I've presented are not a reflection from any of my current or former employers, and not endorsed.

Lastly, as you go through this journey, always know in your heart that you are worthy and deserving of a seat at the table that is tech, if that is what you want. I know in my heart you have what it takes to be successful. Don't let anyone tell you otherwise.

The Current State of Women of Color in Tech

It is probably no surprise to you that there is a lack of women in technical careers within the United States. If you performed a general web search on "women in technology," you will find numerous articles, studies, podcasts, and more that point out this deficiency. In a 2019 study from the National Center for Women and Information Technology (NCWIT), the number of women in computing professions has remained relatively stagnant at 25 percent since 2007. While tech companies have made great strides in increasing the number of women in technical roles, it's disappointing considering that women make up nearly 60 percent of the total US workforce. What does not get reported, or at least not very often, is the lack of women of color in technical roles.

The Realities

In the NCWIT study, it denoted that the percentage of African American/ Black women in computing professions has increased to 12.9 percent in 2017. This is wonderful in many ways, as the numbers were considerably lower for many years, but there has been a *negative migration* of women in general occurring at some top tech companies. That means that more

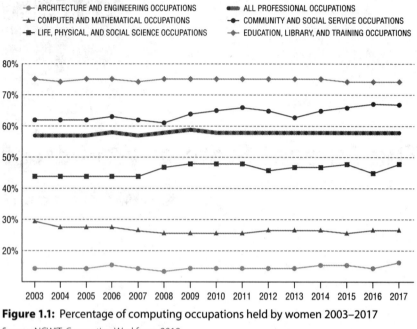

Figure 1.1: Percentage of computing occupations held by women 2003–2017

Source: NCWIT, Computing Workforce, 2019

women are leaving tech companies and careers than staying in them. The Figure 1.1 details the fluctuations of women in the computing professions from 2003–2017.

The Equal Employment Opportunity Commission reports that women only held only 26 percent of computing roles in 2013, a 9 percent decrease from 1990. The breakdown by race is also dismal, as shown in Table 1.1.

In a study of the career and economic progress of minorities in top technology companies by the Ascend Foundation, the number of Black women in technical professions declined by 13 percent over a 12-year period.

Many professional programs exist that aim to educate, nurture, and ultimately keep young women of color in technical careers. Who is it that developed these programs? Colleges and universities? Tech companies and the people within the industry? The answer is all these entities have invested a great deal of time, money, and manual effort to bring more diverse, female talent into technical ranks. Some programs focus on young women as early as elementary school, while others provide educational opportunities, career guidance, and mentorship in college or in the early stages of their professional careers.

Table 1.1: Diversity Challenge by Cohort

TALENT CHALLENGES	ATTRACT AND RETAIN TALENT	
COHORT	CHANGE PROFESSIONAL WORKFORCE FROM 2007 TO 2015	PERCENTAGE OF PROFESSIONALS IN 2015
White men	31% growth	32%
White women	10% growth	11%
Black men	15% growth	1.2%
Black women	13% decline	0.7%
Hispanic men	32% growth	3.1%
Hispanic women	11% growth	1.7%
Asian men	46% growth	32%
Asian women	34% growth	15%

Source: The Ascend Foundation

What's Going On?

While this awareness and the many resources available are wonderful, the lack of women of color in technology continues to persist. Many have said that the problem is that young women in general are not encouraged to pursue science, technology, engineering, or mathematics (or STEM) careers in early in their lives. Others have said that young women of color often don't have access to academic opportunities or resources that will help them develop critical skills necessary for these careers. And others have said that tech workplaces are not cultivating diverse and inclusive environments where women of color feel welcome.

I believe it's all of these things, and much more. Essentially, women of color are "funneled out" of technical careers, starting from early childhood. Although many girls exhibit a natural curiosity and talent for STEM subjects early on in their lives, this curiosity may become diminished over time due to cultural factors, lack of resources, and many other factors.

Early Childhood

The number of young girls interested in STEM fields and activities starts to diminish in early childhood. This can be due to lack of active encouragement in their home and school environments, and the lack of role models who look like them in STEM fields in their lives.

Young girls, particularly those growing up in minority or foreign-born households, are more likely to be encouraged to perform gender-normative activities like playing with dolls or playing "house" and to be encouraged to take on caregiving responsibilities (like babysitting) rather than explore robotics or programming.

Even if girls can invest the time in these interests, parents may not be as supportive as they could be, as they believe that this could be a passing "tomboy" phase they are in, where they are engaging in behaviors and activities that are (perceived to be) normal only to boys. Parental support may be superficial or even contradictory. And some girls are just shamed outright for not conforming to what it means to be a "girl" by their culture and society's standards.

I remember volunteering at a girls-in-STEM career fair years ago—a young Hispanic girl approached the table along with her parents. She was looking intently at the Raspberry Pi that was sitting on the table but hadn't said a word for a few minutes. I eventually asked her if she had any questions about the Pi and how it worked. As I began to explain, she started to warm up and ask more questions. At one point, she stopped herself because she thought she was getting too "geeky." I said, "Not at all"—I loved the enthusiasm and told her that this was a safe space to geek out!

Her parents, on the other hand, were not beaming with enthusiasm. In their defense, all-day career fairs can be energy- and time-consuming. But in general, they didn't appear to share in their daughter's excitement—not that they themselves needed to be interested in computing, but rather they didn't appear to share their daughter's enthusiasm in a possible career fit. When we were done talking and she shared what she had learned with them, they nodded appropriately, thanked me, and then quickly proceeded to another booth. As they moved, it almost appeared that the girl went back to a "shell-like" state, and her enthusiasm had gone away.

Another instance—again while volunteering at a girls-in-STEM event, this time geared toward young Black girls—was when I was watching one of the young girls interact with her mom. There was a break in the program, so she came over to give her mom a hug and kiss. As she ran off, the mother shook her head and said that while she loved her daughter, she was "special" for liking this sort of thing. From her tone, you could tell that she was implying something negative, as if there was something inherently wrong with her daughter having this interest. Studies have indicated that parental influence, encouragement, their own educational levels, and support are major factors in whether a student, male or female, chooses a STEM education or career. Parents who themselves have not studied STEM or are in those careers themselves may not strongly advocate or support their daughters pursuing those paths.

Even in the most supportive of households, however, parents' own feelings and attitudes on gender "norms" (behaviors and attitudes that they consider "normal" for each gender) may influence the degree of support they offer to their daughters. Parents are likelier to support their daughters doing well in their overall studies than directly suggest they pursue STEM education and careers. This may be due to their own perceptions of what they believe women can and are able to do. Parents may not realize that they are engaging in behaviors and patterns that may discourage young women.

Young Black girls who have low parental involvement, as well as less-than-ideal social and economic conditions in their homes, are even less likely to pursue STEM in college—assuming they are even able to go to college.

Primary, Middle, and High School

As girls of color begin school, the number who sustain an interest in STEM may continue to drop. On top of low parental involvement and support, girls in general may not be actively encouraged by their friends, teachers, or school faculty to take STEM classes or participate in STEM after-school activities.

This assumes that STEM classes and activities are even offered in their school or local community. Although as a society it seems we've placed a premium on STEM education, there are still many places in the United States that are "STEM deserts" or a lack of schools that offer STEM education that prepares students for college-level work and careers. According to *Education Week*, STEM deserts are likelier to exist in high-poverty schools (schools where 75 percent or more of the students are eligible for free lunch and breakfast). Almost half of these schools have large Black and Hispanic populations.

This lack of encouragement and access can lead girls to form and hold limiting, confidence-destroying beliefs that these subjects are too hard for them or not meant for them.

For the girls who do stay in STEM classes, they may be picked on or bullied by their male peers—and their teachers. Teachers' own gender and/or racial biases may creep in during classroom lessons, causing them to call on girls less to answer questions in class or even belittle them in front of other students. Bullying or mean behavior from both teachers and peers can compound any doubts and fears girls may have about their abilities.

In my seventh-grade algebra class, I remember getting back an exam from the teacher, where I received 98 out of 100 points. Written next to the score was not a "Great job" or something similar—it was the word "Careless" in very big red letters.

After class, I asked what I had been "careless" about. The teacher commented that I had forgotten to add a negative sign in my answer to one of the equations, in which he took away two points from my overall grade. He continued to say that I needed to not make such careless mistakes if I want to be "any good at math" and that I should review my work more closely.

I was surprised and crushed. I thought 98 was a pretty good score, especially since algebra (and mathematics in general) was a subject where I needed more help and study time with than other subjects. I was proud of myself, as I really worked hard to do well on that exam, and yet when I left the classroom, I didn't feel good at all.

At home, parents or guardians who don't quite grasp the subject matter, or find the value in it, may not offer meaningful or constructive help when needed. Many parents have reported that they have difficulty helping their children with homework, especially in math and science subjects. Although some may have the means to hire tutors or put their children in remedial courses, many may not. For households that are economically disadvantaged, tutoring is a luxury they cannot afford.

Parents may not be aware of free educational resources that can help their children, or they may not know where or how to locate these resources. For one-parent households, parents juggling multiple jobs, or parents supporting other aging or ill family members (often situations present in households of color), there may be a lack of both money and time. Students may try to find or put together solutions on their own to get the help they need or, because they have lack of guidance, may not get any help at all.

College

As young women of color get ready to attend college, they are often at a financial, academic, and general support disadvantage compared to their white peers.

Despite the belief that there are many scholarships for students of color, they are hard to get and are not a given, as there could be hundreds of qualified applicants that a scholarship committee can choose from and they often require copies of academic transcripts, recommendations, minimum test scores on the SAT or ACT, and essays for consideration. Pulling together an application for just one scholarship can be very time-consuming (remember, they still have to go to class and apply to colleges, too), and the expense of transcript fees can add up.

In addition, students of color receive *less* private scholarship money overall than their white peers. Per a 2011 study published by the popular financial aid websites Fastweb and FinAid.org, although white students represented only 62 percent of the overall population of American colleges and universities, they received 76 percent of the overall private merit institutional aid and grants. This is likely since white students may satisfy GPA requirements, as well as participate in extracurricular activities that are of interest to sponsors, versus students of color. While colleges and universities do have need-based financial aid programs that include grants, college aid officers may include a significant number of loans to offset the costs.

Speaking of loans, while many students are eligible for lower-cost federal loans, most young women of color may have one or more part-time jobs to subsidize both their education and their basic needs, as federal-loan funding is limited, and they may not be able to obtain private student loans or rely on relatives. In a study by the National Association of Education Statistics, 85 percent of Black and American Indian/Alaska Native students and 80 percent of Hispanic students received any type of grant. Additionally, 72 percent of Black students received any type of loan—more than any other racial group.

Academically, young women of color may not be adequately prepared for the rigor of some foundational college courses. As mentioned earlier, many US public schools lack college prep–level STEM courses, increasing the likelihood that young women of color haven't gained the knowledge and skills needed to prepare them for college-level courses, let alone courses in STEM.

Coupling this with a professor's biases, a lack of meaningful support at home or within their community, and few to no peers with whom they can identify in their academic programs, many young women of color struggle to get through their programs. In a study by the College Board, of the total number of female students who entered STEM academic program in the United States in 1995 (a low 15 percent), only 4 percent graduated with a four-year degree, indicating that they may have decided to change paths during that time. For the total number of Black students (21 percent), only 3 percent of graduates finished with a four-year degree in STEM.

This makes these young women likelier to take longer to complete their programs, switch to a non-STEM major, or drop out entirely.

The Workplace

For women of color who do make it into a technical career, the workplaces they enter may not be completely welcoming or made with them in mind.

The most problematic workplaces for people of color are the ones that have low representations of people of color in general. For the few present, they are usually in low-level, nonmanagerial positions—positions that require more routine, have less complex actions, tend to pay lower, and have limited opportunities for advancement. You would typically find most of these types of positions in administrative support, facilities management, operations, and customer service.

Almost all employees of color, regardless of their function within an organization, have to deal with *explicit bias* (when someone engages in direct verbal or physical harassment against you based on their held beliefs and attitudes) or *implicit bias* or *microaggressions* (when someone is not conscious enough to recognize that their behaviors and attitudes are harmful yet exhibits them anyway). According to Deloitte's 2019 State of Inclusion (a survey conducted at companies with more than 1,000 full-time employees), 63 percent of African American respondents and 46 percent of women respondents reported experiencing bias at least once within a year from which the survey was taken.

Years ago, at a previous employer, I remember coming to work the day after Christmas. A few minutes after I got settled for the workday, one of my white, male colleagues approached my desk. He asked why I was in the office, to which I replied simply (although baffled) that the office was open. He then replied, "But it's Kwanzaa. Did they make you come in to work today?"

I did not know how to respond. On the one hand, you can argue that the colleague meant no harm and was concerned that my civil liberties were being violated. Yet, it can also be perceived that he was making a slightly racist observation because I was the only Black person in the office. In the interest of ending this episode quickly and without incident, I simply said I don't celebrate Kwanzaa.

This seemingly floored him—how could I not celebrate Kwanzaa? How could I not be knowledgeable about Kwanzaa? From there, he felt it his "duty" to inform me of the background and importance of the holiday by coming back to my desk, at least five more times throughout the day, to tell me why and how Kwanzaa is celebrated.

When I tell this story to friends and others, it's usually in a humorous "Really? Seriously?" tone. But in retrospect, there were many things wrong with this interaction, and because I was a minority in every sense of the word at that place, I did not feel empowered or safe talking about this with Human Resources or with anyone else seriously. When I was let go from the company due to financial budget cuts, I was secretly relieved to never go back there again.

Tokenism, or when someone is hired more for the sake of appearances than whether the organization believes in your abilities, also occurs. This is likelier to happen in organizations that employ affirmative action in their recruiting and hiring methods or look to achieve certain placement goals in hopes of increasing diversity in certain positions.

Affirmative action generates a ton of debate; many argue that race and gender should not be considered in hiring decisions. Only the person who is most skilled at the job should be hired. Yet, as a society, we have collectively more or less agreed that women and people of color have been disadvantaged as soon as they could enter the American workforce and do not have access to the same opportunities that white males do, and therefore, accommodations need to be made for an equal playing field.

As someone who had been told by another previous employer that I was an "affirmative action hire," I can't tell you how belittling and humiliating it feels. While I was doing well in my job and had gotten along with my white male colleagues for the better part of two years, it hurt to learn that I wasn't their first, second, or even third choice and that the only reason I got the position was that Human Resources intervened and insisted that I be hired.

Then, there are the issues of pay and advancement. Historically, women and people of color have made less than their white male counterparts. For every dollar earned, women of color average 64 cents for every dollar a man makes. For Black women, they earn 61 cents for every dollar. It sadly is not much better in technical professions. Men are offered more pay for the same role that a woman takes 60 percent of the time; Black women averaged 89 cents for every dollar their white male counterparts made.

It should not be surprising that women of color are leaving tech jobs. The *Tech Leavers Study*, a study by the Kapor Center for Social Impact, highlighted that the experiences of women of color are dramatically different than their white peers. Thirty percent of women of color respondents claimed that they were passed over for promotions, and 24 percent reported being stereotyped. Thirty-six percent of the women of color cited unfairness as their primary reason for leaving their jobs.

Seventeen percent were subjected to what is called the *cross-race effect*, where they were mistaken for another person of the same race or gender. Although these interactions may be unintended, people who commit these mistakes (usually someone who is not of a person of color) downplay just how harmful and offensive these blunders can be to the person on the receiving end. It can solidify that they are not seen as a person to be valued or respected.

This is not to say that this path (or these experiences) is true for every woman of color. Every woman's path to tech is remarkably different. Some women have fully supportive environments and communities from the time they're born. Others transition into tech after having worked in completely different fields.

But when we examine the entire pipeline of bringing women of color into tech, it's clear that there are significant "leaks" in the pipes. It's clear that women of color are challenged at almost every stage of their journey, and the likelihood of their success is small. Just as there is no single reason for the lack of women in color in tech, there is also no single fix to this complex problem.

Why You Should Be Here

I realize that the picture I have painted so far is a bleak and depressing one. You might be asking yourself why on earth I would subject myself to a field that has typically been non-welcoming to women of color and the support structures are iffy, at best.

For all the negative news and statistics, there really is no greater time for us to be here. I'd like to share with you why by sharing my journey to tech.

My Journey to Tech

Prior to starting my technology career, I was in an entirely different profession and industry. For many years, I worked in mostly administrative and support positions within the financial services industry. My duties were wide ranging and diverse—they ranged from answering telephones, greeting guests, and ordering office supplies to coordinating travel for managers and reconciling invoices.

I was good at my job. My managers and colleagues complimented me often on how hardworking and committed I was to my job, and I was well liked. My pay and benefits were good, I received modest raises, and I enjoyed relatively good job stability, meaning I didn't think that I'd lose my job due to a company not performing well financially.

As good as all of that was, I didn't enjoy my work—at all. Those types of jobs are negatively described as being in the "pink-collar ghetto." Jobs like these are primarily held by women, had mostly routine and, well, boring work to be done, and had limited pay-increase potential or advancement opportunities. In administrative support roles and similar, you have little control in how you perform your work and the type of work you get to perform.

I also did not enjoy the industry. Like the tech industry, sadly, women of color are a minority in financial services. While careers in financial services can pay well, they can also be stressful. There are many rules and regulations that companies in this industry must follow, and in some ways, this limits the amount of creativity one can have in approaching their job.

I mistakenly kept changing jobs, thinking that it was the pay, culture, or some other outside factor that was contributing to my career unhappiness. At some point, I had to stop and ask myself, "Why am I doing the same thing over and over again, expecting a different result?" Why was I sticking to a career path that was not serving me well? Why was I trying to conform to an industry that I had no interest in and in roles that were only going to make me miserable in the end?

It was after my first year in my last admin/financial services job where I had to stop and deeply examine where my interests were, what I wanted and needed out of my career, and where I ultimately wanted to grow. The tech field was always something I had given some thought to but never really fleshed out. I knew that I was always drawn to technology; I always took apart my parents' appliances (much to their annoyance) to see how they worked. I always loved playing on the computer to see what I could do with it, as well as keeping up to speed on technology news.

But I thought to myself, "Was interest alone going to help me land a tech career?" My math and science grades were so-so, and up to this point, I had no formal technology training of any kind. And what kind of options did I have? Was becoming a coder the only route I could take?

The answers to these questions were not going to come overnight or easily. For many months, I thought about my interests, strengths, weaknesses, and goals. I thought about what I knew that I could already bring to the table for an employer, as well as what I needed to learn. I thought about the time and money investment it was going to take. I researched, networked often, and revised my plans repeatedly as needed.

I ended up going back to school while working. I ended up studying a field that gave me a broad overview of information technology, while allowing me to refine my communications skills at Northwestern University. I used much of my vacation and holiday time from work not only to study but to attend conferences, interviews, boot camps, and the like. I did homework during lunch breaks or before the start of a full workday, only to go to class for several hours in the same evening. I did volunteer work whenever possible to apply and strengthen the technical skills I learned in the classroom. I had to juggle family obligations, while also missing out on events with friends and family, and while I was financially in a better position than others with similar situations, funds were still extremely limited. I was lucky if I got six hours of sleep in a given evening, and to say that I was tired was a huge understatement.

I did this for about three years before starting my current job in technology. Was it hard? *Absolutely.* I'd say that my journey into tech was one of the top five hardest things I've ever had to do in my entire life. Was it worth it, and would I do it again? Yes, and yes, with a few changes.

I now get to work with some of the latest, emerging technologies. Instead of following orders without input, my thoughts and contributions are sought after and welcomed. I get to help clients make meaningful technology decisions that will impact their business. I have met some wonderful people who serve as mentors, colleagues, and lifelong friends. I've had great opportunities to share my experiences, mentor people, and travel all over. Finally, the salary for my first tech job was *double* that of my highest-paying administrative job, and I have far more ways that I can advance my career than had I stayed an office manager or a client service representative.

My work can be challenging, and yes, sometimes both my race and gender can make some of those challenges feel more pronounced. But this is the first time in my life where I can honestly say that I am engaged with my work in a meaningful way. I feel that I have a fulfilling career versus having a soul-crushing, dead-end job.

It's (Slowly) Getting Better

It's important to keep in perspective that many great strides and efforts have been made to make tech open to everyone who wants a seat at the table. Although increasing the diversity in tech workplaces may not be progressing as quickly as we'd like, we have come a considerable way since, perhaps, 50 or 60 years ago. In our society, we are having the hard conversations with one another surrounding gender, race, equity, and fairness. We're looking at the undeniable figures that indicate the work that's yet to be done. We're continuing to do the things that we do well and either tweaking what we need to improve or getting rid of ideologies or practices that are hindering making tech hospitable for all.

Support

Women of color have more professional organizations that provide career support than ever before. These organizations offer educational opportunities, networking events, and project collaboration. Here are a few that currently exist:

- **AnitaB.org:** Perhaps one of the largest women in technology professional organizations in the world, AnitaB.org (named after famed computer scientist Anita Borg) offers events, podcasts, and mentoring opportunities for all women in technology. It is the organizer of one of the most popular women in tech conferences, the Grace Hopper Conference, and it seeks to have 50/50 male/female representation in tech by 2025.
  www.anitab.org

- **Black in AI:** This organization seeks to increase the level of participation of Black people working in or studying artificial intelligence.
  blackinai.github.io

- **International Consortium of Minority Cybersecurity Professionals (ICMCP):** ICMCP seeks to address the dual issue of increasing the presence of people of color and women in the cybersecurity field. The organization offers training and mentoring programs, as well as scholarships to study cybersecurity in two-year or four-year colleges.
  www.icmcp.org

- **IT Senior Management Forum (ITSMF):** ITSMF's aim is to increase the number of Black professionals in senior technology positions. ITSMF offers the EMERGE Academy, a one-year intensive leadership program to help mold women of color into future technical leaders.
  www.itsmfonline.org

- **Code2040:** This nonprofit works to provide educational, social, and economic support to Black and Latinx people to fully participate in this new tech economy. Its Early Career Accelerator Program (ECAP) gives training and mentoring to professionals early in their tech career, while its Fellows program give current computer science students a nine-week immersion experience with a local area tech company.
  www.code2040.org

- **CompTIA's Advancing Diversity in Tech and Advancing Women in Tech Communities:** Both virtual communities aim to narrow the gap of the representation of women and people of color in tech. Members can access educational resources and attend local area networking/educational events.
  www.comptia.org

This is not a comprehensive list of all the resources out there—there are many, many more. This is rather to point out that numerous communities exist for you to find help, guidance, and support when and where you need it.

Number of Job Opportunities

Technology is a part of just about every business and educational and governmental institution. Organizations need people who have the technical skills to meet these needs. Table 1.2 shows just a sample of tech jobs that are projected to have the highest growth and most new jobs.

Table 1.2: Projected Growth of Selected Technology Jobs

JOB TITLE	NUMBER OF JOBS IN THE UNITED STATES, 2016	PROJECTED GROWTH FROM 2016–2026
Software developers	1,256,200	24%
Information security analysts	100,000	28%
Computer and information systems managers (includes project managers)	367,600	12%

Source: Bureau of Labor Statistics—Occupational Outlook Handbook

Pay

Tech jobs have the potential to pay extremely well (Table 1.3). While what you're paid can be affected by where you live inside the United States, your level of education, and your experience level, tech jobs boast higher salaries than non-tech jobs.

Table 1.3: Median Salaries of Selected Technology Careers

JOB TITLE	2018 US SALARY—LOW	2018 US SALARY—HIGH
Software developer	$61,660	$161,290
Web developer	$37,930	$124,480
Information security analyst	$56,750	$156,580
Systems architects	$54,360	$142,220
Systems administrators	$50,990	$130,720
Computer and information systems managers (includes project management)	$85,380	$208,000
Sales engineers	$58,430	$165,330
Computer and information research scientists (includes data scientists)	$69,230	$183,320

Source: Bureau of Labor Statistics—Occupational Outlook Handbook

It's Fun

Who says that work can't be fun? Tech is one of the few career fields that allows you to utilize creative-thinking skills to solve problems and create innovative solutions.

Take the fashion industry as an example. Technology has lowered the barrier of entry in creating designs and putting them out into the market. In the past, people who created and sold their own clothing and accessories needed access to physical retail space, access to tools and people to manufacture pieces quickly and in large quantities, and ways to ensure that products reached customers when they wanted them.

These are not small undertakings—this requires a lot of human and financial capital. But with technology, designers can now open online stores to sell their products directly to consumers at a fraction of what a physical retail space would cost. Robotics, which are being used by newer designers, can produce more custom pieces quicker than human hands ever could. Inventory-management and customer-engagement software, when used together, can forecast the customer demand for certain pieces, as well as ensure that there is enough inventory to meet the demand.

One of the things I enjoy about my profession, technical sales, is that I can use technology as a tool to help clients solve business problems. Because these problems don't follow a "one answer fits all" path, I can use both technology and a healthy degree of creativity to help clients get to their desired result. It's a lot of fun when you're drawing out sketches or wireframes of what the client is envisioning, and it's doubly rewarding when your efforts help them to be successful.

Opportunities to Help Others

Being a present and visible woman of color in tech can help give hope to young girls of color. Becoming a tech volunteer or mentor can have many positive effects. For you, it enhances your leadership, teaching, and communication skills, as well as refines your existing tech skills (or teaches you new ones!).

For young girls, they can interact with positive role models that look like them or grew up in situations like theirs. Many girls don't have the good fortune to interact with women who look like them or grew up in similar backgrounds and are current technical practitioners.

As girls of color get older, the idea of a nonwhite female software engineer or data scientist doesn't seem like a weird or foreign concept. They know that women of color in these fields are common and not an exception or anomaly. They can be confident that those career fields are accessible and possible for them.

We Need You!

Simply put, we need more diverse representation at all levels to address the current technological challenges our society is facing as well as future challenges.

In the case of artificial intelligence (AI), businesses are using it more, through chatbots and other means, for low-level tasks—tasks that they believe are repetitive and do not generate a lot of money for them. By automating many of these tasks, and not requiring a lot of human inter-action, businesses can save money on overhead costs, salaries, and more.

That's great for the business, but that isn't exactly great for everyone. Let's take the example of someone applying for a business loan at a traditional bank or lending institution. If a person applies and is, let's say, rejected or offered a higher interest rate than what they expected, a person can speak directly with a lending officer to find out why they took that course of action and could potentially negotiate or compromise to reach agreement.

If a bank or lender uses an AI interface alone to process a loan application, the process to approval or rejection may happen faster. But, if the development team behind the AI application inadvertently programs their own gender and race biases, applicants from specific demographics may experience higher rates of rejection or discriminatory actions than others. As the process is automatic, rarely is there a human being that you can speak to in order to contest or change the decision.

Development teams at these financial institutions, who are likely to be white and male, may not realize that they are entering their own biases when building algorithms to determine whether an applicant should get a mortgage. They may tend to have the same background, experiences, and ways of thinking that may put people who are outside of this scope at a severe disadvantage. Women and people of color are at a distinct disadvantage.

Where major financial decisions are involved, like buying a home and trying to start a business, women and people of color have had a historically difficult time obtaining funding and getting it a low rate. Women-owned companies receive 33 percent loan approvals in comparison to those that are male owned, and those that are people of color get far fewer approvals. In 2017, Black-women-led start-ups were only able to raise .0006 percent of the venture capital they needed for their business (not even a full percent!). Independent decision-making AI systems that have biased algorithms have the potential of making this situation much worse.

One of the best and most effective ways to combat this and to ensure that systems are designed properly is to have diverse development teams, made up of people who come from different educational, economic, and social backgrounds. This ensures that AI systems are designed to serve a wider population, not just a select few.

Tech Career Misconceptions

Technology is a wide and vast career field, and one person's pathway to a tech career is highly unique. There's no one true path to tech. These are just a few widely held misconceptions on getting a tech career.

Tech Careers Require Constant, Hands-On Programming

There's a constant, widely held belief that one must study programming, and excel at it, or become a coder or programmer to have a successful technical career.

It's not true. Understanding programming and knowing how to code in languages like Python, JavaScript, and Java are good skills to have, as it can enhance your understanding of computational thinking (how to break down problems in a way that computers can solve them), help your own problem-solving abilities, understand how applications work, and help you understand how coders and programmers approach problems (you'll be able to speak their language). Taking a programming course or two just for your own knowledge is highly encouraged.

However, it doesn't mean that programming or coding is your only way into tech—especially if you end up not loving it. As you'll find going throughout this book, it's often *soft* or nontechnical skills, like communication, problem solving, and critical thinking, that are perhaps more important than programming.

If you enjoy programming or coding, that's great—keep it up! If you don't, that's okay too!

All Tech Careers Require a Four-Year Degree

Depending on the field, having hands-on, demonstrable professional experience is more valued than an academic degree. Many major tech employers are putting more focus on candidates having experience or certain skill sets, as a traditional four-year bachelor's degree isn't a clear indicator of how well a candidate will do in a job, or even a guarantee that they will do well.

There are different ways to acquire knowledge, skills, and experience. Internship or co-op experiences, apprenticeships, boot camps, hackathons, online courses, volunteer work, and self-study are just a few options that are available and should be explored in addition to a college education.

All Tech Careers Require Studying Computer Science, Computer Engineering, or Another Specific Field

If you decide that a traditional undergraduate degree is the way for you to go, computer science and engineering are not the only paths that you can take. People who are in technical professions have degrees in fields such as mathematics, business, information technology, and even liberal arts.

A computer science or computer engineering degree could place you closer to certain job opportunities and allow you to move into other roles during your career. If you are contemplating a career as a software developer or in artificial intelligence, this might be the more appropriate route.

But when selecting a college major or concentration, you'll want to think about what your overall interests and career goals are and how a program you're considering will best serve those needs. As a possible alternative, you could take computer science or computer engineering as a minor to supplement another course of study. This way, you can explore the field while not committing to a full-blown course of study.

Computer science and computer engineering (CS/CE) programs are not easy nor are they cheap. You will more likely be able to ride out the difficult parts of a CS/CE program and complete it if you enjoy what you're learning, enjoy rigorous learning paths, and are able to bounce back after academic setbacks. You may find it difficult to stick with a CS/CE program if you're doing it for other reasons, like it looks good on your resume.

This is, sadly, not to say that you won't experience "tech elitism" from others. I find that this is more prevalent in software development circles, where those who did complete CS/CE programs in well-regarded colleges and universities try to minimize the education, contributions, and backgrounds of those who studied at "lower-tier" CS/CE schools or coding boot camps. However, you should not allow other people's narrow-minded perception influence what education you pursue. It's usually people who are insecure, are mean-spirited, and have close-minded views that exhibit those types of behaviors and attitudes.

All Tech Careers Pay a Ton of Money

While tech careers can pay more than other careers, you shouldn't approach it with the expectation that you will be making a six- to seven-figure salary right at the start. As you saw in the previous discussion of pay, the low- and high-end salary figures for different types of tech jobs can vary greatly.

A friend once told me that they had a friend who was making nearly $300,000 as a developer for a top technology company in San Francisco. Very impressive indeed.

But after asking a few more questions, I discovered that the friend who is receiving this salary had nearly seven years of professional, hands-on development experience and had many professional certifications under their belt. This made the story more believable versus this being someone who was commanding that kind of salary right after completing a four-year degree or coding boot camp.

Also, certain types of tech jobs will pay more than others due to overall demand. For example, as cloud computing becomes more of the standard for businesses, the need to have dedicated employees to handle and maintain physical hardware is decreasing. Those businesses now need employees who thoroughly understand computer networking and how computers talk to one another over short/long distances versus someone who maintains desktop computers.

As we discussed earlier, as businesses have begun to integrate artificial intelligence in their operations, they will need people who have a firm understanding of data science, machine learning, natural language processing, and more. People with these skills will likely be making more, as there aren't as many people trained in these areas.

Finally, in addition to your education and experience, where you live will influence what you can command salary-wise. Cities that have a higher cost of living, like San Francisco and New York, tend to pay higher salaries than places in less populated, more rural areas. In 2018, the average tech worker salary for the San Francisco area was $113,629, compared to Baton Rouge, Louisiana, at $69,212.

That's not to say that major cities are the only places you can go to be paid well as a tech professional. Many professionals are leaving San Francisco and New York due to how expensive it is and are heading to growing tech cities like Nashville, Tennessee; Provo, Utah; and Cleveland, Ohio—cities that all experienced significant growth in tech jobs from 2017 to 2018 (more than 7 percent and up).

We will discuss how to negotiate salary in a later chapter, but keep in mind that you may only be able to negotiate for a limited amount in certain situations.

Tech Careers Exist Only at Top Tech Companies

One common myth is if you are not working at one of the well-recognized technology companies, like Google or Amazon, then you are not really in a tech job. Not so. All kinds of businesses, in many different industries, have tech jobs and need tech professionals.

Let's look at banks and major financial institutions as an example. Knowing that their customers want access to their financial information 24/7, with the ability to securely perform basic transactions any time, all the time, banks and financial institution realize that they need to make significant technology and talent investments to meet these demands.

To build a customer-facing mobile application, you'll need to assemble a team that not only knows how to program an app for a mobile device and deploy it on a cloud-based platform (so that the app is always accessible to the customer), but also has a thorough understanding of information security (so that customer information is secure at all times) and deep knowledge of the regulations that US-based financial institutions must comply with.

Finding people who have these skills and have a good grasp of the business environment and imperatives is difficult, which is why banks and financial institutions invest a ton of time and money on recruiting and pay highly competitive salaries.

Simply put, you want to look for a position that will provide the experiences you want to have and the skills you want to acquire—some of the best tech jobs may be right in front of you in a "non-tech" company.

Tech Careers Are Only for People with Certain Backgrounds, Grades, Etc.

This is not true at all. Your background, grades, and other qualities will limit you only to the extent that you allow them to limit you.

Some of the most famous tech professionals and innovators came from non-tech backgrounds, didn't complete school, and had terrible grades. Microsoft founder Bill Gates, Facebook founder Mark Zuckerberg, and Bloomberg founder Michael Bloomberg are just a few, more well-known examples of people who achieved success despite failure, didn't complete their formal education, or came from a non-tech background.

But there are so many others—people of color—who are thriving in tech despite not having a "traditional" tech background. People like Esosa Igodharo, who left a financial services career to launch Cosign, a successful social-media shopping app. Or Porter Braswell and Ryan Williams, professionals with business backgrounds, who launched Jopwell, a great site that aims to connect more people of color to career and educational opportunities with major employers, including those in tech. Or Amanda Spann, who has built several successful tech app start-ups like tiphub but had a marketing background and knew that she loved technology but also knew that coding every day was not what she wanted.

I don't have what would be described as a "traditional" tech background. As I mentioned, I was in a completely different role and industry before arriving in tech. Even when I went back to school, I studied communications and information technology (not computer science) and was told, more or less, I should not "quit my day job" as evidenced by my grades for my programming projects (they weren't terrible but certainly nothing to brag about). Despite that, I was still able to find my path and transition into a tech career.

I believe that the following qualities are crucial when embarking on a tech career:

Confidence: Above all else, you must believe you can attain and be successful in a tech career. If you can't believe that you will be successful at a tech career, you're almost putting yourself in a self-fulfilling prophecy to fail.

Having self-confidence may be one of the most difficult things to attain and maintain. While sometimes things happen to shake your self-confidence briefly, like a bad grade or work evaluation, I believe that for women of color, it is a bit harder because there may have been many times when they were made to feel they were in some way "inferior" by their communities, educational institutions, and workplaces, and perhaps, not deserving to feel confident. A misinformed comment here, a damaging comment there—over time, these microaggressions add up and feed into the belief that "I'm not good enough."

You are not only good enough, you're more than that. You are smart, are talented, and deserve a great career, whether in tech or another industry. You deserve to be confident in yourself and your capabilities. As you go through your journey, always remember this in your mind and your heart. Believe in your success wholeheartedly and unflinchingly, even on the days when it may the hardest to do so. Thinking anything otherwise may lead to a self-fulfilling prophecy destined for failure.

Self-motivation: This is your journey. You will have advice and help along the way, but no one can force you to act in your best educational or career interests. You must hold yourself accountable for your actions (and inaction). While there may be many things outside of your control, how you choose to act and respond to a situation is in your control.

Perseverance: You must be able to find the strength within to push through tough, and sometimes unfair, situations. While it isn't fair that women of color must work exceptionally harder to obtain tech jobs, as well as respect and equal pay, you need to be able to continue your path as obstacles and hardships are presented.

To get where I am now, I had to deal with minor setbacks—a disappointing project grade, multiple job rejections, and the like. I also had to deal with more pressing things, like caring for an ill relative or figuring out how to continue my education while rent and other obligations needed to be paid.

I've also had to deal with the stuff that just, well, isn't right. Sometimes at past jobs or at school, people make direct and unkind remarks about the texture of my hair or the color of my skin. I've had people avoid taking me seriously at work because they assumed that I was on the "mommy track," meaning likely to take maternity leave and not return to work afterward. I've had male peers and colleagues talk down and "mansplain" things to me, as they assumed that I wouldn't be able understand a complex concept.

I have, unfortunately, had these and many more crappy things happen to me not only as a result of my race and my gender, but just life in general. While I took action and fought back in situations where I believed I could, ultimately I had to keep moving to achieve my goals.

I hope that you don't encounter experiences like this. I hope these experiences are nonexistent or few. Always keep in mind what your end goal is and what your goal is to move forward. Do not let experiences like this rob you of your momentum or power.

A commitment to continuous learning and improvement: Tech changes rapidly and at an exponential rate. Technologies, programming languages, ways of doing things, etc., can change rapidly and with little warning. Only those who put in the time and effort to continuously improve their skills and learn new ones tend to be successful in their tech careers.

Patience: Learning new skills, especially ones that you may initially struggle with, takes time. Often, you may not grasp material quickly, or at all. You must be willing to embrace a long-term approach to your skills development. Shortcuts rarely, if ever, will give you what you need.

Embracing failure and avoiding perfection: Successful people in tech know that perfection is a myth and can be a barrier to action and personal and professional growth. If you are always waiting for the right moment to present a pitch or start a project, you run the risk of never actually doing anything!

Although experiencing failure is not a wonderful feeling, it is better to experience this early on so that you can learn from mistakes and improve quickly.

Prioritization and time management: There are only so many hours in the day; you must be able to prioritize what is important to you and firmly commit to how you spend your time. While you should always incorporate downtime and rest in your day (self-care is a must!), you may need to choose between studying or going to a party, attending a school networking event with complete strangers or hanging out with your friends, or thoroughly preparing for a technical interview or playing video games.

Only you can determine what is important and should be a priority, as well as how much time you can and should devote to any one activity. Time management and task prioritization are skills you need in just about all aspects of your life.

Resourcefulness and tenacity: You may need to find people and resources to help you. Knowing how to find these resources without much direction or guidance will help you immensely. And when you hit a brick wall, do you give up, or do you find another path or way forward?

A common refrain that I hear from people, entry-level and experienced professionals alike, is "Someone should have told me," and it is usually in relation to their school not telling them the exact classes to take or an employer not telling them explicitly that they should be studying up and improving certain skill sets.

While I can agree with this complaint to some degree, I largely hate when it is said. Your career is your responsibility, and with that, the responsibility lies with you in understanding where you should be spending your time, even if your school, employer, or otherwise is not proactively providing the information. If you find that you're not getting the information you need, ask. Ask as many people and as many times as you need to get the information you need to make informed decisions.

You will come up against many obstacles. Those who take setbacks as temporary rather than permanent ones, and keep trying, are likelier to reach their goals.

A willingness to work beyond "normal" hours: Our society has become conditioned to expect products and services to be available and working 24/7. While technology has automated many functions and reduced the need for humans, humans still need to be available should things not be working properly or if disaster strikes.

It isn't uncommon for software engineers at top tech companies and critical industries (e.g., financial services, insurance, retail, etc.) to work 60- to 90-hour workweeks. Some tech jobs may not be as demanding and subscribe to a regular 40-hour workweek, but there may be times where your day will end well beyond "quitting time."

Creating a Blueprint

We've pointed out that the level of participation of women of color in tech is underreported when there's a larger discussion of the lack of women in tech overall. The reason why this is important to point out is because of a concept called *intersectionality*. Intersectionality describes that while people may be of the same gender, how they experience the world is influenced by their race, ethnicity, age, sexual orientation, and other factors.

The experiences of women of color at home, in their schools, and in their workplaces are different—sometimes significantly—than those of their white peers. They are likelier to face more negative social interactions than those of their white peers and have lower self-esteem. They are less likely to have access to certain educational or professional opportunities as well.

With that in mind, the standard career advice in popular books, blogs, and social media platforms does not address the unique challenges and needs of this community. For example, many people loved Sheryl Sandberg's *Lean In* when it was released in 2013. Many felt that Sandberg had adequately addressed the roadblocks women were having in gaining leadership positions in their organizations, and offered good, practical advice on how they can move their careers forward.

The central problem with the book, which Sandberg herself later acknowledged, is that it assumed that the reader had certain privileges that many women of color do not have: completely supportive households that don't require much of their time and attention, work cultures that allow expression of their thoughts without fear of being fired or held back, and access to career mentors to help them become stronger leaders. This lack of understanding of where the reader may be coming from and experiencing caused much of Sandberg's advice to ring hollow for women of color.

The challenges women of color face in landing a tech job are unique and great in number. In this book, we will address many of these challenges, whether you are just starting out on your career journey or you are transitioning into a new career after years in another role or industry. We'll be covering subjects such as these:

- Finding your tech path—What tech career would best serve your strengths and interests?
- Building and growing a supportive network—Finding your "tribe."
- How to gain skills—How do you prepare to get these jobs?
- Demonstrating your skill in resumes, interviews, and social media.
- Coping with difficulties in your personal, academic, and work lives.

With that, let's get started on your journey into tech!

Summary

- While seeing an uptick in the number of women of color in tech than previous years, many women of color are also leaving the field as well.
- No one factor alone is contributing to the lack of women of color in tech and why they may be leaving; there's a confluence of social, economic and cultural issues that are contributing to this persistent scarcity.
- Despite these negative statistics, women of color are not just surviving, but thriving, in tech. Tech opportunities are plentiful, pay well and give you opportunities to be creative (and hopefully have fun in the process).
- There are many pathways to get into tech; and there are many diverse tech fields one can get into. There's no one "right" way to get in to tech.

The Different Flavors of Tech Careers

In this chapter, we'll look at some popular career paths you can take within tech. For each, we'll look at the following:

- General overview of the field
- Typical job roles and titles
- Average median wage
- What they do
- Top skills needed
- Educational requirements
- Where to seek additional information

The positions, salaries, and responsibilities outlined will vary greatly between organizations and geographic locations. The information is more to help you have a general understanding of the careers.

For many of these jobs, you'll notice that they require several soft skills, including communication and interpersonal skills. While developing technical skills is no doubt important, some of these roles may be more business or customer-service oriented, and the type of technical skills you need will vary greatly.

The career fields and positions outlined assume that you have basic computer and information technology skills, specifically:

- **Computer hardware:** The internal parts of a computer, what these parts do, and how they work together to perform operations. Important parts include the motherboard, memory, and the processor.

- **Mobile devices:** With tablet and smartphone usage outpacing the use of traditional computers, understanding how mobile devices work will become important.

- **Operating systems:** Software installed on computers that allow you to execute programs, as well as manage a computer's resources, like memory. The three most used operating systems are Microsoft Windows, macOS, and Linux.

- **Computer networking:** Connecting multiple computing devices to allow people to communicate with each other and share resources. You can think about the Internet as a massive network of interconnected networks.

- **Security:** Understanding best practices to protect the hardware, software, and data from thieves, damage, and destruction.

- **Software:** This includes understanding how operating systems function on a computer or mobile device, as well as the software development life cycle (SDLC) process.

Some positions may require more advanced skills, but just about all require a good understanding of how computers work and communicate. There are many resources available online, through your public library, and through other local resources if you think you need help in this area or a refresher.

Another good reason to have a basic understanding of IT is that it will help you should you decide to pursue another field down the line. Careers are rarely linear, meaning that they don't follow a straight line. You may find that your interests change with time. Having this understanding can help make career transitions a bit easier.

Business Analysis

Business analysis, in general, is understanding the goals of a business, identifying the challenges that may be keeping the business from progress or success, and then finding the appropriate solutions to address them.

Taking this further, technical business analysis focuses on identifying and addressing business issues within a process, product, or service, and using technology to address them. Business analysts may be tasked with helping an organization choose a new software system, helping with the building of a new software application, or improving an existing process within the organization using technology.

Technical business analysts balance the needs of the business, users, and what is technically possible; they must have technical skill as well as a good understanding of their business and industry.

Technical business analysts may work in the context of a traditional IT department or as part of a software development project team.

Typical job titles: Technical Business Analyst, IT Business Analyst, Computer Systems Analyst, Systems Analyst

2018 average median wage (per the Bureau of Labor Statistics): $88,740

What They Do

To understand what challenges exist and what the desired end result is, technical business analysts may spend a great deal of their time interacting with many stakeholders (someone in or outside the organization that will be impacted by the end result of a business analyst's project) at different levels in an organization. These can be in the form of one-on-one interviews, focus groups, brainstorming sessions, or surveys. They'll spend a considerable amount of time asking stakeholders how they are currently interacting with the existing process or service, the problems that they're having, and why they need these problems to be fixed. This process may be referred to as *requirements gathering* or *requirements elicitation*.

Technical business analysts also spend a great deal of time documenting and analyzing the data they receive. Business analysts may be responsible for any of the following:

- **Business requirements list:** From the requirements gathering or elicitation, this document details the features or fixes that must appear in the final version of the proposed solution.

- **Use cases:** These detail the steps or actions that a user or actor must take to complete a task or achieve a goal.

- **Diagrams:** Rather than using words to describe a process, a business analyst may use several different diagramming techniques to show a current process—this may make it easier to identify parts of a process that should be fixed or eliminated (see Figure 2.1).

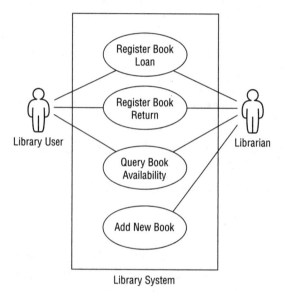

Figure 2.1: Example of a use-case diagram

Once their analysis is complete, business analysts will have to report back to stakeholders on the appropriate course of action that should be taken. What that will be will vary, depending on the business, the issue being addressed, the timing, etc. They may recommend that custom software be created to address the issue, minor adjustments in the process itself be made, or perhaps retraining users—they can even recommend that no action to be taken at all.

Depending on the organization or the project, business analysts may be expected to implement, or help carry out, the proposed solution. As such, they may be tasked with helping with programming, project management, and/or training duties.

Top Skills Needed

Communication: Analysts must interact and interview many different people—managers, end users, architects—with different backgrounds and ways of thinking/working. Being able to ask great questions to better understand stakeholders is crucial. Analysts must also be prepared to present, and sometimes defend, their recommendations to stakeholders and their coworkers.

Because much of their responsibility is documenting information, they must be comfortable with their business writing ability, as well as how they visually present information.

Critical thinking and problem solving: Analysts must review and summarize lots of quantitative and qualitative information and be able to suggest what they think is the best way forward.

Diagramming and modeling: Analysts are often tasked with creating different types of visual diagrams, including the following:

- **Flowcharts:** Represents the steps involved in a work process
- **Entity relationship:** Often used when modeling and creating databases
- **Data flow:** Represents how data flows within a specific business system

Understanding when to use which, as well as the proper symbols, is helpful. Having working knowledge of how to use diagramming software like Microsoft Visio, or online sites like Lucidchart and Draw.io, is also helpful.

Interpersonal: Being able to build and foster good relationships with stakeholders will be incredibly helpful when attempting to ask them for information. Stakeholders who trust and like you will likely be more responsive to your requests and offer helpful information.

Educational Requirements

Most technical business analysts have an undergraduate degree in a computer-related field, but there are also analysts with degrees in liberal arts and social science fields who received their technical training through additional coursework or on-the-job training.

For Additional Information

The International Institute of Business Analysis (IIBA), based in Canada, is one of the leading professional organizations dedicated to the business analyst profession. There are more than 60 chapters within the United States, and they offer professional development opportunities through mentorship programs, certifications, webinars, and other offerings. At the chapter level, they may also host job and volunteer listings on their chapter website. See www.iiba.org.

Bridging the Gap, run by Laura Bradenburg, a certified business analysis professional with more than 15 years of experience, is a site geared for people looking to start or transition into business analyst careers. The site offers free and paid training opportunities. See www.bridging-the-gap.com.

Here are some other resources:

BA Times: www.batimes.com

Modern Analyst: www.modernanalyst.com

Consulting

Consulting can be similar to business analysis, and there is often overlap between the two. Both fields seek to understand a challenge a business is facing and guide them on reaching their desired outcome.

The difference between the two is that most technology consulting tends to focus more on a general strategy or direction that a business should take versus addressing an issue that may require deep, specialized expertise.

For example, a business that has largely operated with physical computers and servers is thinking about putting some or all of their applications and data "on the cloud" or using a cloud service provider to manage applications and data for them. A technology consultant would come in and try to understand, among other things, the following:

- What is occurring in your current environment that is causing you to consider such a move?
- What is your timeframe in moving your operations to "the cloud," or how quickly are you looking to move?
- What is your projected budget for this migration?

The consultant acts as a trusted advisor to the customer as they navigate their project. The solutions that they recommend to their clients are *vendor agnostic* or *vendor neutral*, meaning that proposed solutions can come from any company that is deemed best; they are not tied to or favoring any one company in their recommendations.

Many consulting firms exist and offer a broad array of services to clients. From a tech standpoint, tech-focused consulting companies tend to fall into two areas: *IT strategy*, meaning helping companies create a strategic roadmap from where they currently are from a technical perspective to where they would like to be, and *IT operations,* where firms will help the companies understand where they can make improvements in their infrastructure and systems, and then implement proposed solutions. In both cases, consultants will need to have business and technical expertise.

Entry-level consulting internships and jobs with major firms, like CapGemini, Accenture, and IBM's Global Business Services division, are *highly competitive.* They have strict requirements on grade point averages and the types of courses taken, and they tend to focus more of their recruiting efforts on certain colleges (i.e., nationally ranked colleges).

They also usually have fixed recruiting processes and timelines. Depending on the firm, expect the timeline to take anywhere from *four to six months* and to span several interviews that seek to understand how you behave in certain situations (behavioral), how you would try to solve a project problem (case), and your understanding of certain technologies and concepts (technical).

Experienced candidates (usually someone who has two or more years of professional experience after college or university) are recruited year-round, with about the same number and types of interviews.

Boutique consulting firms—firms with fewer than 100 employees total and that focus on local clients—may have somewhat relaxed recruiting requirements and timelines.

Typical job titles: Technical Consultant, Technical Analyst, IT Consultant, Technology Consultant

2018 average median wage (per the Bureau of Labor Statistics): $83,610 per year

What They Do

"The 'day in the life' will vary greatly," says Hereford Johnson, an IT strategy and big data implementation consultant with Deloitte.

Indeed, a consultant's work depends on the work they have been asked to perform per the *statement of work* that was agreed to by the client and the consultant/consulting firm. Johnson recalled that his assignments varied greatly; one project sought to improve the ergonomic efficiency of technology for people with disabilities, while another was helping a large bank move their data from physical resources to cloud resources. No two projects are ever alike.

Consulting projects can last from weeks to several years and could require the consultant to work in the client's office, whether they are in another city, state, or even country. Consultants have reported that they spend anywhere from 60 percent to 80 percent of their workweek traveling and work very long hours. Although he did have the opportunity to work from home, "I would wake up at 7 a.m. for my first phone call, and then I would be done around 8 p.m.," Johnson said.

Top Skills Needed

Critical thinking and problem solving: Consultants review and summarize lots of quantitative and qualitative information and must be able to find and recommend the best course a client should take. Consultants may also be tasked with writing any number of reports, memos, presentations, etc.

Communication: Consultants are expected to conduct many meetings with clients and coworkers and be able to present information to any type of audience. You may also come across times when you and others will have a difference of opinion on how to move forward in a project—consultants must be able to convey a differing opinion in a way that is respectful for everyone involved.

Continuous learning: Consultants are often considered to be subject-matter experts in their domain or field by their clients. To be a subject-matter expert, this requires a consultant to stay in the loop on any developments or advancements in their domain constantly.

Alternatively, a consultant may be put on a project where they have little or no exposure (obviously not ideal, but it does happen). In those cases, they will have to quickly get themselves up to speed on a subject through self-study or classes (if time allows). "If you're in a room full of developers who [program in Python] for a living, you're not expected to perform at their level," Johnson says. "But you should be able to speak to them intelligently about what they do."

Interpersonal: Consultants often work in small teams that contain members from both the consulting firm and the client's organization. Building good relationships internally and externally will be important to the project's progress.

Time management: Between travel, analysis, reporting, and implementation, consultants are often working within strict, fixed timeframes. Knowing how to manage your time and minimizing disruptions is important.

Educational Requirements

Even with extensive industry experience, an undergraduate degree is an (almost) universal requirement to obtaining a consulting position. Per Johnson, it's a challenge to be hired into larger consulting firms without one—"I've seen people with 20-plus years of experience get shot down because they don't have that 4-year degree."

While having a technically focused degree is helpful, consultants often hold degrees in a wide variety of subject areas, including economics and English.

For certain advancement opportunities, a master's degree or a master of business administration (MBA) is needed for consideration. There are several firms that are willing to subsidize or pay the full cost of this type of education for promising candidates, usually on the condition that they will stay with the firm for three to five years after the completion of the program. Otherwise, the candidate will have to pay back the cost of what the firm contributed.

For Additional Information

A consulting firm's own website is often the best place to start to understand their strategy, values, and what they are looking for in candidates. Often, they have sections dedicated to entry-level opportunities as well as detailed information on their recruiting practices and timelines.

The following is a brief list of some of the better-known technology consulting firms:

- Capgemini
- Accenture
- Deloitte
- IBM Global Business Services
- Cognizant

- Tata Consultancy Services
- Slalom Consulting
- Bain & Co.
- Boston Consulting Group

Other resource:

Consulting magazine: www.consultingmag.com

Computer Networking

Computer networking focuses on how computers communicate and share resources with one another, whether they are physically or wirelessly connected, in the same room or across the world.

As we become more and more reliant on the Internet and cloud-based services for work, school, and our personal lives, understanding how computer networking works becomes important.

Typical job titles: Network Engineer, Network Administrator, Network Architect, Network Specialist, Network Technician

2018 average median wage (per the Bureau of Labor Statistics):

- Network Administrator: $82,050 per year
- Network Engineers/Architects: $109,020 per year

What They Do

Within an organization, network engineers and administrators are responsible for the creation, monitoring, maintenance, and repair of an organization's computer network. Their network can include the following:

- **Local area networks:** A network connected in a smaller area, like an office
- **Wide area networks:** A network that can extend over great distances
- **Intranets:** A private or restricted section of a network
- **Wireless networks:** A network that isn't connected by cables in any way

Network engineers and administrators interact with many audiences in the course of their day. They'll need to meet with business managers to understand what their needs are, employees who may have trouble connecting to their email or other network applications, and outside vendors to understand what tools on the market may improve network performance and availability.

Although they keep mostly standard work hours (about 40 hours a week), network engineers and administrators may need to work on evenings and weekends if there is a network outage or other major technical problem that needs to be resolved immediately.

Top Skills

Computer networking: Careers in networking require a solid grasp of the following:

- Computer-networking devices that help with communications between computers, such as *routers*, *switches*, and *bridges*
- Communications protocols, or the rules that govern how data is formatted and transmitted between devices, like Transmission Control Protocol/Internet Protocol (TCP/IP), Hyper Text Transfer Protocol (HTTP), and Voice over Internet Protocol (VoIP)
- Computer networking security to ensure that others cannot misuse or attack resources on a network

Linux: Linux is a popular *open-source* operating system (meaning software that is publicly available and can be modified and reshared). Many businesses use Linux rather than Windows or macOS because it has built-in tools for managing, monitoring, and fixing networks.

Tameika Reed, a senior infrastructure engineer at Expansia and founder of Women in Linux, is a huge advocate for learning Linux, regardless of your ultimate technical role. "We have people who are getting degrees and PhDs and so on. . . . When it comes down to Linux, which runs in 90 percent of most companies, and it's time to troubleshoot something, they don't know how to troubleshoot the basics of the foundation. I look at Linux as the foundations of getting into tech."

Virtualization: Virtualization allows you to create multiple "virtual" instances of a computer, perhaps with a different operating system, on one computer. For example, with the use of a program, like Oracle's VirtualBox, I'm able to install and run virtual versions of Linux and a Mac computer all on my Windows computer. They will look and act as if I were running them in their normal environments. Companies will often use virtualization to run many applications and operating systems without having to spend a ton of money on buying additional hardware and software.

Cloud technologies: As many businesses move some or all of their applications and data into the cloud, this is adding more complexity for the network engineer, in that they must ensure that resources contained in multiple areas (in physical form or in multiple clouds) can be accessed and protected around the clock.

Problem solving: Network engineers need to be able to quickly identify the causes for network outages or slowdowns so that businesses can operate effectively.

Communication: Network professionals must interact with many audiences, and they need to be able to share information with technical and nontechnical audiences.

Educational Requirements

Network engineers typically have undergraduate degrees in computer science, information systems, or other related programs. Others have been able to transition into networking careers through self-study and hands-on experience alone. In fact, those hiring for these positions prefer that candidates have as much hands-on experience as possible.

For Additional Information

Cisco: In addition to offering highly regarded networking certifications, like the Cisco Certified Network Associate certificate, Cisco also maintains the Networking Academy, an online portal containing entry-level networking classes. They also have hands-on resources, like Packet Tracer, which helps you to simulate network configurations on your own.

Cisco Certifications: www.cisco.com/c/en/us/training-events/training-certifications/certifications.html

Networking Academy: www.netacad.com

Computing Technology Industry Association (CompTIA)—CompTIA is a professional organization based in Illinois, devoted to those in information technology professions. They also administer several vendor-agnostic professional certifications, like the Network+ certification. See www.comptia.org.

VMware Learning Zone: VMware is one of the leading virtualization software companies in the world. It offers a free basic learning subscription to its Learning Zone, where you can learn about virtualization technologies. See mylearn.vmware.com.

Open Source Networking User Groups: Reed also recommends taking part in user groups, especially if you are in an environment where you may not be able to actively apply skills you are learning, such as those connected to the Linux Foundation. "They have ambassadors and different leadership positions within these projects. What happens is that you become the expert in those things—that's where your coding experience and your understanding of infrastructure come into play." These groups also will introduce you to the different people and companies that exist in the space. User groups are open to anyone who wants to contribute. See https://www.lfnetworking.org/resources/osn-user-groups.

Other resources:

The Linux Foundation's free *Introduction to Linux* course: https://training.linuxfoundation.org/training/introduction-to-linux

Women in Linux: http://www.womeninlinux.com

Data Science

The goal of data science is to gain knowledge or actionable insights from data. With the rise of smartphones, tablets, wearables, and other devices, the amount of data we generate has grown exponentially. According to cloud-service provider Domo, the average person will generate 1.7 MB of data *per minute*. During the span of a year, that person will have generated a little over 893 GB of data.

That's a ton of data! But now that we have it, how can businesses leverage this data to improve their products and make service better? How can local governments use this data to make their communities better? This is where data science comes in. Data scientists take all this raw data being generated and transform it into information that can be used to make decisions or take action.

Typical job titles: Data Scientist, Data Engineer, Data Analyst, Data Architect

2018 average median wage (per the Bureau of Labor Statistics): $112,000 per year

What They Do

Typically, data scientists will spend their time collecting and analyzing large amounts of data. They assess whether this data is appropriate for the task at hand or whether *data cleansing* (the removal or correction of incorrect data) is necessary. Using data with errors in it can lead to making incorrect conclusions or assumptions, causing a lot of wasted time and money.

Once the data is considered suitable for analysis, data scientists need to determine the best models or algorithms to use. They'll often use software to help with this, as there's often a ton of data to go through. They review these results to see whether there are any interesting patterns or trends.

Even if nothing surprising or important comes up, data scientists relay this information to their teams, managers, or others with a vested interest in what they are doing. They may do this through written reports, visualizations, or both. Finally, they may recommend a course of action to take based on their analysis.

Teneika Askew, a Business Intelligence lead with Deloitte, described what she enjoys about her job: "Clients are used to seeing reports in Excel, line-by-line data. They don't have reports showing them the art of the possible—what they can do with their data and how to make data driven recommendations from metrics or insights that are crucial to their business. It's exciting for me because I get to curate the data, dashboard or report and demonstrate how data could drive their business."

Top Skills

Analytical: Data scientists must be able to look at a great deal of quantitative data and determine whether patterns or trends are present.

Statistics: Statistics is the study of how we obtain, organize, and analyze data. Understanding the types of statistical analyses that exist, as well as how and when they should be applied, will be helpful.

Programming: Because data scientists often have to review and analyze several hundreds or thousands of numerical data sets, they use languages like Python or R to help model and visualize data.

Structured Query Language (SQL): Data scientists may need to access, manage, or update information contained in a database management system. Knowing how to use SQL commands to access this information will make this task easier. There are different "flavors" of SQL such as MySQL and PostgreSQL.

Communication: Data scientists need to be able to present their findings in a way that any audience, whether technical or nontechnical, will be able to understand.

While clients can sometimes "glow" when presented with positive data, Reed commented that clients may also not be happy when presented with mixed or negative data. "Sometimes it's hard, because you have to say, 'this is what the data says.' Having those tough conversations has to happen as well. Make sure that you are prepared for those conversations—you're prepared to be genuine, and also you're authentic in what you're displaying and demoing."

Educational Requirements

An undergraduate degree in statistics, computer science, mathematics, or a similar field of study is an almost universal requirement for job candidates, with some employers requiring a master's degree or higher to be considered for even entry level positions. As data science is gaining more popularity, colleges and universities are now offering degree and certificate programs in the field.

For Additional Information

Kaggle: Kaggle, owned by Google, is an online platform to help aspiring data scientists connect with others and refine their skills through challenges and competitions. Kaggle also offers free mini-courses in Python, machine learning, SQL, and more. See www.kaggle.com.

Institute for Operations Research and the Management Sciences (INFORMS): INFORMS is an international professional organization dedicated to individuals who work in or are studying analytics and operations research professions. They organize several conferences and career fairs as well as publish helpful journals and articles. See www.informs.org.

Information Security

Protecting computer networks and hardware from attacks or criminals is becoming more important. According to a 2018 study by cybersecurity risk firm Hiscox, small businesses suffered from at least one cybersecurity attack per year. In addition, the average direct cost a small business loses because of an attack is roughly $34,604, not to mention the indirect costs of losing customers.

The types of attacks are also growing in nature. To name a few:

- **Ransomware**: Software that locks up access to your computer files until you pay your attacker money.

- **Denial-of-service attacks:** Flooding a website with fake traffic to the point it stops working.

- **Phishing:** An attacker pretends to be a trusted friend or coworker and attempts to steal personal information, like usernames and passwords or credit card information.

Sadly, there are many, many more ways an attacker will try to disrupt and harm people or businesses. Being able to prevent attacks or detect when attacks are occurring and immediately combat them is becoming a crucial part of a business's or organizations operational strategy.

Typical job titles: Information Security Analyst, Security Administrators, Security Engineer, Security Architect, Security Engineer, Ethical Hacker, Computer Forensic Analyst, Incident Response Analyst, Security Consultant

2018 average median wage (per the Bureau of Labor Statistics):

Information Security Analyst: $98,350 per year

2019 average median wage (per PayScale.com):

Information Security Administrator: $66,852 per year

Certified Ethical Hacker: $79,256 per year

Computer Forensics Analyst: $68,965 per year

Incident Response Analysts: $71,849 per year

What They Do

As you can see from these titles, there are a wide variety of careers in information security. The careers described here are in no way a complete and exhaustive list, but this will give you an understanding of what is available:

Security analysts may be responsible for installing and updating software to protect an organization's network. This usually includes installing a *firewall*, a program or device that monitors and limits incoming and outgoing Internet traffic, and *antivirus software*, which is designed to remove bad programs (or *malware*) that seek to steal information or make computers run poorly.

Analysts also monitor network activity for anything that seems suspicious or out of the ordinary. In Titilayo Robinson's role at a Fortune 100 company, she is responsible for firewall reviews, which check for any firewall weakness and vulnerabilities, as well as exception management, or handling requests that deviate from the company's standard security policy. This includes monitoring all *data egress* (data that is leaving your network) and *identity access management* (guidelines or policies that a company puts in place to ensure that the right people have the right level of access to certain tools or information).

When attacks or security breaches do occur, analysts must document these events along with detailing how the event occurred, what was done in response, and any recommendations they have in improving the response process should it happen again. *Incident response analysts* may be needed when dealing with incidents that require a deeper level of expertise, like malware or virus attacks.

Security consultants help with the creation of a business's disaster recovery plan. This document informs people within an organization of the actions that should occur should some type of negative event occur against the organization. In this case, analysts would define how to respond to ransomware attacks, computer destruction, and more.

Part of Angela Dogan's role as founder and CCEO of Davis Dogan Advisory Services, LLC is guiding businesses on how to minimize their information security risks. "I help businesses build up and out their third-party risk management program." The work that's done will ultimately depend on what the client needs. According to Dogan, she and her firm may be responsible for carrying out risk assessments, helping to identify gaps in their existing security programs, or helping them create and develop a security program if they don't already have one.

No two days are the same for Dogan. "I could be home today, across the country tomorrow. My job does involve travel because I do a lot of face to face with the client and spending time at their organization to understand their culture and ins and outs."

Ethical hackers (or "white hat" hackers) conduct testing and audits to ensure that their networks can handle attacks should they occur. One of the more common methodologies that they use is *penetration testing* (or *pen testing*), where a simulated cyberattack is performed on an organization's computer network to identify both strengths and weaknesses.

Computer forensics analysts are experts who are called in when a crime has been committed using computing devices, digital media, or the Internet. These analysts work closely with law enforcement agencies in gathering evidence that will be entered into police reports or used as testimony in a court of law. Computer forensic analysts may be asked to retrieve deleted data from computing devices, gain access to computing devices that need to be examined but are, for some reason, restricted, reconstruct damaged devices, or even determine whether data may have been compromised or corrupted by outside parties.

Top Skills

Computer networking: Analysts must have a solid grasp of networking devices and protocols.

Operating systems: Operating systems serve as the backbone of computers and computing devices. They manage how a computer uses the limited resources available, like how much of its power it should allocate toward memory management and other processes. It also allows people to interact with computers in a way that doesn't require them to enter lines and lines of code. Knowing how major operating systems work—like Windows, macOS, and Linux—is important.

Vulnerability assessment: Security professionals must be able to quickly identify where there may be weaknesses in their network or computer systems before they are discovered by other people with bad intentions. They must understand the tools and methods available to them to find these vulnerabilities (like pen testing).

Communication: Analysts must communicate with managers and employees from various departments, as well as customers. They must be able to deliver information that any type of audience can easily understand.

Continuous learning: Security threats and attacks change quickly and constantly, requiring security professionals to constantly keep up with new technologies and industry regulatory requirements.

Educational Requirements

Many security professionals have undergraduate degrees in computer science, information systems, or similar fields of study. However, many have entered the field from other disciplines through self-study and other professional development opportunities.

For Additional Information

The International Information System Security Certification Consortium: ISC2 is the professional organization that administers the Certified Information Systems Security Professional (CISSP) certification, one of the most sought after and respected in the industry. It offers many different educational and training opportunities, both online and in person. See www.isc2.org.

ISACA: Formerly known as the Information Systems and Audit Control Association, the ISACA professional organization sets standards on the security and governance of information systems. It also administers several industry-recognized certifications, like the Certified Information Systems Security Professional (CISSP), Certified in Risk and Information Systems Control (CRISC), and Certified Information Security Manager (CISM). See www.isaca.org.

Cybrary: Cybrary is a free online learning platform where users can learn cybersecurity skills for free. Instructors are practicing industry professionals from companies like Cisco and CompTIA. See cybrary.it.

Product Management

Developing a successful product or service is not easy. Great products require a lot of planning, market research, and close attention to how the product gets delivered to the end user. The activities required to make that happen fall under product management.

Typical job titles: Product Manager, Technical Product Manager, Product Development Manager, Product Management Associate

2019 average median wage (per PayScale.com):

Product Manager: $94,002 per year

What They Do

The day-to-day routine for product managers will vary depending on many factors, including the company you're working for and the product or service being developed. Generally speaking, a product manager needs to guide their team (usually made up of people across the marketing, sales, finance, and design departments) through the product development life cycle: idea conception, product design, product build-out, distribution, and servicing.

Although the solution being created may be technical in nature, product managers must address end-user challenges, as well as follow a solid business plan. Project managers must conduct thorough research (technical, market, and financial) and communicate with many different stakeholders, while making sure that a product is made correctly and within budget.

Top Skills

Communication: Not only do product managers have to collect and assess feedback from stakeholders, team leaders from other departments, and their managers, but they must act as an advocate for the customer in their interactions. Product managers need to be able to communicate clearly, effectively, and, sometimes, persuasively.

Analytical: Product managers need to be able to quickly gather and assess the wants and needs of their customers. They also need to analyze whether a specific course of action makes business and financial sense.

Empathy: Product managers need to have deep empathy for their customers. They need to be able to view and understand how their customer will interact with the final product. Because the customer is not actively participating in the product development process, the product manager should act as the closest representation of the customer during the process.

Educational Requirements

Most in product management have four-year undergraduate degrees, but many have reported to have degrees in areas such as business, marketing, communications, or related fields. While having some technical skill is helpful, it's not a strict requirement, as the duties in product management tend to be more business or project management focused.

For Additional Information

Product Development and Management Association (PDMA): PDMA is a professional organization dedicated to the advancement of product development. It is the publisher of the academic *Journal of Product Innovation Management*, and has several chapters and student chapters throughout the United States. See www.pdma.org.

General Assembly: While General Assembly hosts several software engineering and data analytics courses, it also hosts an intensive, part-time course on product development. See https://generalassemb.ly/education/product-management.

Project Management

Before we talk about project management, we should first define what a project is. A *project* is an activity or a series of activities that are temporary and will end in a specific result. A project can be the building of a new product or service, or perhaps the revision or improvement of an existing business process.

Projects can last for a few days to several years, but they have a start date (usually a formal one), and they *always end*. The end can come about because you've achieved the result wanted, or in other instances, the project runs out of money or there is a breakdown somewhere where the project can no longer continue. Whatever the cause, projects are not meant to go on for an unlimited amount of time.

Project management is necessary to ensure that a project achieves its intended goal. It requires planning, organizing, and managing resources effectively, and adjusting as necessary, as few projects ever go completely and exactly to plan.

Projects have *constraints*, or limits on the amount of time, money, and requirements any one project can accomplish. This is often referred to as the *project management triangle* or *triple constraint*—any movement too far in any one or two constraints will affect the outcome or quality of another constraint. For example, a project that grows in both time and scope will increase the overall cost of the project (see Figure 2.2).

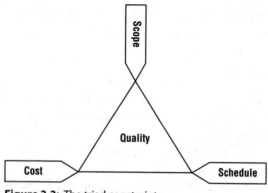

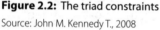

Figure 2.2: The triad constraints

Source: John M. Kennedy T., 2008

Typical job titles: Project Manager, Program Manager, Technical Project Manager, IT Project Manager, Project Coordinator

2018 average median wage (per the Bureau of Labor Statistics): $101,000 per year

What They Do

A project manager's role will vary, depending on their industry or the type of project that is being undertaken. Most project managers, however, will be responsible for a standard set of tasks that align with the Project Management Institute's five phases of project management: initiation, planning, execution, monitoring, and closure.

At the start of a project, project managers help to define the goals of the project at a very broad level. They will meet with the project owners and stakeholders (who can be an external organization, or perhaps an internal department within a company) to determine what they will be able to accomplish, given the time, resource, and money constraint that are in place. The project manager will help the project to define clear and measurable goals, and the timeframes as to when these should occur.

During the duration of the project, project managers will hold regular meetings with stakeholders to ensure that tasks are completed on or close to schedule. The frequency of these meetings may be set by the project owner—meetings can happen weekly by phone, or perhaps once a month in person.

Monitoring and risk management are key responsibilities of the project manager's job—for a project manager, anything that will cause the project to be delayed, out of scope, or over budget is considered a risk. If there is a significant blocker, or something that may be preventing a stakeholder from completing a task, project managers will intervene. If there is conflict among a few or several stakeholders, the project manager will step in to mediate the issue.

Budgeting is also an important function for a project manager. They ensure that all expenses that the project incurs is in line with what was discussed at the start of the project. If there's a chance that a project could go over budget, the project manager needs to inform the owner *immediately* so that they can decide whether they should continue or stop.

Finally, they are responsible for bringing the project to a close—meaning that the project owner confirms that the work performed is in line with the project plan, and that no additional work or rework needs to be completed.

Top Skills

Communication: Project managers communicate with several different project stakeholders, from the people they're performing the project for to the departments and other organizations that need to be involved for the project to move forward. They must be able to share important information quickly and effectively.

Organization: Project managers must prepare and share detailed project plans for everyone involved with the project plan.

Negotiation: Negotiation is essentially a discussion between two or more people or parties to arrive upon an agreement or solution that everyone can work with. Project managers may have to work out agreements with stakeholders and vendors to get work done.

Time management: One of the key components of a project's success is that it be completed on time. Project managers must be able to manage their own time effectively as well as the time for people on their team.

Educational Requirements

An undergraduate degree in business, management, or a related field is a common entryway into the field. Those who want to transition from another career path can also take program management certificate programs that can help prepare them for the Certified Associate of Project Management (CAPM) certification or the advanced Program Management Professional (PMP) certification.

For Additional Information

The **Project Management Institute (PMI)** is the leading professional organization for beginning and experienced project management professionals. It offers several professional development opportunities, such as formal mentoring and educational courses at the chapter level. It also offers many well-recognized professional certifications, like the CAPM and the PMP. See www.pmi.org.

Software Development and Engineering

Building good software and applications that please customers takes thorough planning and time. Software development and engineering focuses on all the necessary tools and activities needed to bring an app or software to market.

Software developers attempt to address a specific user need or problem through the creation of software or applications. While doing so, they need to think about addressing overall user design, security concerns, and app maintenance.

"The main thing I love about my career and job is having the ability to create and build whatever comes to mind without having a key solution," says Ariana Davis, a lead software engineer for the Golden State Warriors and Chase Center in San Francisco. "While there are certain deadlines with assigned tasks, understanding that whatever I build doesn't need to be 100 percent and can be something as simple as a passion project."

As we become more and more dependent on apps, the need for good software developers is growing fast. It should be noted that there is a difference between software engineering/programming and coding. Coding concentrates on the basics and the *syntax* (rules) of a programming language of a particular language, whereas programming requires more in-depth analysis and thinking.

Companies employ software developers in their office on a full-time basis, although they can also work on a freelance or temporary basis through an employment agency.

Typical job titles: Software Developer, Software Engineer, Software Architect, Programmer, Coder

2018 average median wage (per the Bureau of Labor Statistics): $104,300 per year

What They Do

Software developers collect software or application requirements from the people who will be the end users. They attempt to design the "skeleton" of the software and may often use things such as diagrams or prototypes to illustrate ideas or processes.

Depending on the type of *software development life cycle* (SDLC) methodology that they use, development teams may do the following:

- Write the entire code of the application first, test it, and make modifications when finished (*waterfall*)

- Write pieces of code to satisfy a specific function, test it, make corrections quickly, and move on to the next function to be coded (*agile*)

These are the more popular methodologies, but there are many others as well as variations of the ones mentioned.

Software developers create documentation throughout the entire development so that it can serve as a reference in case there is a failure within the program and to assist with any maintenance efforts. They may also assist with installation and with training end users on how to use the program correctly.

You may hear terms like *front end, back end,* or *full stack* developers. These terms denote the area of an application that a developer focuses on:

- **Front end:** Concentrates on the areas of program that an end user will interact with; primarily interested in the user experience
- **Back end:** Focuses on "the guts" of the application—where data is stored (databases) and the application's logic (the workflow, or steps, an application follows when a user interacts with it)
- **Full stack:** Focuses on both front and back ends

Top Skills

Programming: Developers must be able to create programs using a programming language. There are *many* programming languages out; the more popular ones include Java, C, C++, Python, Go, and Ruby. The more languages you understand and use, the more it will help with your marketability, or your attractiveness, to potential employers.

Operating systems: Software developers need to know how their code interacts with any given operating system. How a program behaves in Windows may be vastly different from how it behaves on a Mac computer.

Cloud technologies: Many companies and organizations are creating applications that are *cloud native*, meaning that only cloud services are used in the app's creation and operation. Developers need to understand the tools that are available to them, as well as tools and methodologies to ensure that an app is always available for people to use.

Critical thinking and analysis: Developers need to be able to think not only about the problem they are attempting to solve but about all the different systems and audiences that an app or software may impact. They need to be able to lower any potential risks, bottlenecks, and other issues before they arise.

Communication: Despite popular belief that software developers are quiet loners, software developers need to be able to talk to audiences beyond just other developers. Often they will need to speak to business managers and nondeveloper employees on how their software or app works.

Educational Requirements

An undergraduate degree in computer science or software engineering is an almost universal requirement for these types of positions. While it is true that you can learn coding through self-study and boot camps, there are underlying and complementary concepts (such as networking, computer architecture, and operating systems) that may not get as much attention as they do in computer science programs.

For Additional Information

Institute of Electrical and Electronics Engineers: IEEE is one of the most prominent professional organizations in the world dedicated to engineering professionals and those in similar fields. The IEEE Computer Society is specifically dedicated to students and working professionals in the software engineering and development domain. See www.computer.org.

Code.org: Code.org is a nonprofit that seeks to make computer science accessible to everyone. Its website hosts free online coding classes grouped by grade level, as well as resources to find computer science classes nearby. See https://code.org/.

Cloud Native Computing Foundation: Founded by several major software companies like Google and IBM, CNCF promotes the development and advancement of applications born on the cloud. They host several open user groups, as well as events like KubeCon + CloudNativeCon. See www.cncf.io.

Technical Sales

An organization's sales can make (or break) its business. It is an important function that allows business to operate and potentially grow in the future.

While sales can be a rewarding and lucrative career, it can also be one of the more stressful fields to enter. A salesperson's success almost always comes down to how much of a product or service they have sold.

Technology sales adds a little more complexity to the process depending on the type of technology product you are selling. Technology sales can be anything from selling a small mobile phone app for $10 to a major enterprise resource planning (ERP) software system that can cost millions of dollars. The *sales cycle*, or the total time it takes to sell a product or service to a customer, can take a few days or several months.

Despite the pressure, sales can be fun and pay well. Juliet Okafor, senior vice president of sales at Habitu8, explained, "I really like the idea of hearing a customer's challenge and then finding all the different pieces in order to provide a total solution to a customer—really serving more as a consultant and helping them address both that technical aspect of it, but also the people part of it."

Typical job titles: Sales Engineer, Technical Sales Representative, Technical Sales Specialist, Solutions Engineer, Solution Specialist, Solution Architect, Pre-Sales Engineer

2018 average median wage (per the Bureau of Labor Statistics): $101,728 per year

What They Do

Sales engineers help to explain and ultimately sell complex technical products to customers. Depending on the organization, sales engineers may be asked to give product demonstrations, build product prototypes, design customer solutions, or give presentations to technical and non-technical audiences.

Sales engineers usually work with sales representatives who have already identified a potential customer, although in some organizations, they may also take on the responsibility of *prospecting*, or identifying, potential customers.

Sales engineers, depending on the organization, are paid both a base salary and a commission on any sales that they make. Sales engineers get the opportunity to travel for customer visits, trade shows, and other industry events.

On the other hand, sales engineers' performance is graded almost entirely on whether they make their quota. Sales engineers may be let go from their job if they don't make their numbers repeatedly. Hours can be very sporadic—you may be called to go to a client meeting at any time, and working during the holidays or vacation is not uncommon.

Top Skills

Interpersonal: Sales engineers must build relationships with many different audiences. This includes their clients, teammates, and coworkers who may work in completely different departments.

Communication: Sales engineers will have to communicate with technical and nontechnical clients and audiences as well as with people within their own organization. They are also expected to give presentations and product demonstrations and write reports or other types of technical documentation.

Continuous learning: As technology changes quickly, sales engineers must be able to learn new technologies, products, and services just as quickly.

Educational Requirements

An undergraduate degree is not a strict requirement for this role. Per the Occupational Information Network, only 43 percent of people who are in this or a similar profession have a bachelor's degree, and 24 percent have an associate degree. That said, professionals have been able to compensate for a lack of a degree with several years of industry experience or industry certifications.

For Additional Information

National Association of Sales Professionals (NASP): NASP is a professional organization that caters to all salespeople, regardless of industry. It offers training and networking opportunities to new and experienced sales professionals, as well as certification opportunities. Although a sales engineer's work is more technical in nature, make no mistake that making the sale is a goal. See www.nasp.com.

Mastering Technical Sales: This website is maintained by John Care, a professional with more than 30 years' experience in several sales engineer capacities. Care offers practical advice and resources to new and experienced sales engineers on conducting product demonstrations and advancing your career. See www.masteringtechnicalsales.com.

Technical Support

For all of our technological advancements, things still break or don't work the way that they're supposed to. Technical support teams work to ensure that things get working again and, ultimately, that you stay a loyal customer with their product or service.

Companies need, more than ever, good technical support teams. With so many choices in terms of apps and services, customers are not as loyal to companies or brands as they used to be. Customers are willing to use other companies to fulfill their needs if they have a bad technical-support experience. Think about your own interactions: have you stopped using or thought twice about using an app that didn't give you what you wanted?

Typical job titles: Help Desk Technician, Computer Support Specialist, Technical Support Engineer

2018 average median wage (per the Bureau of Labor Statistics): $53,740 per year

What They Do

Technical support staff members review and respond to customer inquiries and service requests through email, phone, or chat. In most organizations, the goal for tech support is to answer and resolve a query at the first attempt. They will then attempt to walk the customer through the solution together, and if unsuccessful, they will escalate to a senior-level employee or another department. Any follow-up appointments or work that may need to be done, such as scheduling an onsite appointment, will be scheduled by the support professional who originally took the call.

Top Skills

Listening: To be successful, tech support professionals need to be able to go beyond *hearing* what the customer is saying. They need to be able to understand what the customer is saying and not interrupt or offer a solution before they've offered all their information.

Problem solving: After listening to the customer, tech support professionals need to be able to quickly assess what the user's problem is and walk them through the solution or quickly determine whether more help is needed.

Professionalism: Customers may be in bad or less-than-ideal moods when they are calling in for help. They may be genuinely frustrated by the problem, or they may have just had a bad day. No matter the reason, tech support professionals must always interact with customers with respect and patience.

Communication: Technical support professionals may need to interact with customers over the phone, in person, or through electronic chat. In all cases, they must be able to communicate well verbally or through written words.

Educational Requirements

Although there are some companies that require bachelor's degrees in computer science or related fields for their positions, most require only a high school diploma or an associate degree to obtain an entry-level position.

For Additional Information

Help Desk Institute (HDI): HDI is an organization that offers educational and professional organization for people in technical help and support positions. It offers several certifications, including the HDI Desktop Support Technician (HDI-DST) and the HDI Support Center Analyst (HDI SCA). See www.hdi.com.

User Experience Design

When the first iPhone came out in 2007, it was quite a breakthrough. It was the first phone to institute a touch screen and a beautiful full-color display screen. It left a lot to be desired—it was expensive ($499), the call quality was okay, and the glass broke easily. Even with those drawbacks, thousands of people camped outside Apple and AT&T stores to get their hands on one, and they paid the full retail price! The iPhone's success can be directly attributed to an innovative and powerful design that captivated users.

This is the goal of the user experience (UX) design—to design products and services that not only are functional, but that end users are drawn to. Good UX design creates experiences where the end product/service is greatly satisfying to use.

Catt Small, a product designer who has worked with major companies such as Asana, Etsy, SoundCloud and Nasdaq, described why she likes her career field: "I personally really like solving puzzles, and that's why I got into design in the first place. So, it's really fun for me to get to do that as part of my everyday job."

Typical job titles: UX Designer, UX Architect, UX Engineer, User Researcher

2019 average median wage (per PayScale.com): $74,159 per year

What They Do

Much of a UX designer's time is spent making sure that they understand the needs of both the business and the end user of the product or service they're working on. UX designers may attend many brainstorming meetings with business stakeholders to get a better understanding of the business goals they are trying to achieve, while also conducting user research through interviews, surveys, focus groups, observations, etc.

Despite the need to have solid graphic design skills, much of a UX designer's time is spent performing research. Small recalls, "I was pretty much in a room all day with a person who is the business lead on my team; I was collaborating with her and her lead engineer on how we were going to display certain elements on a page based on different requirements. . . . Maybe you're really into drawing pictures, but that's not going to be the most important part of your job day to day. You're going to be doing lots of research, talking to a lot of people, and eventually, you're going to be making the pretty thing."

Once the research has been conducted and analyzed, UX designers can begin to flesh out their design by creating user *personas*. Personas are fictional character representations of end users that are based on the research performed. The more detailed and specific you can be about your persona's personal characteristics, behaviors, desires, and needs, the more designers are able to empathize with them and create products that connect emotionally with the end user.

After feeling comfortable with capturing their user(s), UX designers can now begin creating a wireframe, or a visual blueprint, of the product to be designed. Although there are many digital and online tools for wireframing, like Balsamiq, you can physically draw them using simple pen and paper or a whiteboard. The wireframe should demonstrate how elements (e.g., buttons, text) will be arranged and the flow in which a user would take to complete a process, such as completing a registration process for a website. Once complete, a prototype, or an early sample version, of the end product is designed and constructed as quickly (and cheaply) as possible.

With the prototype complete, the UX designer will conduct *usability* testing. Here, the UX designer will have the end user use and evaluate the prototype. Any feedback or issues that the end user reports, regardless of whether it's good or bad, is recorded and used to make improvements. This process is completed several times until it is deemed by the team that all issues have been met and addressed.

Top Skills

Communication: In addition to being able to interact with several different stakeholders, UX designers must have the ability to convey their thoughts—even if others disagree with them. Per Small, "When it comes to being a real designer, part of your job sometimes is actually pushing back against people and proving that what you believe to be true because of the research that you've done."

Graphic Design: Having working knowledge of Adobe's Creative Suite of products is helpful, particularly Photoshop, Illustrator, and InDesign. But more importantly, knowing how to effectively convey information and stir emotion—using color, shapes, imagery, and typography—is key.

Wireframing: Knowing different wireframing tools available is great, but knowing the important elements that should appear in wireframes, along with when to use a low-fidelity versus a high-fidelity wireframe (i.e., basic versus detailed), is crucial.

Empathy: A popular phrase in the UX community is "You are not your user." This phrase is to point out that UX designers should not build end products that they will use but rather for the actual end user. UX designers must always design from the perspective of the end user.

Teamwork: UX design is not a solo effort; designers tend to work in teams and deal with many internal/external stakeholders. UX designers must be willing and able to accept feedback.

Educational Requirements

Many UX designers hold a four-year degree in human computer interaction, design (graphic, industrial, communication, etc.), or a related field. However, this is not a strict requirement to get into the field. There are many UX designers, however, who are self-taught and have built great portfolios through freelance work and other projects.

For Additional Information

User Experience Professional Association (UXPA): UXPA is a professional organization dedicated to promoting UX best practices, concepts, and techniques. It publishes the free online publications *User Experience Magazine* and the *Journal of Usability Studies* and hosts on online job opportunity board. See `uxpa.org`.

The Design of Everyday Things: Don Norman's book is considered by many in the user design community to be a great book on meaningful human-centered design. See `https://jnd.org/the-design-of-everyday-things-revised-and-expanded-edition,(MIT Press, 2013).`

Usability.gov: `Usability.gov` is a free online portal with best practices and other resources on UX design. See `www.usability.gov`.

Web Design

Web design focuses on the general look and feel of a website. There is overlap here between web design and UX; however, the focus here is the overall design and technical aspects of a website. The focus is not necessarily on the emotions that stir up in the user when they use a website.

When the Internet was new, users were not really concerned about how fast a website loaded, how many visitors a site could handle at a given time, or whether they could securely accept payments for merchandise. Now, making sure that a site can load almost instantaneously, handle all types of traffic, and protect our sensitive information has become incredibly important.

Typical job titles: Web Developer, Front End Developer, Web Designer

2018 average median wage (per the Bureau of Labor Statistics): $69,430 per year

What They Do

Web developers collect information from their potential clients on the type of website they'd like to create. They'll want to know things such as the audience they are attempting to reach, what type of media (video, photos, etc.) they plan to host, or whether they have any preference on a *content management system* they'd like to use, like WordPress. They may also assist the client in securing one or several *domain names*.

Web developers then construct the website according to the client's specifications. This can be an iterative, or continuous, process as the developer will continue to modify the site once the client is happy with the final product. From there, web developers will make updates to the website on an as-needed basis.

Many businesses hire web developers as full-time staff, while others work on their own as freelancers. Those who freelance have usually had several years of experience and a large portfolio of work that they can speak to.

Top Skills

Front-end web development: At minimum, web developers should understand how to create web pages using Hypertext Markup Language (HTML) and Cascading Style Sheets (CSS). Understanding JavaScript can help you to build additional functionality in your website.

Graphic design: Web developers are also expected to help with the overall look and design.

Attention to detail: Writing code for websites require precision, as languages have specific requirements in order to work properly.

Communication: Developers will need to interact with customers to understand their needs for their website.

Educational Requirements

There are no strict educational requirements to becoming a web developer. There are some employers who may prefer that potential candidates have an associate or undergraduate degree for more sophisticated web development.

For Additional Information

The World Organization of Webmasters: WOW is a professional organization for people who create or manage websites in some capacity. It offers advice on best practices, certification opportunities, and a job opportunity board. See `webprofessionals.org`.

W3 Schools.com: W3 is touted as the largest website for web developers. The site provides free tutorials on HTML, CSS, JavaScript, and more. See `w3schools.com`.

Where Do You Fit In?

There's certainly no lack of opportunities in tech. But with all these choices, you're probably wondering what path would be the right one for you. Let's look at your strengths and weaknesses, your work values, and your interests.

What Are Your Strengths and Your Weaknesses?

In your past schoolwork, projects, or work experience, what have you done really well? And what have you struggled with?

Understanding your strengths and weaknesses will be important for your career progression. You will want to leverage the things you do really well, while devoting some time (and possibly more) toward areas you'd like to improve in. You also don't want to possibly put yourself in a career field where you find yourself constantly struggling.

For example, when I decided to go to Northwestern, I picked its Communication Systems program because it had a healthy mix of communication courses that I enjoyed and excelled at, such as public speaking, persuasion, and argumentation. The program also had several technology courses that interested me, but I knew it would require more studying and effort from me, like in discrete mathematics, object-oriented programming, and systems analysis/design.

I also knew that since programming was something I struggled with, and it wasn't something I was passionate about, becoming a software engineer would not have been ideal for me. But because I was really good in business and communication, a career in technical sales was much better for me.

If you're struggling with figuring out what your strengths and weaknesses are, there are few things you can do:

- *Review past feedback*: If you have access to any past feedback you've received for assignments, projects, cases, or anything similar, take the time to review it again. As you're reading, you may notice certain praises or criticisms come up repeatedly. Pay attention to recurring themes, as these will indicate areas you perform well in or may need to give attention to.

- *Ask for feedback*: If you don't have access to previous feedback or the feedback you have been given wasn't descriptive or helpful, ask for it. You can ask a previous or current teacher, employer, teammate, or anyone who has had more than one interaction with you.

- *Take an aptitude test*: If this still doesn't produce anything for you to go off of, you can try an aptitude test. Aptitude tests are designed to measure where your natural talents and abilities lie.

There are many free aptitude tests on the Internet, as well as those that charge a small fee to take. That said, I recommend taking aptitude tests that are administered through local educational or career service institutions. These kinds of aptitude tests, like the US Army's Vocational Aptitude Battery, or ASVAB,[1] have been heavily researched, thoroughly tested, and deemed as a valid and unbiased aptitude exam.

In addition, these exams usually require you to discuss your results with a counselor or professional. This is helpful to avoid misinterpreting your results.

Results from aptitude tests should not be interpreted as "I shouldn't pursue a career in this because my _____ skills tested low." Rather, interpret them as "These are the things that I'm good at, and these are the things that don't come as easily to me. If I do decide to pursue a career in _____, I will have to work a little harder in these areas because I tested lower in them."

What Do You Value?

Are you someone who really enjoys working on your own, or would you prefer to work in a team? Do you want to decide how to perform your work or have someone else determine that for you? Do you want to work from home or from an office? Are you interested in perhaps

---

[1] It should be noted that while the ASVAB is used as a part of the military recruitment process, high school guidance counselors have also used the results from the ASVAB to assist with non-military career counseling.

moving into more of a manager role with the potential for more money but more responsibility, or would you prefer to work as an individual contributor?

These questions and more help determine what your work values are. While no one job will satisfy all your work values, the closer the job satisfies these requirements, the more satisfied you are likelier to be.

The core work values, per O*NET, are as follows:

- **Achievement:** Learning new skills; doing challenging and engaging work

- **Independence:** Using your creativity to solve work problems; deciding how to get work done with little to no supervision

- **Recognition:** The ability to advance your career and obtain leadership positions

- **Relationships:** Being able to work with, and serve, others in a minimally competitive environment

- **Support:** Having nurturing managers or staff; being provided all the tools and resources necessary for you to be successful in your job

- **Working Conditions:** Working in a safe environment; being compensated well for your work; feeling good about the security of your job

A word about money: making a good income is incredibly important and a good motivator for pursuing a career in tech. Chapter 8, "Job Offers and Negotiating Compensation," is specifically dedicated to ensure your able to secure a fair salary. Yet, it should not be your sole motivator and, perhaps, not even your top one.

If you end up working in a career that pays you extremely well but the work itself makes you miserable, you will quickly find yourself on a path to burnout.

Now I don't mean occasional periods of stress—stress is a normal part of everyday life—nor do I mean any other difficult situations that you have with family, friends, or other loved ones, or minor workplace annoyances. I mean, you are *deeply unhappy because of your work alone.* You find yourself crying often, snapping at people for no good reason, always exhausted, not taking care of your body or mental well-being, or just doing things that you know are not like you.

Don't do it for the money alone. It's just not worth it.

What Are Your Interests?

What are the things that you enjoy doing, whether you are at work or school? Do you enjoy building things with your hands? Do you enjoy drawing? Do you enjoy creating and posting things on social media? Do you enjoy tutoring others in different subjects? What about playing games, video or otherwise?

These questions and more can help you determine the tasks you are interested in doing. Just like finding a career field that closely aligns to your work values will increase the likelihood of success, finding jobs that match your interests will also be helpful. Take some time to think about the tasks you enjoy and write them down.

Summary

- Having a basic understanding of information technology will serve as a good foundation for a tech career.

- Tech careers require a diverse set of skills, not just technical skills. Just about any tech career requires you to communicate effectively, analyze information, and problem solve.

- While most tech careers covered here require at least a four-year undergraduate degree, some put greater emphasis on hands-on, field experience or a portfolio of work (such as computer networking, security, and user experience and design).

- Understanding your strengths and weaknesses, as well as what you value in your job, and your interests can help you find career fields that may be a fit for you.

Industry and Other Options

When we think of tech employers, we almost immediately think of what's referred to as the FAANG companies (Facebook, Amazon, Apple, Netflix, and Google). But opportunities exist in many different industries and fields. For example, did you know that at the 2019 Grace Hopper Conference, Bank of America and the *New York Times* were recognized as top companies for women technologists? Bank of America alone employs more than 10,000 technical employees, while the *New York Times* employs close to 1,000 tech employees.

There's almost no industry or domain that hasn't been impacted and revolutionized by tech, and all of them need tech professionals, like, yesterday. In this chapter, we'll discuss tech opportunities within the US government, education, healthcare, and more. We'll also talk about going the entrepreneurial route and starting your own business.

These are by no means the only career fields with tech careers—opportunities across several industries will continue to grow. But the next few sections will give you an example of areas where tech jobs are expected to grow significantly.

Advertising and Marketing

Advertising is a form of marketing communication where a person or company pays money to promote a product or service. Prior to the adoption of the Internet and social media, advertising was mostly done through print, such as magazines and newspapers, or through broadcast media, such as television and radio. These forms of advertising can be incredibly expensive—airing a 30-second commercial during the Super Bowl (historically the most widely watched live sporting event in the United States) cost $5.25 million! There's also no guarantee that commercials will translate into people buying your product or service, or to put it simply, there's no guarantee that you'll receive a return on your investment.

While closely related, marketing differs from advertising in that it consists of the behind-the-scenes work to help bring a product or service to the marketplace. This includes conducting market research to better understand who your target audiences are (as well as your competition's) and developing an overall marketing strategy. Advertising can be an activity that is part of an overall marketing plan or campaign.

Technology has greatly influenced and helped both fields. With the Internet and social media becoming more dominant mediums in our lives, companies realize that they need to devote advertising efforts digitally as well. The challenge for companies then becomes effectively leveraging these different, complex platforms to target the right audience, while not going completely broke.

Although advertising is more art than science—capturing the attention of people who are pressed for time and sometimes have short attention spans has always been a difficult task—technology has enabled advertisers to find and target the right audiences and accurately measure whether an ad campaign has been effective. Rather than making guesses, advertisers now have firm data to make at least educated ones.

Major companies that focus on advertising technology, or AdTech, include traditional advertising agencies such as Omnicom, Publicis, and Interpublic. Digital-native companies, such as Amazon, Google, and Facebook, are also in this space, making it incredibly competitive. Non-ad companies may also have their own dedicated AdTech departments.

For marketing tech, or MarTech, technology has enabled marketers to measure the overall effectiveness of their marketing campaigns and adjust as necessary. Search engine marketing allows businesses to leverage paid advertisements to appear and rank high in search engine results. MarTech has enabled companies to monitor an advertisement's effectiveness and adjust keywords to elevate their search position.

As companies want data to help inform their advertising and marketing campaign decisions, companies are always on the lookout for candidates with strong data analysis skills. There's also high demand for software engineers who can create full-stack applications that deliver great user experiences and for product managers who can create AdTech and MarTech platforms from start to finish.

Here is some additional information:

- **The Trading Desk:** For those looking for training in the AdTech space, the Trading Desk offers an online course, as well as tips and tricks on how to break into your first AdTech job.
  www.thetradedesk.com/tradingacademy

- **MarTech Today:** MarTech Today gives insightful news and research on the MarTech industry and hosts an annual MarTech conference— an event filled with educational workshops, keynotes, and networking events.
  www.martechconf.com

- **American Marketing Association (AMA):** The AMA is a professional organization dedicated to the advancement of marketing professionals. It hosts a two-day digital marketing bootcamp and administers the certification exam for the Professional Certified Marketer Digital Marketing designation.
  www.ama.org

- **Together Digital:** Together Digital leverages its online community, local, and national events, and virtual peer circles to promote the advancement of women in digital advertising and marketing.
  www.togetherindigital.com

Civics and Public Interest

Civics deals with the rights and responsibilities a citizen has with respect to the place where they live (e.g., a town or city). As a citizen of your area, you are afforded certain rights, such as access to public resources, free speech, and due process (i.e. fair treatment in a court of law). With that comes certain responsibilities, such as paying taxes, sitting on a jury if needed, and obeying the laws put in place.

Although we will discuss opportunities in the US government later in this chapter, the roles of tech in government and civics are different. Tech jobs within the government are primarily focused on increasing the efficiency of internal operations and on protecting the data that is contained within. In contrast, civic tech seeks to increase engagement and deepen the relationships citizens have with one another and their respective government.

While civic tech firms serve the public, they are often for-profit or nonprofit companies; they don't have the same restraints and bureaucracy that governments and governmental agencies do. This means civic tech firms can develop and implement solutions quicker than those of their government counterparts. The flipside is that it can be difficult for civic tech firms to keep their offerings free or low cost, as they are receiving funding through a hodge-podge of places—through their business operations, loans, grants, etc. Because of this, salaries and perks of tech jobs in this area may not be as plentiful and may feel the effects of an economic downturn more acutely.

An example of civic tech would be the Code for America program. Started in 2009, the nonprofit seeks tech professionals to design applications for local governments, in the hopes of improving how information and government services are delivered to citizens and, in turn, of increasing citizen engagement. Another example includes Civic Hall, a coworking space in New York City, where tech professionals can contribute to projects that serve the public good.

A role in civic tech can be ideal if you have a love of technology and want a job that is mission driven or where the primary driver of your work is meant to help people versus seeking profit. The job opportunities in civic tech are plentiful and diverse, as organizations need tech professionals of all types. There are no strict requirements in terms of education or experience—just a genuine desire to get involved and help others.

Here is some additional information:

- **Civic Tech Guide:** A community-maintained online resource and a Civic Hall project, this site offers information on civic tech projects all over the United States.
  civictech.guide

- **Coding It Forward:** This nonprofit seeks to inform and get students excited about civic tech, through industry information and a number of internship/fellowship programs that it hosts.
  codingitforward.com

- **Code for America:** As mentioned, this nonprofit seeks tech professionals to design applications for local governments.
  codeforamerica.org

- **Civic Hall:** As mentioned, this nonprofit seeks tech professionals who can contribute to projects that serve the public good.
  civichall.org

Construction and Manufacturing

Construction is the process in which a physical building or structure is created. Construction can range from building homes and apartment complexes to building office buildings to building industrial manufacturing plants and factories. This can also include the construction of roads and highways, utility infrastructures such as pipelines, and telecommunications transmission towers.

When thinking about construction, people may conjure up images of a traditional construction site—hard hats, forklifts, and outdoor work—as well as a lot of low-paying, manual labor. Because of this, people may think it's an industry where technology and well-paying tech jobs are largely absent.

But Micheal Lane, a retired construction professional and president of SheGetItDone, an organization dedicated to helping the disadvantaged explore nontraditional, in-demand jobs in the construction trades, says that modern construction jobs have far more tech than you know. "You can work on a construction site, and you feel like you're in a video game, because we have so many different technologies, like augmented reality, wearable devices, 3D printing, and all sorts of portable technology that we have to deal with."

There is more technology now being used on modern construction sites than there ever has been. Technology has helped to make sites safer for workers; helped reduce the need to perform repetitive, low-value tasks; and helped to speed up the entire construction process. Additionally, construction jobs are expected to grow 11 percent between 2016 and 2026, with 758,000 new jobs added by 2026, according to the Bureau of Labor Statistics.

Manufacturing involves the creation of a product from raw materials, which then can be used or sold. There are many industries within manufacturing, including creating clothes, automobiles, aircrafts, chemicals, electronics, and even food.

The total number of manufacturing jobs has declined steadily over time. From 2000 and 2017, the Bureau of Labor Statistics reports that 5.5 million manufacturing jobs were lost. Many of these jobs were lost to offshoring—the act of moving a company's operations outside the country—or through automation and robotics, effectively getting rid of repetitive, low-value tasks. While it is unlikely that the number of manufacturing jobs will ever go back to previous levels (the highest was 19.4 million in 1979), there are signs of jobs gradually being brought back to the United States. The reasons include the need for higher product quality standards, access to more technological innovations, and incentives being offered to companies to keep producing in the United States. Companies like Apple, Intel, and General Electric have all engaged in initiatives to bring their manufacturing jobs back into the United States.

Many jobs within the construction and manufacturing fields fall under what are referred to as the *skilled trades*. These jobs require specialized skill sets or abilities, which are gained through a combination of attending trade schools and apprenticeships. Trade schools will be discussed in more detail in Chapter 6, "Building Your Skills," but trade school may offer a quicker, cheaper pathway to a successful, well-paying career. "You don't have to go to college and go into major debt," Lane says. "College isn't for everybody."

Many skilled trades are in demand—in fact, for some there are severe shortages—and those who have strong skills in computer-aided design, 3D printing, automation, software development, and IoT, among others, will be highly sought after.

Both construction and manufacturing are heavily male dominated, perhaps more than many other industries. In 2019, the Bureau of Labor Statistics reported that 10.3 percent of construction roles and 29.4 percent of manufacturing roles, respectively, were filled by women. These are the lowest representation numbers for women of the industries and domains discussed. What has contributed to these low numbers are persistent claims by women in the field of harassment, lack of female role models, and inflexible family leave policies.

Lane was candid about the hardships she experienced during her career, including experiencing harassment and microaggressions from her white, male counterparts. Adding insult to injury, there were not many people she could turn to for help or identify with: "There were no advocates. I was alone on a boat, by myself. And now that I'm gone, there is no one of [my gender and color] in that organization."

That said, many organizations exist, like SheGetItDone and Women in Manufacturing, to help support women in these fields and to, in time, increase the presence of women in these fields.

Here is some additional information:

▪ **Associated General Contractors of America (AGC):** AGC is a professional organization aimed at advancing the commercial construction industry within the United States. AGC provides news, research, and information on training resources for those interested a variety of construction fields, including building, utility, and civil construction.

   agc.org

- **National Association of Women in Construction (NAWIC):**
  NAWIC seeks to provide a support network for its members through
  networking and training opportunities, as well as professional
  and leadership development programs.
  www.nawic.org

- **SheGetItDone:** SheGetItDone seeks to promote construction trades
  as a gainful employment pathway for women, people of color,
  youth, and veterans. The nonprofit's site boasts information on
  construction technology and how to navigate working in a male-
  dominated industry.
  www.shegetitdone.com

- **Manufacturing USA:** Made up of 14 national manufacturing institutes, this government and industry-funded partnership is focused
  on manufacturing innovation and providing advanced skills
  training for the current and incoming manufacturing
  workforce.
  www.manufacturingusa.com

- **Nuts, Bolts & Thingamajigs:** This is a charitable foundation by
  the Fabricators & Manufacturers Association, whose mission is to
  help people discover career opportunities within the manufacturing sector. The foundation also offers scholarships and immer-
  sive, hands-on summer camps for high school and college
  students.
  www.nutsandboltsfoundation.org

- **Women in Manufacturing (WIM):** WIM is a national trade organization to support women currently in or interested in pursuing
  a career in manufacturing. WIM provides a job board and networking and professional development opportunities to its
  members.
  www.womeninmanufacturing.org

Education

With employers and educators alike stressing the need for continuous,
lifelong learning, people who want to stay competitive in the jobs marketplace need to seek out resources to keep their skills relevant and sharp.

Before the Internet and other technologies, this was a difficult task,
for both students and educational institutions. For students, in addition
to costs, they needed to devote time to physically attend class. For com-

muter students, they needed to factor in the time it would take to get to and from class. Missing a class could become problematic, as you'd miss out on the material covered and, in turn, negatively affect your grades.

Educational institutions faced challenges too—how could they make classes and learning resources more accessible to different populations of students, not just those who make up their traditional populations? Students with learning disabilities? Students who are juggling multiple priorities like work and home life? Also, how could they make learning interactions more engaging and effective for students? Studies conducted over the last few years have shown that the standard, teacher-led lecture techniques of teaching were largely ineffective. In one study, it was discovered that undergraduate students were 1.5 times more likely to fail a class with the traditional lecturing method versus methods where there was more student engagement. Many employers have criticized educational institutions for not adequately preparing their students for even entry-level jobs.

Educational technology, or EdTech, has removed some of these difficulties. Online learning platforms allow teachers and professors to not only share course information, readings, and additional course resources 24/7, they help to facilitate more engaging student experiences. Many of these platforms integrate chat features, allowing students to interact with fellow students and allowing teachers to ask questions and share ideas. Having this capability is crucial to facilitate group assignments and to help audiences that may not be able to physically attend class.

Designing online educational courses, apps, and platforms takes more than just technical or subject knowledge. We've all probably encountered a person in our lives who had solid subject-matter knowledge but did not have the skill to transfer that knowledge to others. I can't tell you how many lectures and presentations I've sat through, given by incredibly smart people who I've respected immensely, that left me no closer to understanding what the heck they were talking about.

Designing online courses and learning platforms goes beyond being able to effectively communicate. EdTech jobs require an understanding of how someone creates an effective and engaging learning experience for the needs of the intended audience. They must apply different learning strategies, develop meaningful learning activities that measure how well students are grasping the material, and design opportunities for feedback. They also understand that technology is *a tool to enhance* the efforts of teaching professionals, not a replacement for teaching professionals. Meaning, it's not a matter of just posting videos and articles.

There are many pathways into EdTech. Many EdTech jobs can be found in traditional educational institutions (schools, colleges, and universities), as well as at nonprofits, corporations, and government agencies. They need the assistance of instructional designers and implementation experts in creating online curriculums for learners or in offering advice on how to improve existing curriculums. Having familiarity with popular learning platforms on the market, hardware, and software is important, and most employers would prefer that candidates have had some experience in instructional design or teaching. For some, an advanced degree may be required.

There are also opportunities with EdTech start-ups—companies that offer their proprietary software and platforms to educational institutions. In those companies, there are needs for product managers, data scientists, and UI/UX professionals, among others, to create products from start to finish.

Here are some additional resources:

- **EdSurge:** Owned by the International Society for Technology in Education, EdSurge contains the latest news, research, and trends in the EdTech space. In addition to its job board, it hosts several live and virtual networking events and educational workshops. www.edsurge.com

- **EDUCAUSE:** Nonprofit EDUCAUSE's mission is to increase the adoption and use of information technology in colleges and universities. Through its EDUCASUSE Learning Initiative, it hosts several online courses webinars on instructional design and holds conferences and networking events for educators and tech professionals. www.educause.edu

- **EdTechWomxn:** Through its local chapters, conferences, networking events, and social media groups on Facebook and LinkedIn, EdTechWomxn seeks to increase and provide advancement and leadership opportunities for women in the EdTech space. www.edtechwomen.com

Finance

Finance studies how money is both used and managed by people (personal finance) and businesses (corporate finance). The activities that fall under finance can be very broad and can include everyday banking, teaching people how to make the most money out of their investments in stocks and bonds, protecting people from accidents and unforeseen events with insurance, or finding (legal) strategies to lessen a person's tax liability.

FinTech, or the intersection of technology and finance, has transformed how finance activities take place. Fintech has allowed people to deposit checks, send money, apply for a loan or credit, purchase/sell stocks and bonds, and more, using only their smartphones and without ever physically stepping into a bank. For businesses, it has helped to considerably reduce the time it takes to open accounts or decide whether to extend credit to an applicant. These processes would've normally taken hours or days to do. Now they're done in a matter minutes, leading to happier customers.

There are many successful FinTech companies. Credit Karma has allowed consumers to take charge of their credit and improve it by allowing them to access their credit reports for free. Betterment investors can get personalized investment advice from a robo-advisor, at a fraction of what an actual advisor would charge. Services like Venmo and Google Wallet have made it much easier to send money to friends and family.

As you can imagine, traditional financial institutions like banks and lenders are feeling the pressure from these companies and are seeking ways to even out the playing field. While some financial institutions play up the "human factor" and some people's preference of working with a human being on financial matters, they recognize that they need digital offerings for those whose preferences are low cost and convenience. Many need help in modernizing their existing technology systems and in being able to offer the same services and experiences that FinTech does.

Hiring cybersecurity experts is a key focus area for many financial institutions. In a 2017 study, a leading Fortune 100 security software company estimated that financial services firms face 65 percent more cyberattacks than a normal business. As the threat for cyberattacks will continue to rise, the need for cybersecurity specialists has never been higher. Within financial institutions, cybersecurity professionals work with senior compliance officers to develop cybersecurity programs, conduct tests to determine the effectiveness of a company's cybersecurity plan, and help investigate and respond to security breaches.

Application developers are also in very high demand. As banks know that their customers want instant access to account information and the ability to quickly carry out transactions, they realize that having an easy-to-use, accessible-anywhere application is vital. App developers are needed to make sure that these applications are safe, are compliant, and do not require an instruction manual to be used. Additionally, application developers who have experience with integrating artificial intelligence into applications or creating blockchain networks will have a considerable advantage.

Data and quantitative analysts are always in need at investment banks and trading firms. However, those analysts who know how to effectively mine and analyze data, using machine learning tools or statistical programming languages like R, may have a distinct advantage over those who don't.

Although financial firms want to leverage the latest and greatest in technology, they must do so with the thorough understanding of the legal and financial risks of doing so. Businesses need compliance experts to make sure they are following all the necessary rules and regulations, while minimizing their (and their customers') exposure to financial crimes like fraud and identity theft.

Having a background in or exposure to business, accounting, finance, and economics can helpful for FinTech careers, including having an understanding of the industry and its mechanics. This is not a strict requirement, though, as FinTech firms are eager to hire those with computer science, software engineering, information security, and product management education experience (the requirements will vary by role).

Here is some additional information:

- **EFinancialCareers:** This niche job website features finance-centric jobs but offers advice to those looking to build careers in FinTech. www.efinancialcareers.com

- **Black Women Blockchain Council:** The council seeks to inspire and train Black women who are interested in blockchain and the FinTech space. The council provides mentoring opportunities, networking events, and training programs. www.bwbc.io

Healthcare

The healthcare industry includes several businesses and organizations that provide medical services to the public. This includes hospitals and medical facilities, health insurance companies, and medical equipment companies.

Jobs in the healthcare industry will be growing fast over the next few years. The Bureau of Labor Statistics estimates that jobs will grow 14 percent between now and 2028. Doctors, nurses, medical assistants, occupational therapists, and similar roles are expected to continue to be in high demand.

However, there is a growing demand for nonphysician tech professionals in this space as well. The Health Information Technology for Economic and Clinical Health Act (HITECH Act) was created in 2009, and it has incentivized healthcare organizations to adopt and meaningfully use healthcare information technology and protect patient data. Specifically, the act sought to build ways to capture health information electronically, allowing patients to electronically access their patient information and giving patients the means to manage their care—all of this with the hopes that patient care improves, there are fewer misdiagnoses, and communication improves between patients and their healthcare providers.

A result of the act and the US Department of Health and Human Services spending nearly $25.9 billion toward healthcare technology adoption is that it has helped spur the growth of healthcare-focused tech jobs. The Bureau of Labor Statistics estimates that more than 50,000 healthcare tech jobs were added since the act's inception and that the projected job growth between now and 2028 is 20 percent. Critical jobs include business analysts (to design information systems that provide meaningful use to healthcare providers), software developers, and cybersecurity specialists.

There are also emerging fields in healthcare tech, like Biomedical informatics. Biomedical informatics is an approach where data is used to advance medical research. Dr. Tiffani Bright, a biomedical informatician at a leading technology company, explains, "It's a field that focuses on how you use data, information to improve health. The essence is to improve health, improve healthcare. It's a field that truly is an intersection of people, technology, and healthcare." Dr. Bright notes that there are different flavors of bioinformatics, like clinical and public health informatics. Because of the multifaceted nature of the field, understanding data analysis, information systems, human-computer interaction, and healthcare is crucial.

Mentioned by Dr. Bright, AMIA is the professional home for 5,000+ informatics professionals across academia, government, industry and public health. As an interdisciplinary organization, members are students, clinicians, social scientists, engineers, researchers, healthcare executives and many others. AMIA helps members connect, learn, grow and lead through education, networking, professional development and leadership opportunities.

www.amia.org

Here is some additional information:

- **Healthcare Information and Management Systems Society (HIMSS):** HIMSS works to transform the health and medical industries using information technology. It is involved in several initiatives, like the Alliance for Nursing Informatics and the Health Technology Alliance, a learning center where members and non-members can access free webinars. It also hosts the annual HIMSS Global Health Conference and Exhibition.
  www.himss.org

- **American Health Informatics Management Association:** Built for healthcare information management professionals, this association helps to improve the quality of health records. It offers its members several certifications, continuing education, and events.
  www.ahima.org

- **International Association of Healthcare Security and Safety (IAHSS):** IAHSS offers introductory courses and webinars on healthcare security and has a job board for open opportunities.
  www.iahss.org

The US Government

The federal government is the largest employer in the United States. It should come as no surprise then that it is desperately seeking technical professionals. As of December 2019, there were more than 600 open full-time federal tech jobs available across the United States.

Tech jobs in the federal government can include those within the executive, legislative, and judicial branches. Rather than being funded by business revenue, federal government salaries are funded primarily by taxpayers.

The tech jobs that the federal government recruits for are diverse—there are many entry-level, general IT support jobs, all the way to chief technology officer positions. The requirements will vary—some require only a high school diploma, while others may require an advanced degree and several years of work experience.

Among the positions in demand, cybersecurity is perhaps the highest, so much so that there is a website dedicated solely to cybersecurity opportunities. The CIA, FBI, and National Security Agency have their own initiatives to bring more cybersecurity professionals into their fold. To help aid in these recruiting and training efforts, CyberCorps offers scholarships of up to $34,000 toward studying cybersecurity in school in exchange for working for the federal government for a set period after you graduate:

There are plenty of attractive reasons to consider a job in the federal government:

- **Job stability:** Most jobs in the private sector are at-will, meaning that an employer can terminate your employment with little to no advance notice. This doesn't mean you can't be terminated from a government job or placed on a furlough (a mandated leave of absence that is often unpaid) due to government shutdowns. But these happen much less often in comparison to private-sector terminations.

- **Benefits:** Federal workers are provided with comprehensive medical, dental, and vision insurance; life insurance; and long-term care insurance (a policy that helps pay for your day-to-day needs, in case you are unable to work for an extended period).

  Other benefits include retirement plans (specifically defined benefit pensions, where you are guaranteed a certain amount of money once you retire), first-time home buying programs, and student loan debt forgiveness.

- **Pay:** There's a misconception that jobs in the private sector pay more than government jobs. While the salary in private-sector jobs has often been higher, overall compensation for federal government jobs has typically been higher. A 2017 study by the Congressional Budget Office that compared private-sector jobs to their counterparts in the government noted that government workers made 17 percent more in total compensation.

- **Hours and schedule:** For most government jobs, there is a fixed schedule worked that rarely changes. In contrast, private-sector jobs, depending on the role and industry, may require you to work well beyond 40 hours (i.e., nights and weekends).

  Employees receive federal holidays off, currently 10 days throughout the calendar year and, starting out, get nearly three weeks of paid vacation time. With longer service, they can get up to five weeks of paid vacation. They are also allowed to carry over any unused vacation days—up to 30—into the next year for use.

- **Training and development:** Many government jobs provide their employees with on-the-job training resources, rotational programs, and individual career development plans.

As with everything in life, there are a few downsides:

- **Recruiting process:** It can take a long time to go through the federal government hiring process. Depending on the job you're applying to and what agency or office it falls under, it can take anywhere from weeks to months to receive a job offer. Some positions may require you to take a formal examination or go through several background checks. In 2017, it took on average 106 days to recruit and hire a new employee, or roughly 3.5 months. This is a slight improvement from the 122-day average in 2009.

  A senior official with the Federal Aviation Administration noted that having contacts in the department you're applying to helps to increase the odds of your application being referred to the hiring manager versus applying solely on your own.

- **Bureaucracy:** The federal government is huge! Because there are so many federal department agencies (the US government put the figure close to 316), processes take more time than they would in perhaps a private-sector job. Adhering to complex rules and regulations can be frustrating.

- **Pay:** Although overall compensation may be higher in the federal government, those in the private sector may be able to command more salary, or take-home pay (compensation and salary are discussed in greater detail in chapter 8, "Job Offers and Negotiating Compensation"). Most government workers' pay is governed by the Office of Personnel Management's General Schedule classification and pay system. There are 15 levels, and each level has further sublevels and rules governing when you can advance, likely based on the total length of time you've been in a position already. Exceptions can be made in the case of truly exceptional employees to increase pay earlier and beyond the predetermined amounts, but these are granted very infrequently. In a 2017 Congressional Business Office survey, it was discovered that those with master's or doctorate degrees made more total compensation in the private sector.

- **Job advancement:** Rapidly advancing in a government career can be challenging. In addition to length-of-time requirements to advance to another salary, many government jobs may require an advanced degree simply for consideration.

Here is some additional information:

- **USAJOBS:** This is the place to start to research open government tech jobs. Practical advice is also given on how to build a resume

geared toward government jobs and more about the government recruiting process.
www.usajobs.gov

- **Pathways Program:** If you are a student or recent college graduate, the US government provides special internship and full-time opportunities.
www.usajobs.gov/StudentsAndGrads

- **Office of Personnel Management:** Here you can view the current benefits offered for government workers. The site also hosts FAQs on the federal hiring process.
www.opm.gov

- **CyberCareers.gov:** Presented by the Office of Personnel Management, this website offers information on the variety of cybersecurity careers within the government.
www.opm.gov

- **CIO.gov:** Made up of chief information officers in federal agencies, the CIO Council aims to set policies and practices on the design and development of federal information technology resources. It hosts the annual (and free) Women in Federal IT and Cyber Conference, celebrating female leaders in the sector.
www.cio.gov

On Your Own: Entrepreneurism

Perhaps none of the industries or sectors described is quite what you are looking for. Instead of going down a defined career path, maybe you have an idea that you'd like to turn into a viable business. You want to exercise a certain degree of creativity and autonomy. Starting your own business may be an exciting path for you to pursue.

Victoria Scott, founder of WellPower (a start-up organization that she and her classmates at Princeton created to bring clean water to communities that lack it), recalls the difficulty that she and other students had in deciding what to do after graduation, "I was just thinking, 'I don't want to work at a bank, I don't want to work at a consulting firm . . . I just don't want to do that stuff. I want to forge my own path.' But how do I do that? And that's when I found out about entrepreneurship."

The wonderful thing about being an entrepreneur is that there are no strict requirements to becoming one. A degree is not needed, and you don't need to have an office, or much else. You can start building your business at any time. You can decide the product you want to sell, or the service you want to provide, and not have to answer to (mostly) anyone—you're the boss! As the boss, you reap the most benefit when your company is successful.

Of course, just because there are not many requirements or barriers to becoming an entrepreneur does not mean that being a *successful* entrepreneur is easy. An entrepreneur takes on many operational and financial responsibilities in running a business (or multiple businesses). Unlike being an employee at a traditional job, there are no "regular" work schedules—entrepreneurs may work late into the evening, on weekends, and on holidays, as needs arise. If you're entering a business endeavor alone or don't have the funds to hire someone to help you, expect that you will be responsible for wearing many different hats, like dealing with any accounting and marketing functions.

Speaking of financing, although there are options available for financing, such as loans or grants, many entrepreneurs must use their own earnings and savings to launch a business. Finally, you will also likely face stiff competition—you'll need to understand how to effectively market and differentiate your business from your competitors.

What It Takes to Be an Entrepreneur

Talking about all the hard work and pitfalls is not meant to deter you from becoming an entrepreneur but to help you approach the situation with a good understanding of the work involved. According to the Small Business Association in 2019, 30 percent of new businesses fail in the first two years, 50 percent fail in the first five years, and 66 percent fail in the first 10. Twenty-five percent are lucky enough to make it to year 15 and beyond. There could be many reasons a business, even ones with great products and services, could fail—not enough funding, ineffective marketing, not having a solid business plan, or just straight-up bad timing. You can consider starting a business being both an art and a science. Above all else, entrepreneurs have the following qualities:

- **Passion and resiliency:** For Scott, being a successful entrepreneur requires passion for what you're doing and resiliency. "It's so important to be passionate about whatever you are building your company around. If you're not passionate about it, you're not going to work hard for this company. This company might fail. One day, [your] company is going to be doing great, and customers are wanting to buy whatever you're selling, and the investors are really engaged and happy with your progress, and then the next day, you're going to be working 48 hours straight. That's going to be difficult to do for a company you're not interested in."

Continuing the point on resiliency, you will often be faced with tough, and perhaps fair, criticism from potential investors, partners, and customers alike. Entrepreneurs must be able to parse out the valuable information from negative feedback so that they can improve their business. Listening only to the good feedback is a recipe for disaster.

- **A strong tolerance for risk and uncertainty:** While taking the time to do proper planning and market research and having a good business plan will minimize this risk, the risk is not completely gone. Your business may not end up being profitable for some time—is this something that you can accept? If you're dealing with a potential investor, they will (rightly) expect that you have invested a significant amount of your personal funds in your business. Are you comfortable doing that? If the business fails, are you not only comfortable with the tangible losses, like of your money and your time, but the intangible ones, like the hit your pride may take?

- **A strong work ethic:** Exceptional entrepreneurs are willing to put in the time and work needed to be successful. They're out there constantly pitching their company, tweaking and refining their product, and doing so in the face of rejection and certainty. They don't view a "no" as a failure but rather as an opportunity to learn and grow. Simply put, they do not give up.

Getting Started

Before going all in in terms of time and money, there are some key steps you may want to consider taking. Depending on the size and complexity of the company that you are trying to start, additional steps and considerations (e.g., licenses, state, or federal registrations) may be needed.

Research Your Market

You may have a great idea, but is there an audience that will pay money for your idea? Who would your potential market be? Who is already operating in the market, and would they be your competitors? What is your target audience currently paying for the product/service you're planning on offering? Are there any major economic trends that are helping (or hurting) the market you're focusing on? All these questions and more are important to understand before moving forward.

By performing market research, you'll understand if your idea will satisfy a customer need that isn't already being addressed, or perhaps it will help you identify where your idea may need to be tweaked a bit. You can also see where others may have been successful and where they may have weaknesses that you can exploit.

There are plenty of firms where you can purchase market research data, but it is usually very expensive. Luckily, there are several free information resources you can tap into online to discover this information. You could also consider doing small in-person or online interviews with your intended audience to find valuable information.

Write a (Solid) Business Plan

A business plan is a formal document that outlines the mission of your business, the business's short- and long-term goals, and the methods and means in which these goals will be accomplished.

If you envision having others invest in your business or applying for loans and grants, a business plan is a requirement. Very few people or organizations will be willing to give you money without one, as they want some understanding of how you intend to make money and, subsequently, how likely they will be to get their investment back! Yet, even if that won't be the case, it is still good practice to have one, as it will help you start and operate your business more effectively.

Many different business plan templates exist, so take the time to learn which ones would be appropriate in meeting your business needs. Your plan should generally have these sections:

- Executive summary—The key points of the plan.

- Company description—Specific details on your company, like its name, location, size, date of operation (or proposed date), structure, etc.

- Products and/or services offered—A discussion of what the business will be offering, its benefits, and key differentiators from existing products and services on the market.

- Market analysis—Who the businesses target market is, its competitors, and a SWOT analysis (strengths, weaknesses, opportunities, and threats) on the business itself as well as the competition.

- Organization—How the business will be legally structured, as well as the names and short bios of people who will hold leadership positions in the company (including yourself) and any discussion on future hiring plans in any areas of the business.

- Financial plan—Outline what initial expenses are needed to get the business up and running and where initial funding has/will come from. If you envision seeking outside funding in the future, you may need to add key financial statements, like income statements, statements of cash flows, and balance sheets.

A business plan takes a lot of work, but the time and effort spent writing and refining it will reap many benefits in the long run.

Estimate Initial Costs

Take some time to research and think through what expenses you'll have to deal with to get started. Seek advice from fellow entrepreneurs as they'll have firsthand experience. Although some costs may be a little more obvious, like marketing/advertising costs, website costs, supplies, and the like, there may be others that may not be top of mind. For example, should you decide to pick a formal business structure, such as becoming incorporated, there are filing fees by state, and they can be several hundreds of dollars. If you're planning to enter a highly regulated industry, like financial services or insurance, seeking outside legal advice may necessary. If perhaps you have the business idea but don't possess the deep business or technical acumen to make your idea a reality, you may need to hire permanent talent or, at the least, hire talent on a contract or part-time basis.

You may also find that certain costs will have to be postponed until you receive more funding. For example, you may need to run your business out of your home or other no/low-cost space before committing to a formal office lease.

Determine Sources of Initial Funding

As mentioned at the start of the section, you will most likely be providing the majority (if not all) of the funding of your business. These funds can come from your job earnings and savings.

Friends and family can also be a resource for funding; they may offer you financial gifts toward your business, or they may offer more relaxed lending terms than that of a bank. They are also perhaps the fastest source of funding, as the other means mentioned can often take weeks or months to secure. If you do go this route, make sure to discuss and outline the nature of what they're giving you (is this a gift or loan?) and detail the repayment terms if necessary. The very last thing you want is to have a misunderstanding about repayment that puts you at odds with your loved ones.

Pitch competitions can also serve as another great source of funding, as well as media exposure for your business. Pitch competitions allow entrepreneurs to (very quickly) share and convince potential investors and related audiences why your business is worth the investment. Competitions are held at colleges and universities, venture capital firms, startup accelerators and incubators (businesses that provide valuable resources and mentorship to select start-ups), and one-off, start-up-oriented events. Because of the competitive nature and what is at stake—a few hundred dollars to several hundreds of thousands of dollars—the competition is fierce. Well organized and put together business plans are necessary, and you must be able to present an interesting, compelling, but brief oral presentation.

Banks and other lending institutions offer business loans. Some institutions offer loans that are backed by the Small Business Administration (SBA). This means that the SBA will guarantee a portion of the loan for the bank or institution in the event you do not pay back the loan. Having a formal business structure (e.g., being incorporated), a business plan, and financial statements are required; many banks will also want to know about your personal finances, so they may check your credit report and bank statements and want to see evidence of your personal savings.

Venture capital firms will give entrepreneurs money, in exchange for equity, or a portion of ownership in your business. They may ask for up to 50 percent ownership of your company. Getting venture capital funding can be very difficult; candidates will need to present strong business plans and show promise of strong future growth. That said, if you do receive funding, that means you may need to share or give up some authority over your business. Before accepting a funding offer, it's important to understand the venture capital firm's terms and expectations and if you are comfortable with what they are asking.

Crowdfunding sites, like IndieGoGo and Kickstarter, allow you to raise funds from the public. Depending on the platform, you may be able to take contributions outright or offer equity in your business. Also depending on the platform, you may be required to submit a business plan and financial statements.

For more help and tips to get started, you can check out these additional resources:

- **Small Business Association (SBA):** The SBA is one of the best organizations to seek free to low-cost help in starting and running your business.
  www.sba.gov

- **Women's Business Centers:** Operated by the SBA's Office of Women's Business Ownership, these learning centers provide training for women on how to start and grow their businesses. There are more than 100 across the United States.
  https://www.sba.gov/local-assistance/find/?type=Women's%20 Business%20Center&pageNumber=1

- **Digital Undivided:** Digital Undivided hosts several programs to help Black and Latinx women build successful start-ups. This includes an incubator program and a variety of networking events.
  www.digitalundivided.com

- **New Me:** A tech start-up accelerator/bootcamp, New Me offers a comprehensive program dedicated to helping businesses that are led by underrepresented groups
  www.newme.in

Keep Going or Stop?

You're putting in the work to start or continue to operate your business, and for a variety of reasons, things are not progressing as quickly as you'd like. Maybe you have fewer sales than you expected, less customer engagement, or mixed reviews. When faced with these signs or other significant challenges, you might wonder if you should just keep pressing forward or if it may be time to throw in the towel.

First, it's important to remember that it takes *a lot of time* for a company to start producing results. While there are few businesses that have launched and become overnight successes, there are thousands that take years to achieve success.

Second, it's important to define at the start what you believe success will look like for your company. I don't want to underestimate the importance of keeping the business's overall costs low while bringing in as much sales and revenue as you can. Businesses need revenue—and specifically, profit—to survive and grow. If your company has been losing money for many years, a thorough review of your strategy and operations is in order.

But it is important to identify other relevant metrics that may be promising signs to continue. Scott mentioned that if people are downloading and using your app or engaging with your social media posts, these can be great ways to gauge overall customer interest and engagement. With time, you will hopefully have accumulated enough data and customer feedback to understand where you're excelling and make tweaks where necessary.

Third, it is important to check in with yourself to see whether being an entrepreneur is still what you want. If you find your passion for your business waning or you're just incredibly exhausted, that may be a sign to take a break or wind your business operations down completely. Should you decide to stop, remember that you can always start again, whether in the existing business or in a new venture.

Summary

- Expand your "pie" of opportunities. Tech job opportunities exist in a variety of industries and domains. Explore opportunities that appeal to your interest, not just the "hot" tech companies.

- Although anyone can become an entrepreneur at any time, a lot is involved to *potentially* be a *successful* entrepreneur. While running your own business can yield many rewards, there are many risks too. Proceed with a solid plan.

Emerging Technologies

In this chapter, we'll talk about the technologies that are poised to impact the way that we work in the future—and perhaps even sooner than we think.

What Is an Emerging Technology?

An *emerging technology* is one that exists but we have yet to fully use or experience its true potential. Additional research, application, refinement, and even regulation are necessary before we can consider it an *established technology*—a technology that has been in existence for some time, is used by many, and is considered a standard by just about everyone.

Emerging technologies may also have the power to become *disruptive*, meaning they have the potential to replace an established technology or have the power to change how an entire society does things.

Let's take email as an example. Before email, documents, cards, and similar items had to be sent physically, and it took days for recipients to receive them. With email, your recipient receives your documents in seconds, reducing the time and costs involved.

Although email is now considered an established technology, it was very much an emerging technology when it was introduced into mainstream society in the mid-to-late 1990s. As email became more secure and robust to handle image and music files, people and businesses started using postal services and paper products like envelopes much less.

The Future of Work

Many research organizations and studies have pointed out that the adoption and improvement of emerging technologies will cause *structural unemployment,* or people losing their jobs because their skills have become out of date. Artificial intelligence and automation have been widely cited as technologies that will likely cause the most disruption for jobs worldwide.

There's no question that certain roles will feel this effect more than others. Roles that have routine and low-value tasks will face more phase-out than roles involving highly complex work. But tech will not replace the need for humans at every job—at least for right now. Emerging technologies will help people be even better at their existing jobs and will create many new ones, as businesses will need people who understand and can use them.

I was a contract worker at McKinsey's Digital Capability Center (DCC) in Chicago a few years ago. The goal of the DCC was to show small and midsize original equipment manufacturers (OEMs) how they could utilize emerging technologies like the Internet of Things (IoT), augmented reality, and autonomous vehicles to make their manufacturing operations safer and more efficient.

Fun fact—it was here that I earned a Class III forklift license to operate an automated vision–guided vehicle (AGV), which is a forklift that can carry supplies and maneuver around a manufacturing floor on its own using cameras and sensors. The vehicle needed little to no user guidance or intervention.

For clients, the center would simulate a fictional manufacturing floor, where workers were creating compressors by hand. Daily inventory and any production issues that came up were recorded with pencil and paper. If equipment broke down, operators would need to find paper manuals for answers. Any malfunctioning equipment would stop assembly, possibly for the entire day or several days, and require the operator to call for outside service.

The center would then quickly transform itself into a manufacturing floor outfitted with technology, where production data was automatically captured using a variety of sensors, cameras, and cloud-based applications. Using augmented reality–enabled glasses, operators could fix equipment quickly through the onscreen instructions. To ensure that workers spent more time on the assembly line versus getting materials, the AGV could be called through a smartphone or tablet application to bring the materials over, while always checking that the environment was safe to do so (for example, checking to see whether the AGV's path was clear of people).

As the center went from tech-less "current state" to tech-enabled "future state," at no point were the human operators replaced. The technologies used helped to enhance worker productivity and the quality of their output. I thought this was important to highlight—people are still needed to implement and operate the technologies being used. Rather than replace employees, companies can provide learning opportunities for them so that they are able to move into these new jobs.

You can learn more about the McKinsey Digital Capability Center at `www.mckinsey.com/business-functions/operations/how-we-help-clients/capability-center-network/overview`.

In the next few sections, I'll provide a general overview of each emerging technology area, why it's worth becoming familiar with, and places you can go to learn more information.

Artificial Intelligence

In the broadest sense of the term, *artificial intelligence* (AI) is the ability of computers or programs to think and learn like a human being would. A computer or program is considered to be employing AI if it is able to simulate how a human would think and behave in a given situation—applying logic, reason, and ethics and enacting the best way to address the situation.

While we may not have realized the full potential of AI, we are using AI now in places you probably didn't expect. Look at Table 4.1 for examples of how you've probably interacted with AI recently.

Table 4.1: Examples of AI in Common Use

SOURCE	HOW AI IS BEING USED
Ride sharing (Lyft, Uber)	Determine cost of ride, minimize wait time
Email (Gmail)	Mail filtering, spam elimination
Banking (most major US banks)	Credit decisions, fraud detection
Shopping (Amazon)	Product recommendations, fraud detection
Social media (Facebook, Twitter)	Determine which posts and articles appear in your feed

Source: *Everyday Examples of Artificial Intelligence and Machine Learning*, Emerj.com

The Difference Between Artificial Intelligence, Machine Learning, and Deep Learning

People may use the terms AI, machine learning, and deep learning as synonyms for each other. But each term has a specific definition and can be considered different subsets of one another.

At the very highest level is artificial intelligence. To illustrate this point, think about chatbots, which are programs used to simulate conversations, either through voice or text, between a human and computer. You may have commonly interacted with chatbots on shopping websites like Staples or Starbucks or over the phone on customer service telephone lines.

Humans need to program chatbots to work; they need to know the different types of users who may use their chatbot, the type of information they might want to know or tasks they'd like to complete, and how to integrate the chatbot within existing systems. They then need to develop scripts and prompts that the chatbots will use based on this information.

When a user interacts with the chatbot, they are interacting with prebuilt scripts that human programmers have developed. If the user asks a question or makes a request that is unclear or one that hasn't already been programmed, the chatbot will not respond or will return an error message. The chatbot can't make this adjustment on its own, so the programming team must step in to adjust. In simple AI, everything must be programmed by humans; the computer or program does not have the ability to learn and adapt.

Machine learning helps to address this limitation. Using the chatbot example, when the chatbot encounters a request or question that it doesn't understand, the chatbot learns from the exchange (using data and statistical algorithms) when you tell it that's not what you meant or inform it that it wasn't being helpful. When it encounters the same request or question again, it will have a better, and ideally right, answer next time. No reprogramming is necessary for this to happen—it all happens on its own with machine learning.

You can commonly see this type of AI in action in virtual assistants like Amazon's Alexa and Apple's Siri.

There are three different types of machine learning.

- **Supervised learning:** The user takes the lead in training the computer or program. The user will introduce training data to the computer program. When it's given new data, the computer or program will use the training data to make predictions.

- **Unsupervised learning:** Here, the computer or program takes a bit more of an active role in its learning. It's given data with no labeling, and on its own, it will make observations and assumptions on the data and begin organizing data in way that the program thinks a human likely would.

- **Reinforcement learning:** In this type of learning, the user rates how well (or badly) a computer or program is doing in making its predictions. A user will introduce data—if the user feels that the computer or program produced great output, the user will "reward" it. If the user feels that the output was bad, it will "punish" the computer or program by taking away its reward. The computer or program continues to learn through this process until the maximum possible reward is achieved.

Deep learning takes machine learning much further. Here, *neural networks*, or sophisticated algorithms that loosely mimic a human brain, are used to complete a task. Given the huge task that machine learning is attempting to take on, it requires a lot of data and computing power. An example would be self-driving cars, like Waymo, Google's self-driving car project.

Why Does It Matter?

AI is becoming more ingrained in our everyday lives and will not stop anytime soon. As it becomes more accessible for businesses, in terms of costs, ease of use, and implementation, they see the many ways that it can add value for them. Companies can use AI to do the following:

- Analyze and gain more insights from their data
- Make more accurate predictions
- Aid workers in performing tasks that require critical analysis
- Minimize repetitive, low-value work that humans currently do

Figure 4.1 and Figure 4.2 shows examples of AI smart assistants.

Figure 4.1: Smart speaker from LG

Figure 4.2: Japanese company Line's take on the smart speaker

Where Can I Learn More?

You can learn more from these resources:

- **AI Topics:** AI Topics is a directory of the latest research, news, and events centered around artificial intelligence. The site is maintained by the Association of the Advancement of Artificial Intelligence (AAAI), a professional organization dedicated to the advancement, as well as ethical use, of artificial intelligence.

`aitopics.org`

- **AI Trends**: AI Trends is a website devoted to applying artificial intelligence in the business world.

  `aitrends.com`

- **Google AI:** Google hosts a free site where people at all skill levels can complete courses, tutorials, and interactive exercises on AI and machine learning. It also offers a guide on what is considered ethical uses of AI.

  `ai.google/education`

Augmented, Virtual, and Mixed Reality

Augmented, virtual, and mixed reality aim to offer users interactive experiences (see Figure 4.3). The level of interactivity and immersion for each of these is different. Let's explore each one.

Figure 4.3: Having fun in a virtual world

- *Augmented reality* (AR) is where the actual environment you're in is enhanced with computer-generated objects. Your actual physical environment remains the same, but digital objects enhance that environment. Examples of this include those cool stickers you put on top your selfies and videos on Snapchat and the *Pokémon Go* app, where users attempt to capture virtual versions of their favorite Pokémon monsters in their local environments

- *Virtual reality* (VR) allows you to be completely immersed in a computer-generated, artificial environment. This environment may be a digitized version of the one you're currently in, or it could be a completely different one. Facebook's Oculus VR headsets, as well as Sony's Project Morpheus, are major examples of VR.

- *Mixed reality* (MR) is, as the name implies, a combination of both AR and VR. It is like AR in that your environment is enhanced with computer-generated objects. The difference, however, is that there is a level of interactivity possible with these objects. Think of it as an "enhanced environment" of sorts. An example would be Microsoft's HoloLens 2 and its apps HoloBlock and HoloBrush. In these applications, you can digitally paint or build simple block structures, which are overlaid on your physical environment.

Why Does It Matter?

Although AR, VR, and MR have been relegated to mostly video games and social media, they can be hugely beneficial to, many industries.

In manufacturing, AR and MR technologies can allow operators to be more efficient and produce higher-quality output, as the technology can help them in their work. When you need to make repairs, rather than trying to find a manual, AR and VR technologies can bring up the instructions in no time and physically guide an operator through the steps of repair.

VR is already actively used in flight and driving simulation. For those who are relatively new to using a vehicle, simulations allow them practice as much as they'd like before using the real thing. This helps makes the new pilots and drivers feel more comfortable, while saving on time and fuel costs.

In advertising and marketing, AR and VR give businesses an opportunity to create memorable experiences for audiences. For example, IKEA has an AR app where, using your phone's camera, customers can virtually see what a piece of IKEA furniture would look like in their home. The app allows users to place a virtualized version of IKEA furniture overlaid in your bedroom, living room, kitchen, etc. The app allows you to see what a piece of furniture would look like in your home well before going all the way out to an IKEA store, buying it, and realizing that it's all wrong for your home.

AR can even be helpful in real estate. Instead of spending time and effort to look at multiple properties, you can use a real estate agency's app to view what an apartment or house looks like. This offers a fuller experience than looking at a bunch of photos and does not require you to leave the comfort of home.

Where Can I Learn More?

You can learn more from the following resources:

- **Google Cardboard:** Using your smartphone and a cardboard viewer (which can be purchased on the Google Cardboard site for $9–$17), you can experience and experiment with AR and VR yourself in a low-cost way.
  `arvr.google.com/cardboard`

- **VR Scout:** VR Scout is a website with the latest news and events in the AR/VR world. It offers a weekly newsletter called the *Scouting Report*, which is a roundup of the most popular VR and AR news.
  `vrscout.com`

- **Enter VR:** Although much of Enter VR's articles and podcasts talk about the using VR in gaming, it devotes content to VR's application in other industries, like medicine.
  `entervr.net`

Blockchain

Blockchain is a ledger or registry, shared by two or more parties, that contains transaction information—usually when an asset has changed hands from one party to another—that is permanently stored. Once the transaction information is entered into the blockchain and time-stamped into the ledger, it cannot be altered by anyone.

Blockchain solves several problems that can come up when people and businesses are engaged in transactions. It is mostly commonly associated with financial transactions, but blockchain has a variety of use cases in different industries.

For example, if each party in a transaction is maintaining their own transaction records, whose ledger should be trusted if each one is showing different or missing information for the same transaction, especially if they're paper records? How do we know that someone didn't alter their records fraudulently or just simply forgot to enter information? Blockchain removes that uncertainty in the following ways:

- **Decentralization:** No one member of the blockchain owns or controls the network. All members of the network are considered peers.

- **Consensus:** Using very sophisticated algorithms, called *cryptographic hashes*, transactions are checked in the order they occurred, which ensures that the ledger posts the same information for all members.

- **Immutability:** Once the transaction is confirmed and posted on the ledger, it cannot be deleted or altered by anyone in the network.

- **Digital signatures:** These ensure that no one was posing as one of the network's members when the transaction posted.

Blockchain technology can help remove some of the anxiety of doing business with people who you may not know very well. Because consensus handling is automatic and no one person or organization controls the network, it gives more confidence that you can trust the records completely. As the transaction information is available to all members, there's far more transparency, and it allows people to view information at any time.

Many blockchain frameworks are currently available; some of them are *open source*, meaning they are freely available for individuals and organizations to use and alter for their purposes (see Figure 4.4). These include Hyperledger Fabric, Openchain, and Multichain. Major technology companies also offer blockchain technologies at a cost.

Blockchain should not be confused with *bitcoin*. Bitcoin is a popular *cryptocurrency* (a form of currency that is available only in digital form). Bitcoin and other popular cryptocurrencies use blockchain as the foundation of their respective platforms.

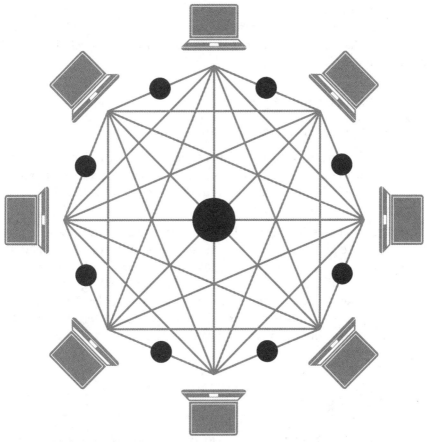

Figure 4.4: Example of a blockchain network. The dots signify each participant's equal ownership over the blockchain.

Why Does It Matter?

Blockchain can be helpful for people and businesses that need to protect high-value assets. When we say assets, this could be money or deeds/leases to physical property. Financial services companies have been very interested in blockchain technology, as it gives them a solid means to reduce fraud and their overall risks. This could lead to financial services being able to send payments faster and reduce the fees they charge to customers.

Assets can also be noncash items, like food or supplies. In the case of supply chain–based businesses, a blockchain will allow them to monitor from start to finish where their goods are and identify whether the goods they are receiving are genuine.

For all industries, especially those that have heavy regulatory requirements, having a blockchain-based system makes it easier to verify and audit records, and this reduces the overall time and costs involved with audit activities.

Where Can I Learn More?

You can learn more from the following resources:

- **Blockchain at Berkeley:** Headquartered at the University of California at Berkeley, this blockchain-focused organization offers virtual classes on blockchain fundamentals and technology. `blockchain.berkeley.edu`

- **The Hyperledger Project:** Started by the Linux Foundation in 2015, the Hyperledger Project is a collaborative project aimed at making blockchain technologies, like Hyperledger Fabric, widely adopted by business communities. Major technology companies continue to invest money and time into the project. The project's website offers free beginner online courses and tutorials on blockchain, as well as project news and developments. `hyperledger.org`

Cloud Computing

The term *cloud computing* can cause a lot of confusion. Many organizations and companies define cloud computing differently from one another, and the use of the word of *cloud* may conjure images that there is some grand computer in the sky where services are accessed. It's misleading, as there are no actual clouds, or computers peeking behind clouds, involved.

Cloud computing isn't a technology per se. Rather, it's more a business concept that utilizes several existing Internet technologies (see Figure 4.5). What makes it emerging is that it has radically changed how people and businesses consume computing resources.

For clarity, I use the National Institute of Standards and Technology's definition of cloud computing; the reason is that NIST is a US government agency that governs standards regarding measurement in several different areas, including technology. This helps compare apples to apples when talking to others about cloud computing.

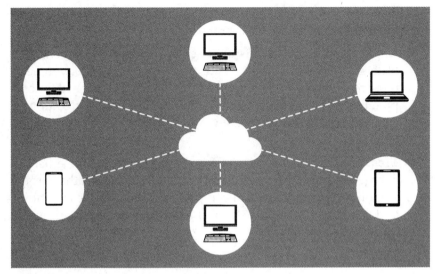

Figure 4.5: Devices accessing the cloud

The NIST definition is as follows:

> **Cloud computing is a model for enabling ubiquitous, convenient, on-demand network access to a shared pool of configurable computing resources (e.g., networks, servers, storage, applications, and services) that can be rapidly provisioned and released with minimal management effort or service provider interaction.**
>
> *The NIST Definition of Cloud Computing, Mell, et. al, September 2011*

Let's take a moment and drill down further into NIST's five key characteristics of cloud computing:

- **On-demand self-service:** When users want to use cloud services, they can provision, or create, them on their own, and they're available automatically or near instantly. Users don't need to reach out to a third party to get the service going—they start it up when they need it.

- **Broad network access:** If you have access to the Internet and a device that can connect to the Internet (e.g., a computer, smartphone, or tablet), you will be able to access the cloud service.

- **Resource pooling:** Because cloud providers have a considerable number of servers and processing resources, they are able to offer their products and services to many customers, or *tenants*, at the same time. Resources can be dynamically assigned according to the demand of their customers.

▪ **Rapid elasticity or expansion:** Users can consume as much, or as little, of a service as they need or want. If you find that you need more resources, you can add them. In contrast, if you need to completely stop or take a break, you can reduce your utilization or discontinue service completely. You can, of course, always come back at a later date.

▪ **Measured service:** Like a telephone or electricity bill, a user is charged only for the service that is actually used. All their usage is monitored, controlled, and reported. This provides visibility and transparency to both the user and the cloud service provider on costs.

Service Models

NIST takes the definition further by defining three distinct service models, or the types of services that cloud providers can offer to people and businesses: Infrastructure as a Service (IaaS), Platform as a Service (PaaS), and Software as a Service (SaaS).

A traditional IT department for a business organization is typically responsible for purchasing, maintaining, and servicing all software and hardware, as shown in the far-left column of Table 4.2.

Table 4.2: Comparison of Cloud Computing Service Models

BUSINESS	IAAS PROVIDER	PAAS PROVIDER	SAAS PROVIDER
Applications	Application	Application	Application
Data	Data	Data	Data
Operating systems	Operating systems	Operating systems	Operating systems
Servers	Servers	Servers	Servers
Storage	Storage	Storage	Storage
Networking	Networking	Networking	Networking

Shaded: Managed by the customer

Clear: Managed by the cloud provider

When a company agrees to work with an IaaS provider, they are asking the provider to give them access to their servers, storage, and network capabilities. The provider is responsible for ensuring that these resources are available just about all the time, as well as maintaining the physical equipment necessary, upgrades, and, to a certain extent, security. The compromise is that the company has little to no control over how the provider gets this done.

Going further, when a company agrees to work with a PaaS provider, the provider is giving the company IaaS services, in addition to providing a platform to create new applications or run their existing applications. This allows the company to make applications that can scale to demand and to make applications available anytime, anywhere. Upgrades for applications, as well as operating software, can happen automatically. This can be good for businesses that have apps where their demand can vary—an example would be retail store apps that have to maintain normal usage patterns throughout the year, but their demand spikes during the holiday season.

Finally, when a company uses a SaaS provider, it is using the provider's complete stack. The software is available for use on the cloud and usually isn't downloadable onto the company's computers, and the company can't change the underlying code or other aspects of the software. All software upgrades are automatically performed by the provider and do not require intervention from the company. The company pays a recurring fee, usually referred to as a *subscription fee*, on a monthly or yearly basis. SaaS is sometimes called *on-demand* software and is the most widely used cloud service model.

Table 4.3 shows examples of different examples of IaaS, PaaS, and SaaS providers.

Table 4.3: Examples of IaaS, PaaS, and SaaS Providers

IAAS PROVIDERS	PAAS PROVIDERS	SAAS PROVIDERS
Amazon Web Services	Amazon Web Services	Adobe (e.g., Adobe Photoshop)
Google Cloud	Google Cloud	Google (e.g., G Suite)
Microsoft Azure	Microsoft Azure	Microsoft (e.g., Office 365)
Rackspace	Salesforce	Salesforce.com

It should be noted that the number of cloud service offerings are increasing. For example, interest is growing in *serverless computing* because it allows users to manage servers or run applications when needed using code. This allows them to use services only when they are absolutely needed and to be charged accordingly.

Deployment Models

Adding to the complexity, there are three main deployment models, or environments in which you can access cloud services:

- **Public cloud:** Resources that are available in a public cloud can be accessed by anyone; they are not exclusive to one person or organization. Costs for services in public clouds tend to be cheaper, but quality may be negatively impacted, as you're sharing resources with a bunch of people.

- **Private cloud:** Resources in these types of clouds can be accessed and used only by a single person or organization. Availability and security are of the highest priority, but the associated costs increase considerably.

- **Hybrid cloud:** Using both public and private clouds, the resources from both are tightly integrated with one another.

Why Does It Matter?

Cloud computing has allowed people and organizations alike more control over the costs and investments that they make in computing resources. Businesses can access more computing resources than if they tried to purchase equipment and maintain that equipment on their own. This also decreases the overall amount of money they must spend on hardware, software, security, electricity, and physical space.

Businesses can create, or *spin up*, resources when there is a need for them and then either decrease resources or get rid of them depending on the current needs. This is the opposite of buying hardware and software outright; rarely can businesses return hardware and software once purchased. They may only be able to sell it at a price that is much lower than what they paid for it.

Businesses today can't afford not to be on the cloud, as the landscape has become far more competitive. Our society has become very reliant on apps for travel, food, banking, communication, etc. Because of this, we have been groomed to expect what we want or need to be available, when we want or need it. A business that wants to remain operational, let alone competitive, will need to understand how to leverage the cloud to meet the market's demands and needs.

People also consume software applications much differently. In the past, users needed to purchase a software license—anywhere from a few dollars to several hundred dollars—and were typically allowed to install the software on only one device and pay a separate fee for any upgrades. You couldn't access that program and its data from any other computer but the one you installed it on. Now, people can pay a small monthly subscription fee for a program and can use it on any device they own that has Internet access. When they no longer need the application, they can cancel the subscription at any time.

Where Can I Learn More?

You can learn more at the following resources:

- **NIST publications:** NIST offers perhaps the most comprehensive, *vendor-neutral* information on cloud computing, or information that does not show favor to any one cloud provider. NIST provides general education publications, as well as overall advice on how organizations can adopt cloud computing while minimizing risk.

  `csrc.nist.gov/Projects/Cloud-Computing/publications`

- **Major cloud service provider platforms:** Each of the major cloud providers provides education via general cloud computing overviews, tutorials, and access to free credits or trial versions to experiment with their services. For those attending school, additional free credits and extended training are available Sites like A Cloud Guru offer instruction on how to access free trials, as well online training on the major platforms.

  `acloud.guru`

- **The Cloudcast:** The Cloudcast is perhaps one of the most comprehensive podcasts currently out there on cloud computing. The podcast interviews leaders in the cloud computing space, as well as providing information on new trends and career advice. It's produced weekly and is available on Apple iTunes, Google Play, Spotify, and other platforms.

  `thecloudcast.net`

Internet of Things

The Internet of Things refers to devices, big and small, that share data with other objects or people. This data is being shared automatically and without any human or computer interaction or intervention.

A device can be any electronic device that can access the Internet. This can include the following:

- Fitness trackers
- Smart watches (Figure 4.6)
- Smart TVs and speakers
- Home appliances
- Sensors

Figure 4.6: Example of a smart watch

According to the software company SAS, there will be more than 150 billion IoT-enabled devices used in the world by 2025; they will also produce 175 zettabytes of data by that time. To put that into perspective, 1 zettabyte is equal to 1,000,000,000,000,000,000,000 bytes.

To illustrate how IoT works, we will use a fitness tracker, like a WiFi-enabled Fitbit, as an example. A user puts on the fitness tracker at the start of a workout. The tracker records certain aspects of the user's workout, as it has several sensors on it that can detect heart rate, body temperature, motion, etc.

As this data is being collected, the fitness tracker is using its internal Internet connection to transmit this data to Fitbit's servers. This connection happens instantly, without the user entering commands on the tracker to do so.

With this data, Fitbit is now able to keep a running tally of your fitness metrics and habits and make suggestions to you on how you can meet your fitness goals much faster. You can access these records and suggestions through Fitbit's app at any time. If, for some reason, the Fitbit is noticing irregular heart or health activity, it will immediately notify you that you should see a doctor right away.

Rather than using the commonly used HTTP (how we typically access web pages), IoT can use one of the following protocols to communicate:

- Messaging Queue Telemetry Transport (MQTT)
- Constrained Application Protocol (CoAP)
- Data Distribution Service (DDS)
- Advanced Messaging Queueing Protocol (AMQP)

The major reasons that these protocols are used is that they send information faster than HTTP and in a manner that is optimized for devices that have limited battery life and that may not always be connected to the Internet.

Why Does It Matter?

Many industries can reap the benefits of using IoT devices. When patients use wearable technology, like fitness trackers, medical professionals can better treat and diagnose patients because they have a more accurate record of a patient's vital records. IoT can also be used to tag medical equipment and determine where it is physically located.

Media and entertainment companies can also offer more engaging content for audiences through IoT devices by analyzing what audiences are viewing or listening to through them.

In manufacturing and utilities, companies can use sensors to predict when machines or other equipment is failing and determine whether preventative maintenance (fixing an item before it is likely to break down) is necessary.

IoT offers organizations the ability to perform their tasks in a well-organized way that minimizes wasted time and increases the likelihood of customer satisfaction.

Because there are tons of these devices collecting and transmitting data, businesses will want to take every opportunity to analyze this data. This ideally will lead businesses to be able to get actionable insights. Also, as sensor technology improves, different types of data will be detected.

For those interested in cybersecurity, IoT offers a wealth of opportunities too. Cybersecurity company Auth0 estimates that more than 20 billion IoT devices are at risk of a cyberattack, as many of these devices have vulnerabilities and don't have native security software in place. Securing these devices will become more and more important as time progresses.

Where Can I Learn More?

You can learn more here:

- **Eclipse IoT:** Eclipse IoT is an open source project that allows users to build their own IoT solutions. The site allows users to experiment in sandbox environments.
  `iot.eclipse.org`

3D Printing

3D printing, or *additive manufacturing*, is the ability to create a solid, three-dimensional object from a computer file. 3D printing can make just about anything—from jewelry to entire houses!

3D printing is referred to as *additive* because objects are built in layers. This is different from typical manufacturing methods because no materials are being cut, drilled, or ground down. No materials are being wasted, and there is very little human interaction in the process. Once the computer file is introduced to the printer, the printer will work on its own.

At a high level, a user will create the object to be printed using computer-aided design (CAD). Once complete, the user will set up the printer for use. This includes making sure that the printer materials have been carefully added to the printer. After the user sends the file to the printer, the user confirms that everything is the way they'd like, and the printer starts. Depending on the complexity of the object being printed, it can take anywhere from a few minutes to many hours. It is best to leave the printer undisturbed and away from places where printing can be interrupted. The last thing you want is all your hard work undone by someone accidently bumping into the printer.

When 3D printers first came out, the printers and materials needed to print were very expensive and too big to fit into a normal room. Now, printers can be purchased on Amazon for less than $200 (see Figure 4.7). Additionally, the number of materials that can be purchased and used has also increased—3D printers can use ceramics, plastics, and metals, among other materials, to create objects.

Figure 4.7: Examples of 3D printers

Why Does It Matter?

Rather than purchase expensive materials or wait for suppliers to provide parts, people and organizations from just about any industry can print out what they need. By being able to print their own materials, construction and manufacturing companies can save time and money on purchasing materials.

For example, the homebuilding and construction company ICON, in partnership with the San Francisco nonprofit New Story, built what could be the first livable, 3D-printed home for $10,000 and in under 24 hours in 2019. This was done in the hopes of addressing the housing issues that are prevalent in San Francisco and other parts of the world. They did this at a fraction of the time and costs it would take to build a home. The site HomeAdvisor says that the average 2,000 sq. ft. home, like the one ICON built, costs $303,488 to build and takes roughly four to five months, depending on overall complexity.

3D printing can also reduce the cost of creating prototypes. A user can quickly create and build out a product prototype, without a huge investment in materials or time. Manufacturing-based businesses have been exploring how to integrate 3D printing more and more.

Where Can I Learn More?

You can learn more at the following resources:

- **Makerbot:** Makerbot sells 3D printers to businesses and educational institutions. It also hosts the 3D Innovation Center for universities that provides training and guidance in utilizing 3D printers in different industry applications.

  makerbot.com

- **3D Printing Industry:** This site hosts a short, free beginners guide on 3D printing.

  3dprintingindustry.com

- **AM Basics:** AM Basics provides a good overview of 3D printing and its implications for industry.

  additivemanufacturing.com

- **Tinkercad:** Tinkercad is a free, easy-to-use CAD app that's available online.

  tinkercad.com

Keeping Up with Technology Trends

There is no shortage of technologies yet to be fully utilized, and that won't change. If you intend to work and stay in tech, staying on top of, or even ahead of, the technology curve is important. The last thing you want to do is invest too much time and money on a technology area that is becoming obsolete. How then can you stay informed, while not feeling completely overwhelmed?

The first thing to realize is that you don't have to be an expert in every single technology area. It's impossible to do so. The best approach is to have a general understanding of what is out there, and you can do a deeper dive into the areas that interest you or resonate with you the most.

You want to strive to be a T-shaped tech professional, having the benefit of both generalization and specialization (see Figure 4.8). This means you have a broad understanding of current and emerging technology area, as well as skills, while at the same time, you are a subject-matter expert in one or two key areas. Not only is this attractive to prospective employers, but it gives you a variety of topics you can speak to beyond just one.

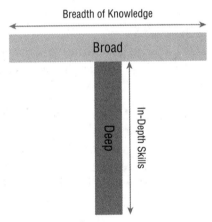

Figure 4.8: The T-shaped professional

Information Sources

Here are some information sources:

- **Your network:** Your network can be an incredible source of information on what's new and can perhaps help you sift through the hype, which there is no shortage of in tech.

- *MIT Technology Review:* Published by the Massachusetts Institute of Technology, the bimonthly magazine offers the latest information on emerging technologies. It also maintains several free newsletters, ranging in topics from AI and blockchain to space technology.

Articles on the website are free to access. A yearly issue is dedicated to the top 10 technologies they believe will have the most impact in the future.

`technologyreview.com`

- **TED Conferences:** Short for "technology, entertainment, design," TED conferences are talks on a variety of tech topics. While the conferences occur all over the world, video versions of TED Talks are available on the website for free.

`ted.com`

- **ThoughtWorks' Technology Radar:** ThoughtWorks, a global technology consulting firm, publishes a free semiyearly report that offers the company's thoughts on what technologies you should be paying more attention to and which ones may not be worth investing in.

`thoughtworks.com/radar`

- *Wired* **magazine:** Published monthly, *Wired* magazine covers emerging technologies and their effects on business and our society.

`wired.com`

- *Wall Street Journal (WSJ) Tech*: Although much of the content here is written from a business perspective, *WSJ Tech* does provide the latest in tech news and where tech investments are being made for the future. While *WSJ* requires a subscription, *WSJ Tech Weekly* is a free newsletter filled with tech news highlights.

`wsj.com/news/technology`

Tools

The following are tools to use:

- **Google Alerts:** Google Alerts is a free tool where you can tell Google to email you every time new and relevant articles, blogs, etc., are published on a search term you enter. You can set up alerts on phrases, companies, and people—just about anything. You can specify which sources you are interested in as well as how often you want to be notified.

`google.com/alerts`

- **Social media:** Using LinkedIn and Twitter specifically, you can follow certain hashtags that are of interest. The following are examples of hashtags you can subscribe to on LinkedIn:

  #artificialintelligence
  #cloudcomputing
  #blockchain
  #future
  #iot
  #innovation
  #technology

When you sign up for them, your newsfeed will start to have content on those subject areas. You can unsubscribe from them at any time. Also, on both platforms, you can follow tech leaders and companies.

Summary

- An emerging technology is one that is in existence but its full potential has not been completely realized.

- Emerging technologies can have disruptive effects to jobs and industries. However, emerging technologies can also produce new jobs and industries. We are not at a place in our society where technology will completely replace humans.

- Staying aware of technology trends will be an important part of your tech career. In addition to keeping your skills sharp, pay attention to which technologies are becoming popular.

Building Your Network

To paraphrase 2020 presidential election candidate Elizabeth Warren, no one person is successful on their own. No successful person in tech—or in any other industry—would be where they are without the love and support of their network.

A network can comprise many different people. Aside from your family and friends, your network can be your coworkers, mentors, sponsors, professors, teachers, coaches, counselors, and loved ones—essentially anyone you look to for knowledge or advice.

The Importance of Building Your Network

Your network will become increasingly important as you progress in your career. While getting high grades and marks in class is wonderful (and encouraged) and doing well at a job or internship is great, those things alone are unlikely to get you job opportunities or promotions. On the contrary, numerous surveys and studies have indicated that people have found their current jobs through networking efforts. Many jobs aren't even advertised because they are filled either through referrals or from internal applicants. Coupling this with the fact that applicant-tracking systems weed out many job applications and resumes before they even cross a recruiter's desk, the case to use networking to find your job becomes more compelling.

Your network isn't just for getting leads for jobs, though. Your network can give you concrete advice about the type of skills you should be building, what schools or academic programs are worth attending, what events may be of interest . . . the possibilities (and opportunities) are endless.

Perhaps more importantly, your network is there for you during times of success—and difficulty. The path to becoming a technical professional and advancing your career can be challenging. Being able to lean on your network during those times helps you stay positive and focused on your goals.

I remember how a mentor in my network helped me get through what was, at the time, a challenging period. I worked at a small company and was tasked to do many different functions; among them was helping with their website design. The colleague who gave me these tasks was smart but had no strong understanding of how web design worked, nor did this colleague care to.

One afternoon, my colleague asked me to update a portion of the company website with new newsletter content. I did so to the best of my ability as I'm not a website designer by trade—I had no formal training on WordPress, and everything I had learned was on the job. After looking at my work an hour later, he was not pleased with how it looked. At all. The colleague angrily called me into the office and accused me of being "lazy" and not caring about my work.

I was mad as hell. While this was not one of my favorite tasks and I already was stretched thin at this place, I always prided myself in being able to deliver high-quality work and in being professional. As he kept criticizing my work without offering specific examples to back up what he was saying, I did something I almost never do—especially to avoid being labeled as the "angry Black woman"—I yelled at him. A brief but fierce argument ensued. It got so bad that I walked out of his office as he was talking.

Immediately after, I cried. I got angry at myself for giving this person the power, in a sense, to get me worked up and angry, and over something so minor. I then started to second-guess myself that maybe I hadn't given it my best. I was about one week into my two weeks' notice of leaving this place, so maybe I had "checked out." I was a wreck.

I decided to reach out to my project management mentor and just spilled my guts out over email. I'm not sure why I reached out to her specifically—this had absolutely nothing to do with project management—and there wasn't anything she could do to remedy the situation. When I look back at this moment, I think that I just wanted to be heard and understood by someone.

I sent her an email later that night, writing about what happened in excruciating detail. I told her I felt awful, that this is not normally something that I would do, and that I didn't respond in the best way. But I was just *so freaking mad* that me yelling and storming out was a far better outcome than what could've happened. I hit Send and collapsed into bed.

Surprisingly, an hour later, my mentor sent me a reply. First, she said that she was so sorry that it happened. Second, while not the best way to handle the situation, she explained that it happens to the best of us, even people with years and years of work experience. Third, she said I should take whatever opportunities I could to learn from the experience. Lastly, she said to enjoy the weekend because I work hard and deserve some time for myself.

My problems were not resolved. I still had to see my colleague first thing Monday morning. I still had to make website updates and do a job that I didn't particularly like or want to do. Nothing changed for me. But that email calmed me and made me feel better in ways I can't describe in words. Knowing that my mentor cared enough to walk me through what at the time felt like a crisis meant the world to me.

Having a well-cultivated network helps you through tough moments. Difficult moments. Moments where there are more gray, ambiguous areas than black and white ones. Or times when you don't know what to do. While it's possible that you can make career transitions without a network, why go it alone if you don't have to?

Where to Network

Networking doesn't have to solely take place face to face. There are plenty of avenues where you can do this online. That said, you'll want to employ a mix of different networking venues and platforms.

In Person:

- If you are in school, your career services office may host networking sessions where you can meet other students and/or faculty and find out about future events. Even if your school doesn't offer networking sessions, classes, school clubs, and organizations provide a solid means for you to meet new people.

- Tech incubators and accelerators—businesses that often provide financial resources and shared workspaces to start-up technology companies—often host a variety of events that have networking sessions in their agenda. These are great events to learn more about up-and-coming businesses and learn about potential job opportunities.

- Conferences, seminars, and similar events allow you the opportunity to not only get a deep dive in a subject area, but the opportunity to meet with professionals, educators, students, representatives from tech companies, and many others. A great example of this is the annual Grace Hopper Conference (GHC) produced by AnitaB.org. GHC has been called the largest gathering of women in the computing fields.

- Meetup.com allows people to form informal groups around topics or hobbies. While there are many tech-focused Meetups, there are several, more socially minded groups that you can take part in as well. It's free to join, and you can join as many public Meetups as you'd like.

- Many professional organizations, as part of their member benefits, host networking events throughout the year. To continue to build their membership base, they will often let nonmembers attend for free or for a fee so that guests can see what they offer, meet other members, and determine whether membership is right for them.

Online:

- Social media platforms like Facebook, Twitter, and LinkedIn can be used to meet and reach out to people to potentially network with. While you can use Twitter to follow tech news and influencers, Facebook and LinkedIn groups give you more of an avenue to share your knowledge and expertise with others. You can even build your own groups that are focused on a specific topic, like cloud computing or diversity and inclusion in tech.

- Many organizations use Slack, the collaboration and messaging tool, to better communicate with others internally. But many organizations host public Slack channels that anyone can join. For example, Blacks in Technology and We Build Black host free public Slack workspaces where you can introduce yourself and meet professionals across the world.

Mentoring

In the traditional interpretation, mentoring describes a relationship between a less experienced person and a more experienced person, with the goal of sharing knowledge, expertise, and personal/professional growth for both parties, not just the mentee.

Mentoring relationships can be formal, where you could be matched with someone through a corporate-or a professional organization–backed program, with required learning and exercises, or it can be informal, where mentor and mentee meet and discuss issues as needed. Whatever form mentoring takes, it can be one of many resources you can use to build your skills and to broaden your professional network.

Where to Find Mentors

Schools, professional organizations, and others host formal mentoring programs. In these programs, a mentee (usually someone who is new to a career field or is looking to acquire certain skills) is paired with an experienced professional who can offer guidance and feedback. Formal mentoring programs can last a few weeks to a few months and often have a prescribed curriculum/agenda, several required touchpoints between mentor and mentee, and a measurable goal for the mentee to achieve.

You can also just reach out to mentors through informal means via your school, your job, your community—just about anywhere. I gave a talk on mentoring (mentioned in more detail in Chapter 7, "Demonstrating Your Skills"), and a few minutes after speaking, one of the audience members came up and just asked me if I would serve as a mentor, to which I'm glad I said yes because she's an awesome mentee. If there's someone you admire because of their skill set and leadership ability, don't be afraid to ask them if they could serve as a mentor to you.

Blueprints for a Beneficial Mentoring Relationship

Mentoring requires a tremendous amount of effort and energy, from both the mentor and the mentee. When considering entering a mentoring relationship with someone, whether formal or informal, you spend some time reflecting on where you are, where you'd like to be, and whether you can commit to a mentoring relationship at this time.

Also consider whether your potential mentor has the ability, time, attitude, and skills to effectively mentor you. Someone who may be experiencing significant life changes or a high amount of work demands may want to help you but may not have the availability that you want or need.

Here are some questions you should ask as a potential mentee:

- *Why do you believe that you need a mentor now?* What are you hoping to gain out of this relationship? Can your needs be addressed by other means, like courses or other types of opportunities?

- *Do you have the time to devote to this relationship?* The answer to this question will have great importance for a formal mentoring relationship, where you may be asked to create agendas, participate on regularly scheduled calls, and, perhaps, write reports or give presentations. With your current school or work obligations in mind, would this be something that you'll be able to do on top of everything else?

- *Are you self-motivated?* Mentors can't do the work for you in terms of completing tasks or following up on specific items. They shouldn't be expected to either. As mentioned, this is your career journey, and the responsibility of getting things done and pushing through challenges is ultimately yours.

- *Are you willing to be challenged?* Mentors want to see their mentees succeed and grow. This means that sometimes they will need give you critical feedback. And sometimes that feedback may sting or not what you want to hear. Whether the mentor is skilled at giving feedback is another matter—the question becomes, can you accept the feedback as it is, learn from it, and move forward?

- *Can you respect your mentor's time and resources?* Mentors willingly and gladly give their time and resources to be in service to others, but that doesn't mean that they have an infinite supply of time and resources. They are often mentoring on top of their professional work and personal obligations. Being on time to agreed-upon meetings, as well being an engaged mentee, will go a long way in building a solid relationship.

- *How do you prefer to communicate?* Do you prefer face-to-face communication, or are you fine using tools such as video conferencing, email, or online chat? Would you prefer more constant communication (once a week), or would occasional contact (once a month) work better? Understanding your preferred methods and frequency of communication and knowing your mentor's preferences will increase the likelihood of successful outcomes.

When looking for potential mentors, consider the following:

- *Why do they enjoy mentoring, or why are they interested in mentoring?* Understanding their motivations in wanting to mentor isn't necessary to know, but it can give insight into who they are and what they value.

- *Are they available and committed?* While there are things that happen in our personal and professional lives that are beyond our control, the last thing you want is someone who cancels agreed-upon meetings often or is distracted or not paying attention when they are in your presence. A good mentor must be both available to help you and committed to giving you their attention.

- *Can they offer constructive feedback?* As mentioned, mentors will sometimes give you feedback that may be hard to hear. However, feedback should never be given in a harmful or embarrassing way.

- *Do they hold you accountable?* You don't want a mentor that tells you that everything you do is great all the time. One of the central themes of mentoring is growth, and in order to grow, feedback on areas of improvement is necessary. Only hearing positive feedback can be just as detrimental to your growth as (if not worse than) unnecessarily harsh feedback.

- *Can you trust them?* You may find that as your relationship with your mentor grows, you may begin to share very sensitive and personal information with them. You want to feel that you are in a safe space and that private information will stay private.

- *Are they forgiving?* You may end up running late for a meeting or find that you may not be as prepared for your meeting as you should be. While a good mentor will not let you completely off the hook (they'll call you out on it), they will also recognize that you're human and that things happen.

- *Does this person have authority over you?* This can be tricky. While there isn't anything wrong in having a mentor that is either a supervisor at your job or a current professor, you'll want to exercise some extra care. Because this person has some influence or position of authority in your career path, you may "edit" what you say much more or just avoid saying things altogether, which you might not do if this person had no authority over you.

Additionally, there is the potential that the mentor in this situation may try to take advantage of you. Proceed carefully.

You've Found a Mentor—Now What?

By this point, you may have formally agreed to a mentoring relationship with one (or more) people. To begin to build a great relationship with them, it is important that you both get to know each other and lay the foundation for the work you'll do together.

- *Have a low-pressure "meet and greet," if possible.* This meeting should ideally happen before any actual "mentoring" happens. This is especially important for mentoring relationships where the contact will be sporadic or the mentoring is occurring long-distance.

- *Thank your mentor for their time, as often as you can.* Most mentors have very busy and full schedules—they mentor on top of all of their other obligations. Saying thank you is deeply appreciated and makes mentors feel valued and appreciated.

  One of my career mentors, Joanna Vahlsing, senior vice president at digital marketing services firm Centro, says the best way to say "thank you" to a mentor is to stay committed to learning and growing as a professional—"That's the best gift that you can give." If you do feel like getting them a tangible gift, it doesn't need to be a lavish gift. Rather, make it personal. If you know that there's something that they like, like coffee or books, a small denomination on a gift card will work.

- *Provide feedback.* It is perfectly okay and encouraged to share constructive but fair feedback with your mentor. This can help you make adjustments or ultimately decide that another mentor may better suit your needs.

  For example, if your mentor has been for the most part helpful but their feedback isn't so great, you can approach them like this:

  "Mary Jane, I appreciate your feedback as my mentor. Sometimes though, your feedback can be harsh. In our last conversation, when I asked you what [term X] meant since I didn't know it, you commented that I should know that and I wasn't trying hard enough in my studies. I felt hurt because I assure you I'm trying my best and I genuinely wanted your guidance."

  Once your mentor is made aware of their behavior, they can take corrective actions to ensure that they don't do it in the future.

Listen, This Isn't Working Out

Sometimes mentoring relationships get off to a great start, and the potential for a strong, lifelong relationship is possible. You have great chemistry, you understand each other's communication styles, and you respect each other. That's great!

Sometimes, however, some mentoring relationships are not meant to be. Your personalities conflict, you don't like their feedback style, they're unavailable, etc. Sometimes, you may outgrow the relationship, meaning that you did get valuable insights and experiences when your relationship started, but now that's no longer true. All of this is okay and normal.

Before ending a mentoring relationship, examine your reasoning for doing so. I believe that people think that mentors should be their friends first and have an instant rapport or chemistry. While I think that it's great if a mentor is a friend, a mentor isn't necessarily supposed to be your friend. Above all else, a mentor's primary concern should be helping you to grow and get better, even at the risk of not being considered a friend by the mentee.

When choosing to end a mentoring relationship, lean more on objective criteria (facts) versus subjective (emotions). If the relationship is truly not helping with your skill growth or the mentor doesn't possess the skills necessary to be successful, like being respectful to you, then ending the relationship may be a good move. If it's because the mentor isn't outgoing, you may want to examine this further.

Whether in a formal or informal program, here are some tips to approach ending the relationship:

- *Be direct, be honest, and be respectful.* You don't need a long, detailed explanation. Just explain that you're ending the relationship and the reason why. If your career situation or goals have changed or you just do not feel like the current relationship is fulfilling your needs as a mentee, say so. What you do not want to do is say things like "because you suck as a mentor." Whether the relationship was a good fit or not does not excuse you from being professional when dealing with them.

- *Thank them for their time.* Again, even though it may not have been a perfect fit or the relationship may not have remained beneficial, this person did take time from their schedule to attempt to help you.

- *Reflect positively on the experience.* Try to remember any positive outcomes that came from your time together.

You Need a Sponsor, Not a Mentor

Finding a great mentor is hard. Many of the women I interviewed for this book stated that they had few to no mentors when entering their chosen profession. Being able to find a mentor, let alone a great one, can be difficult.

For some women, while they have a mentor or no shortage of mentors around them, they feel like they are "stuck." They are not making the career progression they'd like to be making, or they are having difficulty being recognized for their skills and contributions. Mentors can be helpful in giving advice to fix this, but in these instances, a sponsor may be needed.

I consider sponsorship and mentorship as two very different things. A mentor can provide advice and general guidance. A *sponsor* can provide those things as well but can be seen more as your career champion. Sponsors publicly advocate on your behalf in and outside of the organization. They also have the authority to either create opportunities for you or heavily influence others to consider you for projects and opportunities.

Another key difference between mentors and sponsors is the amount of reputational risk they take on when advocating for you. A mentor may point you in the direction of where to find opportunities, but when a sponsor advocates for you, they are staking their reputation on the belief that you will excel in a specific opportunity. If you end up not performing to expectations, the sponsor's reputation may be at risk.

I believe you need both in order to make progress in your career. The question is when the right time is to ask for a sponsor. According to Catt Small, senior product designer for Etsy, the best time for sponsorship is when you have a specific goal in mind. "My goal, when I met this person who sponsored me, was that I wanted to do public speaking. I knew that I wanted to get on stage, and I knew that was my very specific goal. If you know what you want to do, you've given it a shot, and you're not 100 percent sure of what the right route is, it may be worth reaching out to some people who may get you closer to that goal or point out opportunities where they can actually exercise their skills."

I also recommend it in times where you feel a bit "over-mentored," meaning you have been receiving (and following) great advice from many people, but for all of your efforts and patience, you are not getting hired or promoted.

You also want to be sure to build a strong relationship with a sponsor before asking them to advocate for you. Demonstrating to your sponsor what you are capable of makes it easier, and likelier, that they will take on the risk of recommending you.

Overcoming Social Anxiety

While networking certainly offers several amazing benefits, this is not to say that it comes easy to those of us who have social anxiety! Social anxiety is the fear of any type of interaction with other people. People who have social anxiety are concerned—or downright worried—that they will be looked upon negatively by other people. Many people struggle with this over the course of their lives.

This should not be confused with social anxiety disorder. The distinction between the two can be hard to pinpoint, but people with social anxiety disorder tend to experience severe physical symptoms that keep them from living a normal life.

It's completely normal to feel anxiety during networking events. But remember the following:

- *You're not the only one feeling this way.* Yes, there are many people who say that networking energizes them, and they feel confident. But there are just as many people who worry about looking foolish or dumb. It's okay to have these feelings. But . . .

- *You have plenty to offer to the conversation.* Don't take the feeling you are feeling as "the truth." Meaning, you can and should acknowledge the anxiety, but don't believe the negative thoughts. You are smart, and you bring a lot to the table in terms of skills and life experiences. Anyone in the room would be lucky to get to know you.

As someone who struggles with social anxiety often, I know it can be hard to turn the negative thoughts off and to use the anxiety as a reason not to attend or participate in networking events. But your career is too important to leave it to chance or to hope that someone will notice how awesome and talented you are on your skills alone. It's a competitive job market, and any way that you can help your efforts will make life easier.

Here are some strategies that may be helpful:

- *Put your phone on silent and put it away.* You can't engage in meaningful dialogue with people if you are staring into your phone. It can also be a crutch that prevents you from interacting with people. Put your phone on Do Not Disturb, turn it off, and do whatever you need to do to keep your phone time to an absolute minimum during the event.

- *Bring a friend.* You don't have to do this alone. Ask a friend or two to accompany you so that you won't be by yourself. You can chat with them during low points of the event, but don't stay with them all night. Make sure to move around the space where the event is being held and talk with others.

- *Bring several friends.* There's strength in numbers! With a group of friends, you can strategize where one or two of you can go out in pairs to network and then return to your "hub" to report on your interactions. You may get a better sense of who you may want to talk to and who you may want to try to avoid.

- *Let your partner do most of the talking.* If you are at a loss for what to say, ask other people open-ended questions. You can ask things like, "How are you enjoying this event so far?" or "What projects are you working on now?" You don't want to hammer them with questions all evening, but you'll get to learn more about the person you're talking with and ideally engage in a deeper-level discussion.

- *Don't feel like you must talk about tech, work, or school.* You can talk about movies, television, major cultural events—it's completely up to you. Plus, if you're at an all-day event focused on one topic area, you may want to talk about an entirely different topic later in the day.

- *Make a networking goal.* If you're someone who gets physically drained from constant networking, it may be best to set goals and pace yourself during the event. For example, at the start of the event, you could decide that you will meet one or two people. After that, you are free to do as you please for the remainder of the event.

- *Talk to everyone, regardless of title or position.* Talk to people who truly interest you—you share common interests or hobbies or work in similar professions and can relate to each other. Don't focus on only talking to recruiters, managers, or C-level employees, as you may miss out on meeting great people.

I met one of my dearest friends through a student recruiting/mixer event for a Chicago tech company a few years ago. She was also a student, but at Loyola University, and I was incredibly impressed with her skills and experience that I referred her for a position at my company at the time. Heck, she did my job better than I did. But our friendship has transcended employers, life events, and more. I couldn't tell you anything about the company, who worked at the company, or what exactly they were recruiting for, but I know that I'm thankful that I went and met her.

▪ *Know when to, politely, walk away.* You end up engaging with someone, and it's clear that this isn't someone that you want to keep talking to. You don't want to be rude, but at the same time, there are others for you to meet. In those instances, politely (and honestly) excuse yourself. You don't have to make up a wild excuse about a sick relative or work emergency. If you are attending a networking event, then there should be no hard feelings when you indicate that you'd like to mingle with a few other people.

▪ *Avoid or limit alcohol.* While alcohol is regarded as a "social lubricant" that makes people calmer and "more fun to be around," nothing could be further from the truth. Alcohol tends to break down people's inhibitions, but to the point where they are engaging in reckless or unprofessional behavior. If you're underage, don't drink, and if you are of age, enjoy it responsibly. The last thing that you want to do is leave a bad impression with potential future colleagues and employers.

Strengthening Your Connections

You've been going to events and conferences, joined some online groups, and are making connections online and off. That's fantastic! So, how do you keep the momentum going with your newfound connections?

The first thing is to follow up after your initial contact. Your follow-up should not be an "ask" like, "Can you refer me to a job in your organization?" or "Can you write a letter of recommendation on my behalf?" It gives your newfound contact the impression that you view theirs as a purely transactional relationship or a relationship that you feel is only worth having if you get something out of it.

Rather, adopt a giving mind-set, and think about what you can offer to your new connection. Think that you don't have anything to offer? Trust me, you have plenty of things to offer, including (and not limited to) the following:

▪ Congratulating them on a major accomplishment or life milestone (getting married or having a baby)

- Recommending a book, website, article, or other resource that you think they'd find useful

- Introducing them to other people who you'd think they'd like to talk to

- Inviting them to an event they may be interested in going to

- Helping with a project they are working on or problem they are having

There's no limit to what you can offer, and not all offers need to be monetary in nature. Knowledge is a powerful currency, and those who can help people connect with others or resources are highly valued.

Summary

- Creating and cultivating a good network is not only great for helping for future job opportunities, but it makes the difficulties of the job (and life!) much easier to withstand.

- Conferences, events, professional organizations, school, and LinkedIn are just a few of many great places to meet new people and grow your network.

- It's okay to be anxious about networking! Just don't let it get in the way of you meeting great people.

- Mentoring can be beneficial to mentors and mentees alike, if both are willing to put in the time and effort a mentoring relationship requires.

- Mentoring can be great for general career guidance and advice, but a sponsor may be necessary to advocate for you and advance your career.

- Adopt a give versus take mind-set when developing your relationship with your new network connections. You have more to give than you know.

Building Your Skills

In the previous chapter, I discussed potential career paths. In this chapter, I'll talk about assessing your current skill set, the different methods and means you can take to get the skills you need, and the different ways you can subsidize your educational and professional pursuits.

Skills Gap Analysis: Where Do You Need to Be?

Now that you have a better understanding of the types of skills needed for each field, it would be a good idea to do a thorough skills gap analysis so that you can create a plan.

Just as it sounds, a skills gap exists when there is a difference between what skills a company or organization advertises as needed for a position and your skill level. For example, if your knowledge of the programming language Python is basic or limited and the job requires a proficiency in Python, then a skills gap exists.

You can do your own skills gap analysis by comparing your skills to the current job market. Look for two or three descriptions for jobs that you are considering. As you're reviewing, make note of the *soft* and *hard* skill examples.

Soft skills are the skills that are tied to the communication, interpersonal, and professional skills you possess. Soft skills aren't quantifiable, meaning they can't be measured in numbers, and someone's proficiency in a soft skill is subjective, meaning it's influenced by someone's feelings, opinions, and biases. Because of this, they are not easy to prove. Examples of soft skills include the following:

- Time management
- Problem solving/creativity
- Ability to work as part of a team
- Ability to adapt to any situation presented
- Ability to lead others

Hard skills can be acquired through formal and informal education and can be measured in some way. Examples of hard skills include the following:

- Programming ability
- Mathematical skill
- Data analysis
- Foreign language skills (knowing multiple languages)

Using the job description of a technical support specialist as an example, these are their soft skill requirements:

- Customer service
- Oral and written communication
- Time management

These are the hard skill requirements for the job:

- Proficiency in Microsoft Office software (Word, Excel, etc.)
- Experience writing and updating SQL scripts
- Experience with issue-tracking software

After identifying these skills, you'll next want to look at your past and current experience. A resume is helpful for this, and we'll take about resume creation in the next chapter, but it is not a requirement. You'll want to think about *all* your experiences—whether paid, academic, or volunteer—and think about the work you've performed. If you can connect your work to the skill, then you have met that skill requirement. If you've been using Word and Excel consistently throughout your academic and work projects, then you are likely very proficient.

If you haven't demonstrated a skill through current or past experiences, then this an area you may want to spend time developing. For example, if you are unfamiliar with SQL, then you may want to take a course to learn the basics.

There are, however, exceptions to keep in mind.

Exception 1

You may not be able to address all skills gaps directly or immediately. Our sample job description asks for experience with issue-tracking software, such as JIRA and Zendesk. Although some software companies allow you to try trial versions on your own, you may only get access and hands-on experience on the job.

Exception 2

Even if you don't believe you possess every requirement, I strongly encourage you to apply for a job if you possess most of them. Per a 2019 study from LinkedIn, women feel that they need to meet every requirement of a job before they apply, while men will apply even if they have only a third of the requirements. Let the employer decide if you're a good fit or not. You will never know until you apply, and the worst thing that an employer can do is say no.

Formal Education (Is It Worth It?)

Formal education is defined as structured instruction you receive in a classroom and from a professionally trained educator (like at a high school or college). Though not always, students receive a certificate or degree at the successful completion of a program of study.

Many companies, both in and out of tech, realize that having a college or university degree is not an indicator that a person will be successful in the role. Many employers complain that college graduates do not have the practical skills needed for the roles they are hiring for—since new hires need more training upon hire, employers may be reluctant to spend the time and money on them. Some employers place more value on any hands-on, professional experience over classroom learning.

However, you'll find that many of the professions I discussed in Chapter 2, "The Different Flavors of Tech Careers," require, at a minimum, a four-year undergraduate degree. For those that don't, the positions typically have limited earning potential and advancement opportunities.

So, why the disconnect? If we say that we value actual experience over classroom learning, why is the degree still a requirement? I can't speak for employers, but it was something that I remember hearing in a lecture at Northwestern University that still resonated with me, and perhaps may resonate with employers as well: trade schools teach you a specific skill, whereas college teaches you how to critically think. By this, the lecturer didn't mean that trade schools are not challenging—they are. But trade schools tend to challenge you in one subject area or domain, while college is challenging due to the variety and types of courses you would be taking. Because of the nature of most American undergraduate programs, you may be expected to take several courses in writing, communications, history, mathematics, and sciences in addition to coursework for your major.

I can see both sides of this argument. At Northwestern, I took just as many courses in business and communications as I did in Java programming, computer networking, and systems design. Those courses were just as challenging—sometimes more so—than my technology-oriented classes. Writing and giving my final graded "crisis speech" (a speech where you are asked to respond to a fictional yet catastrophic event) for my public-speaking course was just as nerve-wracking as writing and compiling my Java-based budget calculator app.

At the same time, while I did have foundational knowledge of how computer hardware and software work and how they communicate with one another, and many of my instructors had worked previously in the tech industry, my knowledge was mostly limited to the classroom and my textbooks. I had no working experience of what occurs at an enterprise level.

I knew that I preferred the formal education route. Although there are many self-paced, online learning resources, having a knowledgeable, experienced, and live instructor was helpful when I had questions. I also enjoyed the opportunity to network with students from all over the school. The biggest factor for me was career advancement opportunities. The career services office was a great resource for me to attend networking events, practice my interviewing skills, and have access to unique career opportunities that I may not have found in my own job-searching efforts.

Ultimately, whether formal education is worth it is up to you. When considering this route, here are some things you'll want to think about:

- Would you be able to take a few courses to fill in the skills gaps, or is it necessary to commit to a full program?

- Would you be able to commit to a program that is two to four years or potentially longer?

- Would you be willing to take challenging courses that may not have a direct connection with your primary course of study?

- Would you prefer to take courses that have more emphasis on technical skill?

- Costs—while colleges and universities provide the most financial aid opportunities, including federal and state grants that don't need to be repaid, you may still need to take on (significant) debt to afford the cost. Would this debt responsibility be something that you are willing to take on?

Trade Schools

Trade, or vocational, schools teach students skills that they will need to enter specific career fields. The key differences between trade school and other formal education institutions are that the length of time to complete study is shorter (usually two years or less), and you take fewer classes in other subjects.

There's a negative perception surrounding certain nationally accredited, for-profit vocational schools. Credits earned usually can't be transferred to other institutions. If you decided that you wanted to get an undergraduate degree from a traditional four-year college, the credits earned would not transfer over, meaning you'd have to complete the program from the beginning. The quality of curriculum of these schools, as well as the costs (sometimes higher than traditional college), have also come under fire.

Take the ITT Technical Institutes, which went completely out of operation in late 2016. ITT Technical Institutes were for-profit educational institutions across the United States that offered students technology-based undergraduate and graduate degrees. They charged high tuition rates to their students (most of whom were lower income and nontraditional college age), who in turn incurred a massive amount of student loan debt.

ITT's programs of study, as well as their recruiting and administrative practices, did not undergo as much review or scrutiny as other, traditional colleges and universities. The lack of oversight gave many employers and others pause, making it difficult for ITT graduates to secure employment after graduation. In written, collected testimony from 700,000 New York area ITT graduates and former students from 2003 to 2017, many stated that their education was deemed "worthless" by employers. Many reported not being able to find entry-level employment and that just the mention of ITT on their resume meant automatic rejection.

Because of ITT's lack of regional accreditation, credits earned at ITT schools would not be accepted at other colleges. This meant that even if ITT students wanted to transfer to a new school, they would have to start their degree studies from the beginning, and with all of the debt they accumulated from their previous school.

There are excellent trade schools out there that offer quality curriculums, are cost conscious, and assist with placement with jobs after graduation. If you're considering one, here are some things to look out for:

- Accreditation—In the accreditation process, a school or institution voluntarily demonstrates to a neutral third-party organization that their academic programs meet certain standards. An institution can be regionally or nationally accredited, and more weight is given to regionally accredited institutions, as they tend to have more stringent standards. Whether regional or national, you'll want to make sure that the school has gone through some impartial review process.

- Job placement—Exercise caution with any institution that guarantees a job for you upon completion of a program. No institution, no matter how prestigious, should promise you that you will have a job once you're finished. Whether you're able to secure a job afterward is dependent on several factors, many of which are beyond your (and the school's) control.

- Costs and financial aid—Give close attention to the tuition and fees that a school charges. If they seem higher than what an equivalent program at a community college charges, you may want to investigate why. Also, if the admissions department heavily pressures you to take out federal, state, or private loans to attend classes, run away. This indicates that there's no regard for your overall financial situation and that they are not concerned about you acquiring massive amounts of debt.

- Student complaints—I'm a firm believer of "where there's smoke, there's fire." If many former students complain that a program was too expensive or they're unable to secure well-paying work in their field after a reasonable amount of time and effort, then something is off. You can check with your local attorney general's office to see if there are any complaints against the institution.

Massive Online Open Courses

Massive online open courses (MOOCs) have made it easier for anyone to pursue an education, any time, anywhere, and (sometimes) at a fraction of the cost of going to a brick and mortar school. Two of the most popular MOOC platforms, Coursera and edX, boast more than 50 million registered users and may have a course that has more than five hundred thousand registered users alone.

MOOCs allow learners to pursue a course of program of study mostly at their own pace. Students can view lectures and submit assignments when their schedules permit. If you have access to a computer and a good Internet connection, you can access a MOOC course at any time. While most MOOCs are delivered through individual, private contributors, some courses or programs of study on the platforms may be sponsored or developed by colleges, universities, and employers. Some courses can be used for college credit or toward a professional certification.

While MOOCs offer many benefits (increased accessibility to higher learning, flexibility, and affordability to name a few), there are some drawbacks. The primary one is that anyone who participates in a MOOC must be disciplined in completing their work. It can be argued that this is an issue with traditional degree programs, but MOOCs specifically have a low completion rate. Per a 2015 study done by University of Cambridge researcher Dr. Katy Jordan, the average completion for a MOOC is somewhere between 5 percent to 15 percent. There is still a reluctance on the part of some academic institutions, employers, and other organizations to accept MOOCs as a viable learning option, although this is gradually changing.

MOOCs can be a great alternative to costly classes and when your schedule just doesn't permit you to travel to and from a physical location. You'll want to consider MOOC platforms that have established track records, have made partnerships with academic institutions and employer organizations, and offer refund options should your schedule change and attending class won't fit into your schedule. You can sign-up for classes now at Coursera and edX at the links below.

www.coursera.org

www.edX.org

Boot Camps

Boot camps are training programs that focus on teaching important skills in a short duration of time. They focus on technical skills that the boot camp organizers believe are relevant and will allow students to make an immediate impact with employers upon hire. These boot camps can last anywhere from three to 15 months and can be completed full- or part-time, in person or online.

While the majority of boot camps available focus on learning one or several programming languages, there are boot camps devoted to learning data science, user experience design, and artificial intelligence, for example.

Boot camps are typically run by private organizations, although some colleges and universities are creating boot camps as well. Instructors are typically professionals who are currently working in the industry. Many boot camps offer job placement services; some even have deferred tuition where you don't have to make payments until you've secured a job.

When evaluating potential boot camps, pay attention to the following:

- Your overall career goals— If you are not intending to become, say, a full-fledged professional software developer, you may want to skip boot camps altogether. You may be able to gain programming knowledge and experience through free online courses, self-study, and practice.

- Admissions—Some boot camps require testing and an admissions interview before they accept you. While this can be time-consuming, this will help both you and the school determine whether this will be a mutually beneficial fit. Are the classes geared toward your goals? If you're attending in person, are the classes offered at convenient times and locations for you? Do the teaching methods work for your learning style? These (and more) are important questions to ask.

- Time—For full-time boot camp programs, it is important for you to attend all or most of your sessions. Missing one can be detrimental, as boot camps cover a lot of material in a short period of time.

- Program of study—Be sure that the curriculum is teaching you the latest technologies and languages for enterprise software, not the ones that are falling out of favor or obsolete. For a coding boot camp, learning Java, JavaScript, and Python may serve you better than learning COBOL. TIOBE, an organization that rates software code quality, maintains a Programming Community Index, which measures monthly the popularity of programming languages in the world. You can check it out at `https://www.tiobe.com/tiobe-index`.

- Costs—Like the other forms of education mentioned, boot camps also cost money. Because these are privately run, they are usually not eligible for federal or state aid. While some boot camps do offer scholarships or reduced or free tuition to groups that are underrepresented in tech, this is not true for all.

Hackathons

Hackathons are an excellent way to build your skills and your network. Hackathons are short, competitive events (anywhere from a few hours to two or three days) where individuals and teams collaborate to develop a solution to a problem presented by the organizers. Hackathon organizers can be a mix of tech companies, schools, and other organizations.

As hackathons tend to focus on coding challenges, like creating an application to benefit a local community, software developers and designers tend to participate in these events. However, there are many noncoding hackathons as well, where the focus is on solving a specific business challenge.

There are prizes associated with winning a hackathon, anywhere from cash to receiving a full-time job offer at the organizer's company. There may be a small fee to participate, and that is usually to cover event space, marketing, and food fees.

Unless stipulated by the organizers directly, registration is open to anyone who is interested, and you don't need to be a professional developer to participate. In fact, if you are new to programming, you will probably learn more at a hackathon because you'll be working with and learning from others with more experience.

You can find upcoming hackathon events at the following sites:

- Hackalist (`hackalist.org`)
- Hackevents (`hackevents.co`)
- DevPost (`devpost.com`)

Conferences and Seminars

There is no shortage of conferences and seminars that you can attend. There are literally hundreds held in the United States every year, and that number will continue to grow.

Conferences and seminars are not meant to turn you into technical subject-matter experts by the time they end. Rather, they're designed to introduce you to new subjects, entice your interests to do further research and investigation when they're over, and help you connect with professionals within the field. Some conferences also allow for opportunities to interview with potential employers.

Conferences and seminars cost money to attend. Although many events give discounts or scholarships to students and other audiences, the cost alone can be a major barrier in attending. This is especially true if the event is being held in a different city or state than the one you live in; travel, hotel, and meal costs must also be considered. If you are working or have caretaking responsibilities, taking any time off can be difficult.

A few years ago, I was invited to attend a multiday conference for young leaders in engineering and technology for IEEE USA. The conference was held in New Orleans, Louisiana (in the middle of summer, no less!). The organization agreed to reimburse me for some of the costs, like registration and meals, but other costs, like transportation and hotel, were out-of-pocket costs. I ended up paying somewhere between $600 and $700. Although I found the conference worth my time and part of my costs were reimbursed, it still required an initial outlay of money at a time when I was also juggling tuition payments and other financial obligations.

Given the time and money commitment, consider the following first:

- Attend free or low-cost local events—Sometimes the best events are in your own backyard. You can do a general search on Eventbrite to find local tech events or subscribe to city-specific tech event newsletters like *Gary's Guide* for New York events (garysguide .com) or *Chicago Tech Events* (chicagotechevents.com).

- Utilize student, professional organization, and other discounts available to you—The discount offered may or may not be significant, but you will still spend less money in the end. Event organizers may have certain requirements, like being enrolled in school full-time versus part-time, and may ask for proof. But be sure to use applicable discounts whenever possible.

■ Review the events agenda—An event agenda can give you a better understanding of the topics that will be discussed and what type of audiences the topic is geared toward (e.g., introductory, intermediate, expert). You can assess if you're interested in the topic.

■ Have your attendance sponsored—Your school, work, or other organizations may be willing to pay for event registration, travel, and meal expenses. You may need to provide documentation, essays, and other materials to justify the expense, but it would be worth the effort if it's a conference you really want to attend. Also, be on the lookout for any event-specific scholarship opportunities that the organizers may be offering.

Internships, Externships, and Co-ops

Internships, externships, and co-ops are great ways to get professional experience. These terms are often used interchangeably, but let's examine the key differences:

■ Internships—An internship is a professional learning experience within a fixed time frame, usually four to 12 weeks and coinciding with a school's academic period (e.g., fall, spring, or summer). They may be full- or part-time, and being enrolled in a degree-granting, academic program isn't a hard requirement (although this varies by employer). Interns engage in practical, low-level work in exchange for either pay or academic credit, and based on good performance, an intern could be considered for a full-time position at the organization.

■ Externships—An externship is a learning experience that occurs in a short time frame, usually a day to 12 weeks. Externships can be full- or part-time. Externs observe and shadow people in positions that they are interested in versus performing professional, low-level work. Externships are typically unpaid, do not receive academic credit, and usually do not lead to full-time employment at the host organization in the end.

■ Cooperative education (co-op)—Co-ops are learning experiences that tend to occur over more than one academic period and place an emphasis on full-time working experience. Depending on how they are structured, students will alternate between working full-time and attending classes. Being enrolled in an academic program is typically a hard requirement, as the work being performed is closely tied to what a student is studying. Co-ops usually grant academic credit and are paid.

These opportunities are great ways to get experience, but not all opportunities are created equal. When determining which ones to pursue, think about the following:

- Type of work—Because internship, externship, and co-op opportunities run for a limited length of time and students may not have years of experience in certain skills, host organizations are not likely to give you mission-critical tasks to perform. That said, you don't want to be completely relegated to clerical tasks (e.g., answering telephones and/or opening mail) or doing someone's personal errands. While this helps the host organization and helps you get certain types of skills, these tasks don't help in acquiring technical or complex analysis skills. When you read the opportunity's job description or speak with the hiring manager, try to get as much information as possible on the work you'll be doing.

- Pay—For opportunities where you'll be performing many duties on behalf of the host organization (particularly if the duties generate money for them), you should be compensated fully for your efforts. Getting academic credit is one thing, but students and other audiences have living expenses just like everyone else.

- Potential exploitation—States like New York have passed stringent laws recently making most unpaid internships illegal, and other states will be following suit. It's because, sadly, some employers have taken advantage of unpaid interns in the past.

- Expectations based on gender—Women may be expected to perform certain types of work for free and/or without expectation of being promoted. If you are performing solid work, you should be paid for it.

- Advancement—If possible, the host organization should provide advancement or full-time hire opportunities for top performers. During the interview process, ask the host organization what career paths or opportunities are available to people who do a great job.

- Value—For opportunities that are unpaid and have no predefined pathway to advancement, like externships, assess how the experience will add value to you. Understanding a day in the life of someone in your desired career can prove to be an invaluable experience. Additionally, exposure to certain tech companies can give you an understanding of whether this is an organization you would want to spend part of your career with.

In addition to a school's career services department and general job search sites like Indeed and LinkedIn, you can find internship, externship, and co-op opportunities on WayUp (`wayup.com`) and Internships.com (`internships.com`).

A note of caution—beware of any job listings or organizations that require a fee to "access" opportunities. These are signs of a scam and should be avoided altogether. You should never have to pay a fee to get a job.

Volunteering

Volunteering is a wonderful way not only to get hands-on experience, but also to provide critical services to organizations that don't have the resources to hire professionals outright.

To improve my web design, WordPress, and conference organization skills, I volunteered my services for a leadership conference being held by IEEE Women in Engineering for four months in 2016. I helped to build and maintain the event website using WordPress, as well as helped people with registration and refunds. This experience greatly improved my understanding of web design, search engine optimization (SEO), event promotion, and collaborating with remote teams (I was based in Chicago, while much of the event team and registrants were based in and around Detroit, Michigan). In the process, I learned more about the different fields of engineering and broadened my network with incredible engineering students and professionals.

Through volunteer work with Black Girls Code, I was able to help facilitate technical workshops for young girls in a variety of topics, like artificial intelligence and robotics. These workshops not only increased my understanding of the technical topics and allowed me to meet industry professionals, but it helped to improve my communication skills, as you have to communicate with different audiences.

For volunteer opportunities, you will want to think about the following:

- Type of work—Again, you will want to make sure that the opportunity is closely aligned to the skills you are looking to acquire or improve. Opportunities where you can improve your technical skills may be better suited than those where you are performing administrative or clerical work. You can look for skills-based volunteer opportunities through organizations like VolunteerMatch, the Taproot Foundation, or Catchafire.org.

- Type of organization—You'll want to check if the organization is an actual charity. You can verify if a charity is real through sites like Give.org, Guide Star, or Charity Navigator. You'll also want to make sure that the organization's mission closely aligns to your personal values or is something you are passionate in.

- Level of responsibility—Much like making sure that you are not being exploited by a private employer, you will want to make sure that a volunteer organization doesn't take complete advantage of you and your time. Certain volunteer positions require more time and commitment than others—examples would be serving on an organization's board of directors or serving in an elected position like a president or treasurer. But general volunteer opportunities should not require a significant amount of time or resources on your part.

- Length of commitment—If you have many work, school, or family obligations, you may want to seek volunteer opportunities that don't have ongoing time commitments. Rather than serve on a committee, you can volunteer for a few hours or a day of service. Organizations are thrilled to have the help, no matter the length of time.

Certifications

Professional certifications can be an important part of advancing your career. Technical professional certifications are given to an individual when they have demonstrated a minimum level of knowledge and experience of a product, technology, or specific set of skills. To verify this knowledge, an individual may need to demonstrate a certain level of academic and professional experience, as well as pass a proctored, third-party exam.

Some technical professional certifications last forever, while others require continuing education or additional exams to keep the certification from expiring. Certification exams cost money, ranging anywhere from $50 to as much as $1,000. These fees are nonrefundable, so if you miss your scheduled exam or do not pass, you will have to pay the exam fee again. This is not including any test preparation costs, which include assessment exams, study guides, and required courses to sit for the certification exam.

Do You Need Certification?

Choosing to get a professional certification is a huge commitment. Whether you need to pursue certification will largely depend on the role you are pursuing and an employer's requirements. For example, there are many tech companies that require their technical support agents be certified in CompTIA's A+ certification program—an entry-level certification that demonstrates that an individual has basic knowledge of maintaining and repairing computers and servers. Many employers use certifications to quickly identify potential applicants they want to hire.

Professional certification alone is not enough to get (or keep) a job. Many certifications, like a traditional undergraduate degree, simply demonstrate that you have working, foundational knowledge or experience in a specific technologies or skill areas versus deep technical expertise and many years of experience.

Not all certifications have longevity. CompTIA's A+ certification has been regarded as a valuable and solid certification since 2008. Other certifications, particularly those that are product specific, don't have a long history and are often replaced with certifications for newer products quickly.

Finally, not all certifications are as visible, or perhaps as highly regarded, as others. For example, Microsoft offers Specialist, Expert, and Master level certifications for each of its Office offerings. Each exam costs roughly $100. If you are in a position that requires more than just a working knowledge of these products, that's one thing. However, few professions require you to know Office productivity beyond a basic level. Considering the time and expense involved, it may not be worth pursuing.

Consider certification if:

- Your current or future employer is requiring it—Your employer may explicitly say that getting one or several certifications is a requirement for employment. Employers in this case will pay or reimburse for the training and associated exam fees on your behalf.

- The certification in question makes sense for you career goals—According to training company Global Knowledge, the highest-paying technical certification is Google's Certified Professional Cloud Architect certification. The average compensation for these certification holders is $139,529. However, the people who get this certification are those who have at least a year's experience using and designing cloud solutions on Google's Cloud Platform. This means not only understanding Google's platform inside and out, but having a good handle on intermediate to advanced cloud computing concepts too. The exam is also $200, and you'll have to pay it again if you don't pass.

■ There's no denying that you have the potential to make more money and get more visibility from potential recruiters. But if you are not interested in the role, pursuing the certification may not be worth the money, time, or effort.

How to Pay for Skills Training

While there are free courses, events, training programs, and certifications available, you will likely need to pay for many of these opportunities on your own. Let's review a few ways you can go about this.

Loans

Simply put, a loan is a sum of money that you borrow to be paid back. The company that lends the money to you (the lender) charges you interest—a certain percentage that is charged on top of the monthly payment, in exchange for lending you the money.

There are many types of loan products, but we will be concentrating specifically on student loans and consumer loans.

Student Loans

Student loans are available to students who are enrolled at least half-time in an approved degree or certificate program. The proceeds for the loans can be used to paid for tuition, housing, meals, books, and other expenses that are associated with attending and completing the program.

Student loans typically fall into two categories:

■ Federal—The William D. Ford Direct Loan Program offers students low-interest loans. The amount a student can borrow is determined by the student's current year in school, how many courses they are enrolled in, and overall lifetime limits. For example, an undergraduate student enrolled in an approved four-year college can borrow up to $12,500 and $57,500 for the entirety of their undergraduate career.

Most loans offered under the program are non-credit-based (meaning your credit score is not checked, nor is it a factor in whether a loan is given to you). The overall interest you are charged is lower than with a private lender, and repayment normally does not begin until six months after you graduate or stop attending classes.

- Private—Banks, credit unions, and other nonbank lenders offer student loans too. Private loans are mostly credit based, meaning that the lender may require a minimum FICO credit score in order to be considered. Because most young people have not built a credit history, a cosigner (someone who will agree to take loan repayment responsibility should you not pay, or default) is required. The interest rates tend to be higher than federal loans.

Loan limits tend to be higher, and there are fewer restrictions on how the money is used. The lender will send the money directly to the school, and if there are funds remaining, those will be given directly to you. When you graduate or stop attending classes, you may be given a grace period, but that is entirely dependent on the lender.

Personal Loans

A personal loan is a sum of money borrowed for, as its name states, personal reasons. The money received from this loan can be used for any purpose that the borrower likes, including educational expenses, travel, etc.

Personal loans can be either unsecured, meaning based on your credit score and overall financial picture (current income, debts, etc.), or secured, meaning using your property as collateral for the loan.

Personal loans are expected to be paid almost immediately after being taken out, so there is no grace period. They tend to be more expensive than student loans.

Credit and Charge Cards

Another financing option are credit cards. Credit and charge cards allow individuals to purchase goods and services on credit, where the individual promises to repay the bank or credit union that gave them the card in full.

Credit cards have spending limits, meaning that there is a specific amount of money that you can charge up to. Although used interchangeably, credit cards allow you to pay a small amount of what you owe each month (with interest), whereas charge cards are expected to be repaid in full each month.

Use Credit Responsibly and Sparingly

I am not a fan of debt. Debt can be very debilitating, financially and mentally, and more so on people of color. People of color are typically an underbanked population, meaning they often do not have access to traditional financial products and services. When they do have access, they are generally charged more in interest and fees than wealthier, white populations.

Sometimes, though, taking out a loan or charging your credit card may be the only way that you can make your tuition payment for the semester. Additionally, avoiding credit works against you. Having no credit history can be detrimental when you're applying for an apartment or mortgage.

If you choose to use loans and credit cards, use only what you absolutely need. Avoid taking cash advances out on your credit card, as the interest you end up paying is usually higher. Make sure you pay your bills on time—not only do late payments hurt your credit, but if a friend or relative agreed to be co-signer, their credit is impacted as well.

Grants and Scholarships

Scholarships are a form of financial aid that are used to help students continue their educational pursuits. Both grants and scholarships are considered "gift aid" in that they do not need to be repaid. They can range from a few hundred to several thousands of dollars.

Grants are mostly given using needs-based criteria, like an individual's total yearly household income. Federal and state governments offer educational grants, as do private organizations. Grant funds are limited, and there may be strict cutoff limits as to which individuals and populations are eligible to receive them.

Scholarships are given using mostly merit-based criteria—an individual's overall academic record, community service, extracurricular activities, course of study, and many more. Scholarships are offered by companies, private organizations, and many others.

Scholarships can be highly competitive, and while there is a prevailing notion that people of color have an easier time getting scholarships, or that they are automatically given, I can assure you that this is not the case.

While attending Northwestern, I remember I applied for at least nine scholarships—some within Northwestern, others with outside organizations—all of them having stringent academic requirements, and each application requiring official transcripts, multiple recommendations, and well-written essays. I was incredibly fortunate to receive three scholarships, totaling nearly $6,000. This amount covered roughly 8 percent of the total tuition and fees that I paid. The remainder was paid through federal and private loans, as well as through my own job income.

Even in writing that, I realize that I was in a place of privilege. If students are even able to find the time to devote solely to writing quality scholarship applications, they still face stiff competition. I remember many of my student peers—incredibly smart and worthy—worrying about whether they'd be able to complete their studies because they lacked the funds.

Still, every little bit helps when it comes to paying for education, and you should pursue every grant and scholarship that you are eligible to apply for. If you are attending a two- or four-year college or university or an approved trade school, you will want to make sure that you complete and submit the Free Application for Federal Student Aid (FAFSA). For many institutions, this form is required in order to be considered for federal, state, or institutional aid. You will want to pay attention to any deadlines for filing, as you may not receive aid in time for classes. For more information and to file, go to the Federal Student Aid website at `https://studentaid.ed.gov/sa/fafsa`.

To find general information on outside grants and scholarships, check out Fastweb (`fastweb.com`), Peterson's Scholarship Search (`petersons.com/scholarship-search.aspx`), and Scholarships.com (`scholarships.com`). These search sites allow you to find scholarships based on gender and ethnicity, as well as the course of study and other factors. There are also outside organizations that offer scholarships for specific populations. For example, the National Center for Women and Information Technology (NCWIT) and the American Association for University Women (AAUW) offer scholarships for women in technical fields.

Tuition Reimbursement

To keep employee skills competitive, as well as keep them engaged, many organizations offer tuition reimbursement. Under tuition reimbursement plans, your employer will pay you back up to a certain amount for work-related courses. While you still need to bear the upfront registration costs, you may end up having a course partially or completely paid for.

Employer tuition reimbursement plans vary greatly, from the amount of money you can get back (for most institutions, the limit is $5,250), to where you can take classes, to the types of classes you can take, and even to the grade you're required to achieve (for most places, it's B or higher).

Check with your employer's Human Resources department or benefits manager to see whether a tuition reimbursement program exists, as well as its requirements.

Deferred Tuition Plans and Income Share Agreements

Deferred tuition plans and income share agreements (ISAs) are examples of "Buy now, pay later." As educational institutions know that costs can be a major barrier for a student in pursuing a course, certificate, or degree, they remove that by not requiring students to pay any up-front costs. Rather, they require students to pay for their studies after a certain condition is met, which could be the completion of their studies, or when they have secured permanent full time employment.

Under a deferred tuition plan, a student pays back the tuition in installments for a fixed period. Meanwhile, under ISAs, students pledge a percentage of their yearly income, up to 25 percent, for 1–5 years. Some institutions will take payments only if the student secures a full-time job over a certain amount (e.g., $50,000 per year) or will limit the total amount of money they collect from a student.

Educational institutions assume a significant amount of risk by offering these types of programs. Institutions are staking their operational and financial livelihood on the success of their students finding gainful employment. This substantial risk, as well as industry regulations, is part of the reason why few educational institutions offer these as payment options.

There's also risk for students. Some institutions charge students for choosing a deferred tuition plan, almost to a point where taking out a student loan and paying the tuition up front would've been a cheaper option. If a student who signed up for an ISA without a collection limitation ends up with a wildly successful, high-paying job, they may end up paying the institution much more money than what the program was worth.

Crowdfunding

Crowdfunding allows individuals and groups to raise funds publicly and online. People can raise funds for projects, business ventures, personal causes and expenses, charity, and more.

Anyone can start a crowdfunding campaign for any purpose, and there are many crowdfunding sites to choose from. GoFundMe, probably the most popular and most accessible crowdfunding site for personal causes, allows people to launch campaigns quickly and collect funds, less 2.9 percent of proceeds for processing fees.

While there are certainly wildly successful crowdfunding campaigns that gain media attention, the truth is that many personal crowdfunding campaigns do not meet their funding goal or receive any funding. Crowdfunding related to educational causes tend to fair worse than other types of campaigns.

But why? Largely, because most Americans, regardless of race or ethnicity, struggle to pay for educational costs. When comparing education crowdfunding campaigns to campaigns to cover basic needs, like food or shelter, or responding to a tragic event, they kind of pale in comparison.

During a theories of persuasion class, my professor offered to give a $5 bill to a student who could be the most persuasive in convincing her to part with her money. I tried with the argument that I'm a student with tuition bills and student debt. She politely said that while she can relate (she had a master's and doctorate degree after all), having significant debt and bills attributed to education has almost become a way of life and, for some, a typical "rite of passage" for an American adult.

Should you decide to embark on a crowdfunding campaign, make sure you have the following elements to help toward successful outcomes:

- Have a compelling story—It's not enough that you have a need. That may be good enough for your friends and family, who know you well and love you. But for people who do not know you well, or at all, you need to demonstrate a compelling reason as to why they should give and what exactly you'll do with their money.

- Share with your networks and encourage them to share—Share your campaign with your friends and family on social media platforms like Facebook and Twitter and through email. Kindly ask that they share with their networks too. Although you are likelier to receive donations from those closest to you, this "spreading the word" will help increase the overall potential number of donors.

- Share often—Posting or sharing one update will not be enough. You will need to remind people to donate to your campaign more than once. At the same time, be careful not to send or post too many reminders. You may end up annoying your network and turning people off from your cause.

- Say thank you—No matter the size of the contribution or whether you meet your campaign goal, say thank you to everyone who contributed or shared your campaign.

Summary

- Do a skills gaps analysis. Assess where your skills are already strong and transferrable and where you can seek to build your skill.

- Soft skills revolve around communication and interpersonal skills. They are hard to teach or measure. Hard skills can be acquired through formal and informal training and can be measured.

- The decision to pursue formal education is an entirely personal choice. There are many informal and experiential learning options available to gain the skills you need and should be considered in relation to your goals, budget, and other factors.

- Certifications, like formal degrees, are an indication that you possess fundamental technical skill. They can be an integral part of your development, but obtaining the certification itself shouldn't be your end goal. Even after obtaining certification, you must continue to deepen your skill with work experience and additional training.

- Although there are many ways you can pay or finance your education, be sure that you are making financial decisions that you are comfortable with. Seek scholarships, grants, and other "free" forms of money first before using loans, credit cards, and other forms of financing.

Demonstrating Your Skills

In this chapter, we will go over the many ways you can document your experience, ranging from traditional means like resume, online platforms like LinkedIn and GitHub, and other more creative means, like writing, public speaking, or building your own website.

Building Your Resume(s)

Although there are many ways that you can show off your skills and experience, the resume is still relevant, important, and necessary. A resume serves as your "calling card." Resume help employers understand your skills and your educational and employment background, and help determine if your unique mix of attributes could be a potential fit for a job or career with their organization.

You'll notice the heading for this section has *resumes* as potentially plural. You may find that one resume is appropriate to applying to only certain types of jobs; the skills and experiences you demonstrate for a user-experience design job may not be the skills and experiences you want to highlight for a cybersecurity job, for example. Depending on the types of roles you are applying for, you may need more than one resume so that it is tailored to the position you're applying to.

There are many, *many* formats that a resume can take. Let's go over the three most common types: *chronological, functional,* and *combination.*

Chronological

A chronological resume (Figure 7.1), perhaps the most commonly used resume format, lists your work experiences in the order in which they occurred, beginning with your most recent work experience and working backward.

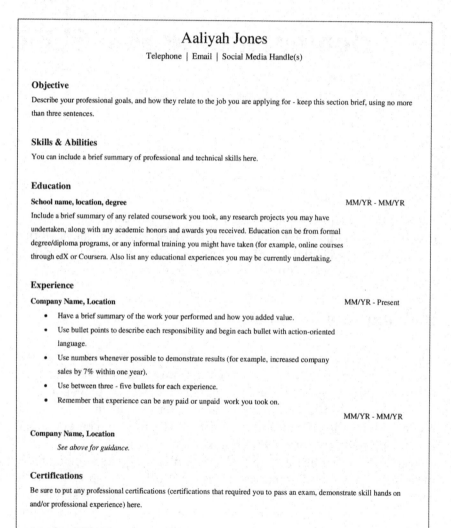

Aaliyah Jones
Telephone | Email | Social Media Handle(s)

Objective

Describe your professional goals, and how they relate to the job you are applying for - keep this section brief, using no more than three sentences.

Skills & Abilities

You can include a brief summary of professional and technical skills here.

Education

School name, location, degree   MM/YR - MM/YR

Include a brief summary of any related coursework you took, any research projects you may have undertaken, along with any academic honors and awards you received. Education can be from formal degree/diploma programs, or any informal training you might have taken (for example, online courses through edX or Coursera. Also list any educational experiences you may be currently undertaking.

Experience

Company Name, Location   MM/YR - Present

- Have a brief summary of the work your performed and how you added value.
- Use bullet points to describe each responsibility and begin each bullet with action-oriented language.
- Use numbers whenever possible to demonstrate results (for example, increased company sales by 7% within one year).
- Use between three - five bullets for each experience.
- Remember that experience can be any paid or unpaid work you took on.

                                                                MM/YR - MM/YR

Company Name, Location

See above for guidance.

Certifications

Be sure to put any professional certifications (certifications that required you to pass an exam, demonstrate skill hands on and/or professional experience) here.

Awards and Honors

Here is a perfect place to brag about any professional or personal awards or achievements you may have had.

Figure 7.1: Chronological resume example

For each experience, you would detail the following:

- The name of your employer
- Your position
- The dates your employment took place
- A few bullet points illustrating the work you performed

Chronological resume demonstrate to employers the progression of your career in an almost linear narrative format. It is the most favored by recruiters because it presents your skills and career progression in a simple, straightforward way.

If you have many work experiences (paid or unpaid)—particularly within the same industry and no or minor gaps between experiences—this may be the best format to use. If, however, you don't have many career experiences under your belt, are in the process of changing career paths, or have significant gaps in your work history, this format may not cast your experiences and skills in the best light.

The emphasis of this resume is on your experiences and the skills utilized. While education, achievements, honors, certifications, projects, and other noteworthy items should be on your resume, they should be listed after your experience section.

Functional

If you don't think that your experiences would reflect well using a chronological format, you can opt for the functional format (Figure 7.2). Rather than focusing on your experience in a linear path, functional resumes allow you to put more emphasis on your skills (applicable to the job you're applying to and transferrable ones) and experience.

- Skills are listed as main headings.
- Examples for how you practiced or demonstrated that skill are listed underneath each heading.
- Employer names and dates of employments can be added, but that is optional.
- Relevant industry keywords are heavily emphasized.

Keep in mind that some recruiters and human resources professionals may not like this format. Although it may do a better job of demonstrating of what you could bring to a position and company, some may find it cumbersome to read through and may misinterpret that you may be less than forthcoming about your background, or rather, you may be trying to hide something from them.

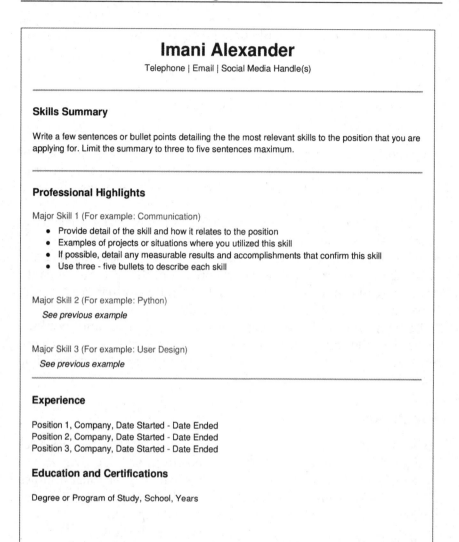

Imani Alexander

Telephone | Email | Social Media Handle(s)

Skills Summary

Write a few sentences or bullet points detailing the the most relevant skills to the position that you are applying for. Limit the summary to three to five sentences maximum.

Professional Highlights

Major Skill 1 (For example: Communication)

- Provide detail of the skill and how it relates to the position
- Examples of projects or situations where you utilized this skill
- If possible, detail any measurable results and accomplishments that confirm this skill
- Use three - five bullets to describe each skill

Major Skill 2 (For example: Python)

See previous example

Major Skill 3 (For example: User Design)

See previous example

Experience

Position 1, Company, Date Started - Date Ended
Position 2, Company, Date Started - Date Ended
Position 3, Company, Date Started - Date Ended

Education and Certifications

Degree or Program of Study, School, Years

Figure 7.2: Functional resume example

Combination

Combination resumes (Figure 7.3) use elements of both formats and may be the best bet for those who are new to the workforce or those who have a wide array of work experiences that span many different industries or job functions with few gaps in employment. This resume demonstrates the relevant skills but also gives employers what they are looking for in terms of a chronological detailing of your work experiences.

Jordan Moore   Telephone
                                        Email • Social Media Handle(s)

Skills and Accomplishments
- **Skill** - Write a brief description of the skill and how you have use it currently and/or in past experiences. Include both hard and soft skills.
- **Skill** - *See above.*
- **Skill** - *See above.*
- **Accomplishment** - Briefly describe any major career accomplishments; emphasize measurable results when possible.

Experience
Company, Location
Job Title   MM/YY - MM/YY

- Have a brief summary of the work your performed and how you added value.
- Use bullet points to describe each responsibility and begin each bullet with action-oriented language.
- Use numbers whenever possible to demonstrate result.
- Use between three - five bullets for each experience.
- Remember that experience can be any paid or unpaid work you took on.

Company, Location
Job Title   MM/YY - MM/YY

See previous example

Company, Location
Job Title   MM/YY - MM/YY

See previous example

Education and Certifications

- Degree, Graduation Year (YYYY)
  College Name, Location

- List additional certifications obtained or trainings completed/in progress

Figure 7.3: Combination resume example

In this resume, relevant qualifications and skills, as well as your education, can be placed before the experience section.

What Every Resume Must Have

We will not spend a great deal of time debating over which style is better than the other. The "right" resume format has been and continues to be a heavily debated issue among professionals that will not be resolved any time soon. Ultimately, you will want to spend some time reflecting on your experiences and then select a format that will present your skills and experience in the best light.

Additionally, you may need to consider known industry or role resume "norms" when crafting your resume. For example, many consulting firms have somewhat strict standards on how a resume should be formatted— chronological order, one-page total, standard fonts like Times New Roman, black font color, and no pictures or distracting images. Conversely, resume for more creative technical fields don't have these constraints, and it is perhaps encouraged to use more colors, fonts, and imagery.

We are going to focus on the elements that *must* be present in your resume, regardless of the format you choose.

The Heading

The heading must include the following information:

- *Your name.* Your legal first and last name should appear. If you go by a nickname or an alias that's different from your given name, you can include this as well.

- *Your contact information.* Include a working phone number and email address where you can be contacted. If you have an email address that might be embarrassing or awkward, consider creating and using a new one from a free email service provider. You can list your home address, but this is not a strict requirement and may free up some extra space.

- *Your social media handles.* You may also list your social media platform handles, like Facebook, Twitter, or LinkedIn. I would *highly stress* that you should share them only if you are comfortable and believe that your profiles convey you in a positive and professional light. Many people have lost opportunities or existing jobs because of what was on their social media proflie. If in doubt, set your profiles to private and do not share.

The Body

The body must include the following information:

- *Your personal statement and career objective.* Many professionals are divided on the importance of this section. I think that it is an important section for those who either are just coming out of school or are changing careers. It's an opportunity to demonstrate to employers what your career goals are and how they align with the job to which you are applying.

This section should be no more than one paragraph, two to three sentences at most. The more detailed you can be about what your career goals are, while stating them concisely (or using as few words as possible), the better.

■ *A listing of your key skills and strengths.* In this section, you'll want to list the relevant skills and strengths that you have that are a match for the position to which you're applying. You will also want to list any technical skills here, like software programs you are familiar with and programming languages you know.

If there are specific jobs or industries that you have in mind, you will want to include as many relevant keywords—or essential phrases or descriptions that apply to a specific job—as possible. Be mindful to not go overboard with using keywords, or *keyword stuffing*, where your text simply comes off as random keywords put together but when read by a recruiter, it makes absolutely no sense.

Also, depending on the role you are pursuing, you may want to omit any skills related to common business productivity software, like word processing, spreadsheets, presentations, and email. Employers, for the most part, assume that you already have some working knowledge of how to use these programs through school and other experiences.

■ *Your education.* You should list any diplomas and degrees that you have obtained or are in the process of obtaining. You should list the name of the school or organization, the dates of study, and the name of the program of study, if applicable.

You can also list any relevant education you may have received through less formal means, like any online courses you may have taken on your own or educational programs offered by professional organizations.

You should list any coursework you have taken that is related to the job for which you are applying. I'd avoid listing your grade point average, or GPA, unless an employer is specifically asking for it as part of the job application process or you achieved a very high GPA (over 3.5 on a 4.0 scale) in a demanding and challenging academic program. List any academic honors you may have achieved like honor roll or making the dean's list.

- *Your work experiences (paid or unpaid).* At minimum, your entries for work experiences should have the following:

  - Your title or the position you held

  - The name of employer or organization where you provided services

  - The dates of your employment

  For each experience, you want to describe the work you performed in detail, in bullets, and whenever possible, describe what positive effect your actions, contributions, and efforts had on that organization. Even better—quantify, or express in numbers, what effect your work has had. This can be anything from increasing something positive (increased overall sales by 25 percent) to decreasing something negative (decreased loss of customers by 15 percent). When you describe your experiences, present yourself as an active, results-oriented contributor who brings value to an organization versus someone is a passive, task-oriented participant.

  Each sentence should begin with an action verb (e.g., *handled, gathered, coordinated*). Table 7.1 shows a sampling of words you can use when describing your tasks. Please note that this is not an exhaustive list, and some words can be used to describe other activities, not just for those in the column in which they are listed.

  Alternatively, you can list separate bullets for achievements or accomplishments while on the job (e.g., "Received recognition as Employee of the Month").

Let's compare the following bullet points for someone in a student internship, where one of the responsibilities they took part in was in the creation of a database.

Example 1
- *Responsible for database design and development.*

  While this bullet point does describe the task that the intern performed, it comes off as passive and not descriptive. What kind of database did the intern design? What tools did the intern use to design the database? For what purpose was the database being designed, and what effect, if any, did the efforts have on business outcomes?

Table 7.1: Examples of Action Verbs

COMMU-NICATION	RESEARCH	DESIGN	TECHNICAL	ADMINIS-TRATIVE	LEADER-SHIP
Authored	Analyzed	Altered	Assembled	Administered	Boot-strapped
Influenced	Collected	Conceptu-alized	Built	Arranged	Chaired
Interpreted	Evaluated	Created	Calculated	Assisted	Conducted
Negotiated	Examined	Customized	Computed	Coordinated	Directed
Lectured	Identified	Designed	Engineered	Implemented	Engaged
Promoted	Investigated	Developed	Installed	Maintained	Executed
Publicized	Measured	Fashioned	Operated	Monitored	Facilitated
Spoke	Reviewed	Performed	Pro-grammed	Organized	Formed
Translated	Summ-arized	Sketched	Trained	Prepared	Headed
Wrote	Surveyed	Visualized	Upgraded	Updated	Planned

Example 2

■ *Using Microsoft Access, developed a company profile database of top biotechnology and pharmaceutical companies, enabling the company's associates to perform competitive analyses.*

This bullet point is stronger, as it details what the intern used to create the database, the issue the database was addressing, and what value this creation brought to the organization.

Not all work activities are going to yield specific outcomes or results. Some work is just necessary to keep the business or organization functioning (e.g., most clerical duties). That's okay. But whenever possible, try to frame your work descriptions with the problems you are addressing, the action(s) you took, and the results of your efforts.

Additionally—and this is especially true for those beginning their careers—experience includes *all* paid and unpaid work that you undertake. This means activities like the following:

- Volunteer and community service work
- Paid or unpaid internships
- Part-time jobs, including caretaking, retail, or food service
- School activities where you had an active leadership role (e.g., president or treasurer)
- Any personal projects you may be embarking on (i.e., entrepreneurial projects or creative projects)

While some of these may not directly relate to specific technical skills, they do demonstrate important transferrable skills. As you progress in your career, you can omit these experiences and replace them with newer, more relevant experiences.

What You Can Leave Out

There are elements that should never be present in your resume. These include the following:

- *Typos, grammatical errors, and misspellings.* As your resume is likely the first (and maybe only) impression you get to leave with an employer, there is no room for error and, honestly, no excuse for one full of these kinds of mistakes. Check your resume as many times as necessary to determine that there are no errors in it. Ask a trusted friend or advisor to review the resume as well, as a fresh pair of eyes may catch things that you didn't.

- *Personal details.* Your height, weight, age, marital status, religion, and similar items should never be listed on your resume. Employers are prohibited by law to ask you questions on any of these topics. Additionally, to protect yourself from identify theft, do not write your Social Security number or tax identification number on your resume and if possible, avoid writing your home address.

- *References section.* People have included this section with either the phrase "Furnished Upon Request" or worse, the actual name and contact information for their references listed underneath. Most employers will already assume you will have at least one person who will be able speak to the quality of your work. Including this section is wasting space that you can use for other, higher-quality information.

  Also, do not list your references' personal information, out of courtesy to your references and to protect their information. When an employer wants to move forward with the hiring process, they will ask you directly for the information. You need to confirm with your references that they are comfortable with having their information shared for this purpose.

- *Empty and overused phrases.* Terms like *results driven, strategic thinker,* and similar phrases should be avoided. These are filler phrases that take up space and do not demonstrate anything that you have specifically done.

  Terms like *hard working* or *skilled communicator* should also be avoided. Most employers will assume that all the applicants applying to their positions have these traits already. Restating the obvious will not help you.

  Don't believe me? Look at the lists in Table 7.2 of the top overused words and phrases from professional networking site LinkedIn, as well as career sites Careerbuilder.com and Indeed.com.

Table 7.2: Overused Words and Phrases, per LinkedIn, Careerbuilder, and Indeed

PER LINKEDIN	PER CAREERBUILDER .COM	PER INDEED.COM
Motivated	Best of breed	*Go-to person*
Creative	Go-getter	*Strategic thinker*
Enthusiastic	*Think outside the box*	*Think outside the box*
Track record	Synergy	*Results driven*
Passionate	*Go-to person*	*Detail oriented*
Driven	*Results driven*	Proactive
Leadership	*Team player*	*Hard worker*
Extensive experience	*Hard worker*	People person
Strategic	*Strategic thinker*	Self-motivated
Successful	*Detail-oriented*	*Team player*

You may notice some overlap between the lists, which are in italics. Try your best to not incorporate these phrases when writing your resume.

- *The words "I," "me," my," and other personal pronouns.* Professional resume should always be written in the first-person. Other than being repetitive to read, employers will assume that everything written on there is about you.

▪ *Hobbies and interests.* Although listing your hobbies and interests can give employers some insight as to who you are outside of work and school, they are usually not interested in this information. There are exceptions, of course—an employer may be asking for this information, or it is incorporated in the resume when applying for college or educational programs. Most of the time, however, employers are primarily interested in your skills and abilities. They can usually ask these kinds of questions during the interview process.

▪ *Significant embellishments and lies.* Resume writing does require a bit of creative writing. But outright lying or severely stretching the truth on your resume is a huge no-no. It's not worth the risk to your professional reputation.

When it comes to work experiences or education, information can be easily verified with either a phone call, an email, or a lookup in a centralized online database. Per a 2017 HR.com study, 96 percent of US employers conduct at least one background check on potential hires. If it's found that you did give false information during the application or interviewing process, you could lose a job offer and harm your professional reputation.

Let's say, however, that someone strongly "stretches the truth" and says that they are an expert in a certain skill but are actually more entry level or, perhaps, have no knowledge of the skill at all. Although many employers can (and do) give tests to verify proficiency levels, we'll assume here that a candidate was able to get around this requirement somehow.

If the candidate, now employee, is presented then with a situation where they need to demonstrate their knowledge for a critical work project, people around them will figure out very quickly that they have no clue what they are doing. Any trust that the employee may have built within the organization will be gone and near impossible to rebuild. Suspension, demotion, or even firing is likely to happen.

▪ *Graphics and images.* While there are those who believe that sharing your photo or embedding images on your resume is not a problem, I believe they should be left out for two important reasons. First, a photo that presents you in a less than professional light (e.g., a picture of you at a party, or when the picture's overall quality is poor) can work against you—even if you've presented yourself as a perfect fit for a position in every other aspect.

Second, images tend to interfere with applicant tracking systems (ATS), thus rejecting your application outright. We will talk about ATS in the next section.

As mentioned, there are different industry and job function norms where putting pictures on a resume isn't an issue. But for most jobs within in the tech industry, it's best to leave them out.

First Impressions Matter

Before submitting your resume for any positions, you want to make sure that it is mistake free, is a positive (and accurate) representation of your skills and abilities, and is "ATS friendly" (or well-constructed for applicant tracking systems). The last part is becoming more and more crucial over time.

Let's first discuss what an ATS is and why it is being used by more employers. An ATS allows recruiters and other hiring managers the ability to find top job candidates quickly and efficiently. Before these systems were available, recruiters and hiring managers had to manually review physical resume and then physically file them. This may not be a big deal when there are only one or two resume to review. But imagine hundreds, maybe thousands, that need to be reviewed for specific skills and experience and then filed and retained—either physically or digitally—and regardless of whether a candidate was given a job.

There was also no way to accurately track who applied for a job and when they applied for it. If a company had more than one office, there was no centralized way for different offices to view candidate information. The job application process was haphazard in this respect.

This is where an ATS comes in. Recruiters and hiring managers, no matter where they are, can quickly retrieve candidate applications from a centralized place and then quickly filter and sort applications to find top candidates. The methods that an ATS uses to score the strength of an applicant—keywords comparisons, minimum criteria, and other mechanisms—will differ by company and system, but these systems allow those involved in recruiting and hiring activities to save a lot of time.

Take the average job posting. The number of applications that one posting may receive will vary because of several factors (e.g., company, location, required skills, etc.), but on average, one job listing will receive 300 applications. A company that is using an ATS may narrow down the total applicant pool between 60 percent to 78 percent through automatic or manual filtering. This means that 180 to 238 of those applicants will be taken out of consideration and perhaps never have human eyes see their application. While some are weeded out because they did not meet minimum qualification criteria set by the employer, some are weeded out because the ATS doesn't like the formatting used in the resume and other minor formatting and style issues. Even the most well-qualified candidates can be taken out of the running because they used a font the system didn't like or the margins were not just right.

For the resume that remain using the example, only 66 to 120 resume/applications remain will be considered and reviewed by humans. Adding insult to injury, the average length of time a recruiter or hiring manager will take to review the resume is between *4 to 7 seconds*. If the first thing they see in that short period of time is a resume riddled with errors or is not connecting how you're qualified for the job, you can be sure that they will not be contacting you.

Additional Tips and Resources for Resume Writing

Although resume writing can be a challenging task, you're not in it alone. Many resources exist to help you write your first resume or perhaps redo an existing one.

- *Get your content down first.* Before choosing a template, think about what you are going to write and what you'd like to convey when detailing your experience. The following exercise may be helpful if you're struggling with what to write:

  - Take a piece of paper and begin writing about one of your experiences. Write down the name of the person or organization you were working for. Remember that experience can be full-time or part-time work, volunteer work, and projects.

  - Write down what work you performed. Don't worry about making it sound perfect or how much you write. The idea here is to start getting your activities down on paper. Write down any specific tools or programs that you used that helped you to do the job.

  - List you performed the work for—Here you'll want to list the people you were actively supporting or providing a service, whether that was internal (inside the company) or external (the public or specific customers). For example, if you were working as customer service in a retail company, you were providing support to your direct manager and to customers for that company.

- If it applies, write down any accomplishments that occurred through your efforts. Did you create something new or novel? Did you receive recognition or an award from your manager? Did your work directly improve a process or help a company save money? Make sure to write these down!

- *Consult your local library, school career services department, or your state's Department of Labor.* If you need one-on-one help with writing your resume, you can connect with the career services departments that may be available through your school, your local library, or your state labor department.

- *Try writing your resume yourself first.* There are professional resume writers and services that can help you to create or revise your resume for a fee. These fees can vary greatly—anywhere from $50 to thousands of dollars!

   There is value to having a professional prepare your resume—they might be more familiar with prevailing industry trends, more familiar with the quirks of applicant tracking systems, or more adept on how to highlight your experiences if you are transitioning from another industry (e.g., military service) or job function. I have used resume writers in the past when I felt that I was having a difficult time best articulating to tech employers that my skills were transferable to their jobs.

   But you often have the best "voice" and intimate knowledge to articulate your experiences. When employers ask you to walk through your resume with them, your answers will sound more authentic, because they were written by you.

- *Take advantage of resume reviews.* Academic institutions, career fairs, and career services offices usually offer a resume review, where experienced professionals will look over a resume and give you their thoughts on what works well and what they believe can be improved. While this can be a humbling experience, remember that feedback they give you is in the interest of getting you the job/career that you want. Whenever possible, have reviewers who are familiar with the jobs that you are applying to give you targeted feedback.

If you can't secure an in-person review, there are plenty of online resources that can help as well. Two services that are particularly helpful are VMock and CV Compiler.

Both VMock and CV Compiler allow you to upload your resume and receive instant feedback. VMock (www.vmock.com) will compare your resume to other uploaded resume (against candidates from top US-based colleges and universities) and score your resume based on the following:

- Impact—How action oriented your work descriptions are

- Presentation—Based on the overall length of the resume (number of pages), formatting, spell check, and other presentation criteria

- Competencies—How well your analytical, communication, leadership, teamwork, and initiative skills are conveyed in your resume

Resume receive an overall score from 0–100. Scores from 0–50 indicate that the resume will need additional review and revision, scores 51–80 mean that they are good but need some additional TLC, and scores 81 and above indicate that a resume is in good shape. Regardless of score, feedback and suggestions for improvement are given in those three core categories and on a line-by-line level.

CV Compiler (www.cvcompiler.com) offers this type of feedback as well but is geared toward technical resume. It offers feedback and additional insights on the following:

- In-demand and niche tech skills—How much does your resume emphasize both?

- Technological proficiencies—Does your resume do a good job emphasizing the skill depth you possess in certain technologies?

- Online presence—What social media platforms, online portfolios, and code repositories would enhance your resume?

Both services offer a free-to-try version (usually one free resume upload) and have different membership tiers depending on your needs.

Another service that may be helpful is Jobscan (www.jobscan.co). It compares your current resume against a job description you provide and offers feedback on how closely aligned your resume is to the description presented. It will present a "match rate" and offer specific suggestions on where improvements can be made in skills and education presentation, as well as tips on how to improve your resume with applicant tracking systems.

■ *Have another pair of eyes review your resume before sending it.* As mentioned earlier in this chapter, have a trusted friend or colleague review your resume for typos and other errors. People are prone to not see their own mistakes after staring at the same document repeatedly.

■ *Keep practicing.* As with any skill, you will improve with practice and time. Resume writing is no different. It is a skill you need, as you'll need to revise your resume for all of the new experiences and skills you'll be acquiring.

LinkedIn

If you are not already on LinkedIn, I strongly suggest signing up for a free profile. LinkedIn is the largest professional networking site in the world, with more than 600 million users worldwide. Of these users, 90 million of them are senior-level influencers (e.g., people who are helping shape hiring decisions), and 63 million of them make hiring decisions outright.

While LinkedIn can be considered a social media site, its purpose is different than that of Facebook, Twitter, and Instagram. There is a social aspect to LinkedIn; you can connect with classmates, coworkers, managers, teachers, mentors—just about anyone. However, the purpose is to show off your professional side. When you post updates or share articles or pictures, you want to be cautious, as you never know when a potential employer could be looking.

A side note for those who are social media averse. I was, and to some extent still am, not a huge fan of social media. I used to joke that having someone who tends to be antisocial (yours truly) on a platform that demands you to be social is not a good idea. For a long time, I was resistant to using social media platforms. I remember talking to a previous mentor about this, to which she said that not being on social media was "totally my choice," but to keep two things in mind in relation to social media and building your professional brand.

First, potential and current employers are *actively* looking at your online footprint, including your social media or lack of it. They are making assumptions and creating a narrative about you based on what is, or isn't, out there. Wouldn't you rather be the person who controls that narrative? Second, social media allows you the flexibility to promote yourself in a "liberating" way that your current job or situation may not allow. Why not use every tool that is available to set yourself apart?

The Difference between LinkedIn and Your Resume

Many people think of LinkedIn as a just another site to add what is already on your resume. Relisting your resume is an acceptable practice, but with all of the features and the audience reach possible with LinkedIn, you could be missing out on making yourself stand out to employers.

Here are some key differences between your resume and LinkedIn:

- *Networking.* Perhaps the biggest draw of LinkedIn is the ability to connect with recruiters and hiring managers directly.

  When you send a resume using normal means, it's what I consider a *push communication,* meaning you send your application materials to recruiters and hiring managers, but there's no way that you can tell if it was received or understood by them. You don't even know who they may be, as contact information rarely contains names, phone numbers, or email addresses. With LinkedIn, there's more opportunity for *interactive communication* with recruiters and hiring managers, with its messaging, group, and online conference capabilities.

- *Length.* A resume should be a specific length, usually no more than one page. LinkedIn frees you from this restriction as you can list as many of your experiences as you like.

- *Flexibility.* You also can take more liberties with detailing your experiences and, perhaps, providing a fuller picture of who you are (including a professional photo of yourself). The language doesn't need to be quite as formal, although you'll want to take care that you're demonstrating how you are bringing value to your work and organizations.

  The prevailing advice is that resume should be tailored to one specific role or industry. This often means having to craft multiple resumes for different career fields and roles. LinkedIn gives you more freedom to tell your "career story" and highlight the things that are the most meaningful to you.

- *Media/proof of past work.* You can add documents, media, links, and other compelling pieces of work history to your profile, giving recruiters more access to your past work than through a resume or application.

- *Skill endorsements and recommendations.* LinkedIn allows current and former colleagues to attest to your past work experience publicly. Recruiters and prospective employers can go to your profile and see this information easily. You have the option of making a recommendation private if you feel like it does not serve your business needs.

Creating a LinkedIn Profile

Getting started with a Linked profile takes only a few minutes.

1. Go to the LinkedIn home page.
   www.linkedin.com

2. Enter your email address and create a password; then click the Agree & Join button.

3. Enter your ZIP code and job interests; then click Continue.

4. You're done! You'll be taken to your profile home page.

Essential Elements of a LinkedIn Profile

You can use your resume as a source of inspiration for your profile, but you want to approach how you construct your profile a little differently than your resume. Let's look at the minimum elements your profile should have:

- *Professional photograph.* You'll want to use a high-quality photo (one that isn't grainy or fuzzy) of yourself in professional or at least business casual attire. The front of your face should be fully visible, and there shouldn't be any distracting images in the background. Figure 7.4 shows an example of a great profile photo.

  If you don't have access to a professional photographer, a selfie can be a reasonable alternative, if it is taken in a well-lit area, with no distracting backgrounds, and while wearing professional or business casual attire. Whenever possible, though, have a friend take the photo of you.

- *Headline.* Your headline will be one of the first things that LinkedIn members will see (along with your photo and your name). If you are starting out, it is fine to list your current position and company or the fact that you are a student at a college or university. Many people on LinkedIn do this.

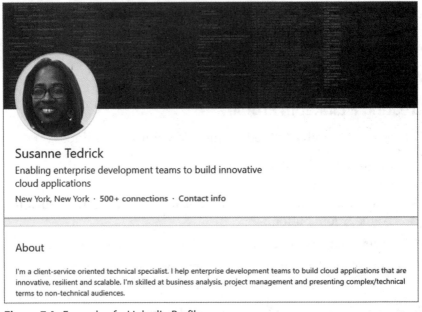

Susanne Tedrick

Enabling enterprise development teams to build innovative
cloud applications

New York, New York · 500+ connections · Contact info

About

I'm a client-service oriented technical specialist. I help enterprise development teams to build cloud applications that are
innovative, resilient and scalable. I'm skilled at business analysis, project management and presenting complex/technical
terms to non-technical audiences.

Figure 7.4: Example of a LinkedIn Profile

There are a couple of issues with this approach, though. First, a title may mean one thing to one employer, but may mean nothing to the people outside of the organization. I could say to you that I'm a *client technical specialist*, but ultimately, what would that phrase mean to you? If you didn't work at my company or in my industry, would that give you a clearer idea of what my job entails and what I do for people? Probably not.

A headline gives you the opportunity to demonstrate what you're known for, what your strengths are, and where you would like to take your career. But even better would be to have a headline that informs potential viewers of your strengths and career goals.

There are many approaches you can take. The first that I like to use is what can be considered a "benefit statement"—what you can do or provide to someone if they sought your help. For example, a headline for an algebra tutor could look like this:

Helping students master the principles of algebra and achieve academic success.

Another way is to list what you are currently doing, where you're highly skilled and what you are seeking out of your next opportunities.

Let's look at two examples:

Example 1

- Computer Science Student at Carnegie Mellon University

Example 2

- Computer Science Student at Carnegie Mellon University | Full Stack Development Specialist | Seeking Challenging Full Time Opportunities

The first example lets people know who you are and what you do, while the second takes this a step further by calling out what you excel at and what you are looking for in your next opportunity. The point is that you can be as creative as you'd like when creating your headline. Just remember that you are limited to 120 characters—make them count!

- *Summary.* Using the headline as the foundation, you want to briefly describe the following (you're limited to 2,000 characters here):
  - Your background and experiences
  - Strengths and skills
  - Career goals

  Whenever possible, use keywords that are synonymous or related to the role you are seeking.

- *Experiences.* Like your resume, list all experiences whether they were paid, volunteer, etc. When possible, list employer names, positions, and dates of employment, as well as the details of the work you carried out.

- *Education.* List all formal and informal education that you have taken part in. If you were involved in any school-specific activities or received any honors, be sure to list them!

- *Skills and endorsements.* LinkedIn allows you to list up to 50 skills on your profile, and you can give others in your network the option to endorse you for those skills if you'd like. You'll want to include skills that are relevant to the types of jobs you are applying for and that you possess.

Additional LinkedIn Tips

Here are some additional tips:

- *Set your profile to public and have a custom URL.* When your profile is set to public, you increase the likelihood of being found in professional searches. Additionally, changing the profile's URL to something customized (e.g., `https://www.linkedin.com/in/ firstname _ lastname`) looks more professional. To customize your URL, go to Settings And Privacy in the main menu and then Edit Your Public Profile.

- *Fill out all profile sections, if possible.* In general, LinkedIn profiles that have a good degree of information in them usually appear higher in search results. This means having a photo, headline, summary, two work experiences, and one educational experience listed.

- *Connect with people!* Send connection requests to current and former classmates, teachers, managers, and others. When sending a connection request, *always* include a personalized message to the recipient, especially if you are not familiar with them. Include a salutation, a bit about yourself, and why you are connecting with them. Here is a sample of what you could send:

  Dear Aliyah,

  I enjoyed your post in the Business Analyst group regarding the need to perform root cause analysis when trying to properly address problems. I'm currently a student at Northwestern studying to become a BA myself and would love to connect and learn to a seasoned professional like you.

  Thank you,
  Susanne Tedrick

- *Join groups.* As mentioned in in Chapter 3, "Industry and Other Options," LinkedIn provides a great way to network with professionals anytime, anywhere. There are thousands of groups that you can join, and they can be affiliated with a school, employer, industry, geography, or profession. While some groups are closed to certain audiences only (and hidden), there are many that you can join just by searching.

  Not all groups are created equal. Some groups have members who post and share great content, while others have inactivity or are just spamming product promotions. Take some time to explore, and remember to be courteous and follow the group's rules on content posting.

- *Get recommendations.* LinkedIn allows others to go beyond endorsements and write detailed recommendations that you can post on your profile. Reach out to current and former supervisors, teachers, advisors, and colleagues who can attest to your work and would be willing to recommend you publicly.

- *Update career interests sections.* Under the Jobs menu, LinkedIn allows you to indicate to potential recruiters and employers that you are looking for opportunities. You can list the types of jobs you are looking for and the locations in which you are willing to work. It's advised that you review these settings every three months.

- *Focus on making quality connections.* When sending out connection requests, your goal isn't to get as many connections as you can. The point is to try to develop meaningful professional relationships with others, to learn from others, and to provide help to others. With that in mind, LinkedIn may limit the number of connection requests you can send if you have many that are outstanding (you sent them, but the recipient has not accepted the request) or too many people in a short time declined your request to connect.

- *Be safe.* You should generally not accept invitations that you do not know very well, or if their profiles give you concern (e.g., the profile contains very little information). Many bad actors use LinkedIn as a means to steal personal information or to try to lure you into an employment scam. Do not send or list personally identifying information on your profile.

Writing

Writing is an excellent way to share your knowledge and expertise with others, from online platforms to traditional print media. Let's explore a few ways you can do that.

Online Publishing Platforms

Online publishing platforms combine many attractive features into one solution. They allow writers and content publishers to submit their work with few restrictions, while giving them access to a wide and varied audience, and the potential to make money from their work.

There is some sacrifice in design decisions—it doesn't give you the complete editorial freedom that having your own website or blog allows (we'll discuss this in the next section)—and depending on the site, there may be restrictions on the subject matter discussed or images used. But because there are already many subscribers, the heavy lifting and time-consuming work of finding audiences and optimizing your content for search engines and similar is not something that you have to worry much about.

Some popular online content platforms include the following:

- Medium
  www.medium.com

- LinkedIn Publishing
  www.linkedin.com/post/new

- ScoopIt!
  www.scoop.it

Academic and Professional Journals

Academic institutions and professional organizations regularly publish journals that may have opportunities to submit your work. Having your work published in an academic or professional journal is a great accomplishment. That said, it can be a competitive and challenging process that requires a lot of time, research, and editing.

Academic journals focus on any primary research that you, or as a part of a team, may have conducted and your findings from that research. Professional journals, or trade journals, focus on the current news or trends that are happening within a specific industry or profession. Articles written for professional journals tend to be written by people who have had a few years of experience within their profession, but this isn't a hard rule.

Here are some tips if you would like to go this route:

- *Make sure you find the right journal.* If you have a topic in mind for a paper, ensure that your proposed paper is the right fit for the journal. If your paper is based on research you've done on human-computer interaction, it may be better suited for a journal centered on user experience and design than a journal devoted to data science. Read a few of the articles in the journal you intend to submit to so that you have an idea of the types of articles that appear in there, and if your topic may be suitable.

- *Follow their submission advice and guidelines exactly.* Although the publisher may call these "guidelines," the truth is that they are likely the minimum requirements just to have your paper considered. Don't ignore them or follow only some of them—follow them as much as possible!

- *Cite your references and sources.* Be sure to give credit where it is due, especially if your research or paper is building from previous research. Additionally, you do not want to be accused of plagiarism or stealing someone's work.

- *Solicit feedback.* Having feedback early and often will increase the likelihood that your work will be accepted. Sites like ResearchGate (www.researchgate.com) allow you to share your research work with other interested peers, from students to professional researchers, from all over the world. They may offer suggestions on how to improve your writing or point you in the direction of previous research that may aid you in your writing process.

Public Speaking

The ability to speak in front of others is a skill that everyone, no matter what they do, needs. It is great to acquire technical skills and be able to apply them in solving problems or creating new products and services. But being able to share information in a clear and confident manner is just as important. Those who can convey information in a memorable and effective way leave a lasting impression and are remembered, and possibly for future speaking/job opportunities.

I had the opportunity to attend the recent Grace Hopper Conference, where more than 25,000 rising and experienced women technologists were in attendance. Visiting one of the vendor booths, I was approached by someone who greeted me and said, "You gave a talk at Portland State University on creating mentoring programs in June, right? I really enjoyed and learned from it!"

I was shocked. I gave a talk for the Advancing the Careers of Women in Tech (ACT-W) on helping hiring managers and diversity and inclusion leaders. My talk was no more than 40 minutes, and there were perhaps 50 people or fewer in the room. It was my first professional speaking engagement outside of my work, and if I'll be honest, it was good, not great. The fact that this young woman remembered me and my talk from a small conference six months ago (in a sea of people, no less) meant that some elements of my talk were on point.

Public Speaking Misconceptions

There are some popular misconceptions about public speaking that persist. Among them:

- *Great public speakers are born.* Not at all. While there are certainly people who have a natural aptitude for public speaking, that doesn't mean they do not need to practice and prepare for each public speaking engagement they have. Even knowing how to effectively give an unprepared (or impromptu) speech takes skill building.

- *Public speaking is all about charisma.* Charisma is one's ingrained ability to attract or charm people. While it certainly can be helpful, your content and delivery are just as important, if not more so.

  Thinking about the act of persuading or to get someone to do something, there are people who may take an action based on someone's charisma. But there are also people *not* swayed this. There are people who may be more swayed by more logical arguments or emotional ones. A good public speaker recognizes how to adjust their content, delivery, and other speech elements for their audience.

- *I must be an expert on what I'm talking about and know the answers to everything.* If this were the case, there would be far fewer public speakers out there. When I gave my talk on mentoring for ACT-W or my webinar on the foundations of cloud computing for AnitaB.org or when serving as a panelist for a women in AI discussion, I was far from an expert in any of those topics. The key in each of these was that I had firsthand exposure in these in areas during my academic and professional career, I was genuinely interested in the subject matter, and I had the desire to share what I experienced. If you're willing to share and are comfortable with sharing that you "know what you don't know," you'll be just fine.

Public Speaking Basics

Whenever possible, I recommend taking a live, in-person public course if it is offered at a local school or engaging with a professional public-speaking organization like Toastmasters. These venues allow you to practice, while peers and professionals can give you detailed feedback on what you are doing well and areas that could further develop. You can find a local Toastmasters chapter at www.toastmasters.org.

The following are general tips you can use when preparing for public speaking opportunities:

- *Define the outcome.* After your talk is over, what is it that you want your audience to do? Are there specific actions you want them to take? Will they be more aware of a community issue than before the talk started? Beyond just listening to you speak, think about what you'd ideally like each audience member to take away once it is over.

- *Prepare.* In addition to crafting the content and message you want to deliver, you also want to know who you will be delivering the content to and adjusting your message accordingly. Preparation will also help address nervousness that may come up once you're onstage.

- *Write a speech outline, not the whole speech.* Writing out your entire speech and memorizing it may lead you to potentially sound robotic, as you're essentially just reciting lines. When you talk, you want it to sound like your natural self and like you're having a conversation with an intimate group of people versus "speaking at" a room full of strangers.

- *Practice; record and time yourself.* Practice as many times as you need to where you feel comfortable and know your material inside and out. Record yourself so that you can listen later and evaluate content or delivery changes you would like to make. Practice in front of a trusted advisor or friend, and ask them to give you feedback. When all fails, practice in front of a mirror and watch for eye contact, verbal tics, etc.

  Also make a note of how much time your talk is taking and adjust as necessary. As a rule of thumb, you want to leave yourself a few minutes of free time for audience questions and answers or to address any technical issues (e.g., need to put your presentation slides on a projector or computer you're not familiar with). So, if you're given 45 minutes to talk, you want to have only 30–35 minutes of speech and content to leave the last few minutes for questions.

- *If you are using presentation slides, go easy on the text and graphics.* This is a huge pet peeve for me and many others. If I am sitting in your presentation and you have two full paragraphs of text on your slide, I promise you that I'm not paying attention to what you are saying. That's because I am spending more time and effort to read what you wrote on your slide.

Your slides are not meant to act as a crutch during your talk. They are meant to illustrate or enhance your talk. Do not read off your slides. Use pictures whenever possible and use the fewest number of slides you can to convey your message.

- *Be prepared for things to not go as planned.* It's great when things go the way they're supposed to, but often that's not the case. For example, the Internet connection goes out, and you can't show your online demo; your computer can't connect with the available audio/visual equipment in the room you'll be speaking in; or a construction crew will decide to start drilling during your presentation (I've seen the last one happen firsthand). Anything and everything can go wrong, and sometimes, it is completely out of your control.

  Before your talk, think about alternatives that you can take if things go wrong. Back up your presentation to thumb drive. Prerecord yourself giving the demo in case the Internet isn't available. Be ready to project your voice should the audio system be down. Make a checklist and try to prepare contingencies wherever possible.

- *Use your nervousness as an asset.* It's normal and perfectly fine to be nervous right before giving your talk. Whenever possible, try to translate that nervousness into excitement for what you're doing. Reframe it as, "Although this is really nerve-racking, I have the opportunity to influence and inspire others. How cool is that?"

- *Breathe!* When I was practicing for my ACT-W speech, my speech coach noticed that I wasn't inhaling and exhaling normally. By not doing so, I was seriously impacting my delivery—instead of sounding confident and enthusiastic, my voice sounded weak; I came off as nervous and unsure of myself. Take notice of your breathing as you talk.

- *Make eye contact.* This isn't to say that you need to engage your audience in a staring contest, but you want to look them in their eyes for a few seconds to convey that you acknowledge them and are confident in what you are saying.

Where to Find Speaking Opportunities

Being invited to speak at a conference can be a wonderful experience, but there are plenty opportunities around that you can use to start building your skills and speaker portfolios. These are some places to consider:

- Schools and other academic institutions
- Local volunteer organizations

- Event and conference "call for speakers" (usually listed on their website)
- Speaker listing websites, like SpeakerHub: `www.speakerhub.com`

Other Creative Ways to Show What You Know

Resume and LinkedIn are the most straightforward ways you can demonstrate your skills, but other options exist and may be better ways to show off your experience.

GitHub

For those pursuing programming-centric professions, being active on code repositories like GitHub may be the best way to go. In simplest terms, code repositories allow users to share code and full programs with others, with the potential to allow others from anywhere to collaborate with them. Code repositories also help to track and manage project code changes (or version control)—this becomes incredibly important working with larger teams.

Often, recruiters are using code repositories to assess a candidate's skill set and what projects they are actively involved in. Code repositories are not a replacement for a candidate's resume or LinkedIn profile, but they can help further solidify a candidate's standing with an employer. As an example, is a screenshot (Figure 7.5) of my GitHub profile.

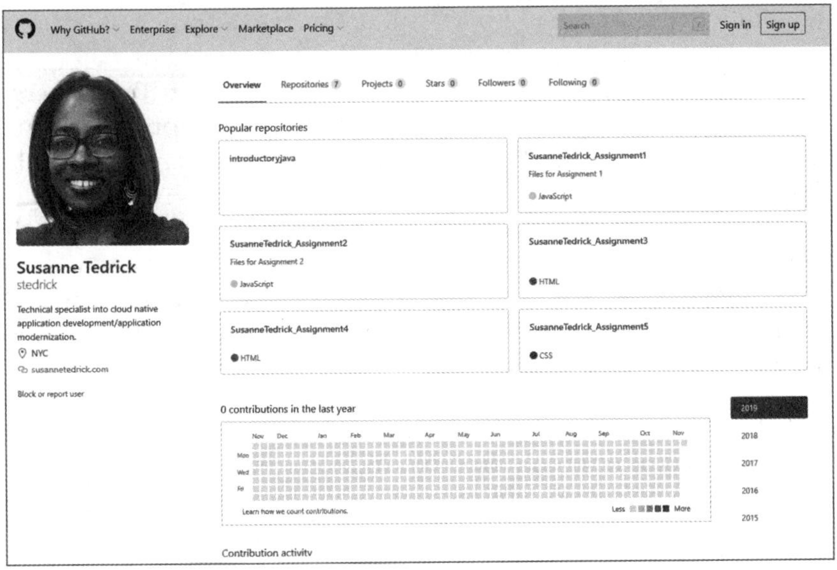

Figure 7.5: Example Github profile

On your profile, you will want to include the following:

- *Photo.* Rather than using a symbol or other images, a good-quality picture of yourself will convey more professionalism. The picture doesn't need to be overly formal, but it should be appropriate and suitable for business environments.

- *Bio and links to other work/websites.* A brief blurb about yourself and the work you have done so far, as well as links to other work or websites, is also helpful.

- *Pinned repositories.* In GitHub, your frequently used repositories will come up on your profile landing page. However, you'll want to "pin" your best work or, rather, the repositories that demonstrate the breadth and depth of your skill. Avoid pinning repositories that aren't indicative of your contributions (e.g., tutorial repositories or cloned repositories that contain little or none of your own original work).

Personal Websites

For those interested more in design-centric or more creative technical careers (e.g., web design or user experience), having a personal website may be one of your best options for showcasing your work. A personal website gives you the opportunity to *show* rather than *tell*.

A personal website is not attached to any company or organization. It's solely yours, and you can brand and design the site however you'd like. The ability to customize is a powerful option, as the previous options discussed do not have much (or any) customization options.

You can use services like Squarespace, Wix, and WordPress to create free personal websites, and with little to no web programming experience needed. With their free plans, you are usually limited to a few prebuilt designs, and the web address you are given isn't customizable. They do offer more options for customizations with their premium plans.

As it is your website, you have total control over what does and doesn't appear. There is no set standard for what a personal website should contain. Here are some sections you may want to consider:

- An About Me or Bio page
- Examples or links to your past work or work in progress
- Testimonials and endorsements of your work

- Your contact information (If you are not keen on having your email address or phone number appear, you can embed an email contact form that hides your information.)

As this website is supposed to be a more of a reflection of your professional work, you should refrain from posting deeply personal information, offensive material, irrelevant work, or design elements that are distracting (e.g., cartoonish-looking clip art or graphics).

I provided a screenshot (Figure 7.6) from the homepage of my own personal website as an example.

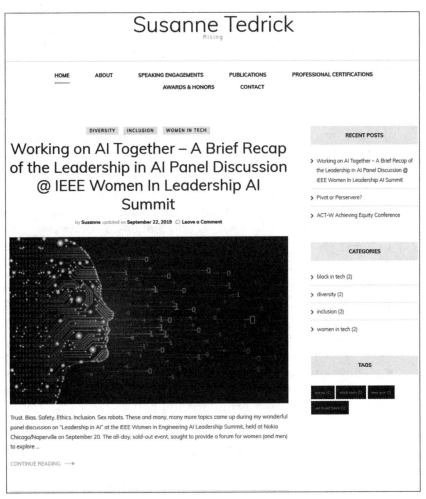

Figure 7.6: Example personal website

Building Your Interviewing Skills

You've managed to bypass the ATS and delighted a recruiter enough with your resume and portfolio to make it to the interview process! Congratulations on making it to this point, as it's no easy feat! You're now at the interviewing stage, and you will want to make sure that you're prepared.

Although the interview process for each organization is different, they may employ any or all of the following interview types:

- *Screening interview.* Screening interviews are usually short in nature—no more than 30 minutes—and are used to both verify that the information you presented in your application is correct and that expectation perspectives (both yours and the employer's) are in sync. The interviewer may ask you to briefly describe your background, your compensation expectations, and how quickly you would be able to work should you be extended a job offer. If this goes well, the interviewer will invite you to advance through the interview process. These interviews typically take place over the phone or by video conference and may be conducted by a recruiter or human resources manager.

  A newer trend in this type of interview is recording video responses to question prompts. Using their computer, tablet, or smart phone, candidates record their answers and submit them for review. Candidates may only be given two or three chances to record their answers, and at no point do they interact with a person in real time.

- *Traditional interview.* In traditional interviews, a candidate meets individually with each person directly or indirectly involved in the hiring process for the position. This includes the hiring manager, people who the candidate would be working with on a regular basis, and other people in the recruiting department. Depending on the seniority of the position and the level of authority the position has, candidates may have two or more individual interviews, typically ranging from 30 minutes to 1 hour.

  Interviewees may ask candidates a variety of questions to assess their behavioral response to certain situations, problem-solving ability, and academic and work credentials. Some take this further and may ask open-ended questions or even brainteasers.

Traditional interviews can take place in person but can also take place over the phone or by video conference.

- *Panel interview.* Instead of meeting with one person at a time, a panel interview is conducted with two or more interviewers in the room with you at the same time. This may be more stressful, but a panel interview can be helpful in that it may present you in a fairer light than an interview with a single interviewer who may be inexperienced or biased. In addition, if all the necessary decision-makers are on the panel, this can potentially make hiring process go faster.

- *Technical interview or assessment.* To confirm that you have the technical skills and knowledge necessary for a given position, employers may administer one (or more) technical interviews to candidates.

Technical interviews vary greatly from employer to employer. For example, an employer may ask you a series of questions to ascertain how familiar you are with certain concepts, while others may take many hours and are administered with pencil and paper or through a computer. Some companies use the whiteboard technique, where they'll ask a candidate to work through a problem from start to finish, using a whiteboard and dry-erase markers.

Becoming a Better Interviewee

Like resume preparation, people become better at interviewing with time and practice. Here are a few recommendations to become better at the process:

- *Practice, practice, practice.* Take advantage of any opportunities that you can to practice interviewing in front of another person. Many schools, professional organizations, and other career service organizations allow participants to do general practice interviews with professionals. Mock interviewers will provide you detailed feedback. They'll assess you on things like the quality of your answers, as well as your tone and body language, among other factors.

Keep in mind that it's okay to not do well in a mock interview. They are designed to show you the areas in your interview technique that need improvement. It is much better to fail, so to speak, in a mock interview than to fail in a real interview.

If live mock interviews are not available to you in your area, several online resources like Pramp (www.pramp.com) and Interview Buddy (www.interviewbuddy.com) allow you to conduct online mock videos and receive assessments from technical professionals.

For technical interviews, there are resources like Interviewing.io (www.interviewing.io) and InterviewBit (www.interviewbit.com) that offer sample technical questions and practice exercises so that these types of interviews are a little less daunting.

In addition, *Cracking the Coding Interview* (CareerCup, 2011) by Gayle McDowell is a highly rated and highly regarded resource in assisting people in coding technical interviews.

- *Prepare answers to common questions in advance.* While you don't want your answers to sound overly rehearsed, there are certain interview questions that come up often, and when they do come up, you don't want to fumble through your answer. The questions that are commonly asked include:

  - *Tell me about yourself.* This question trips many people up! When asked this question, the interviewer doesn't want your whole life story or background, but they do want you to provide enough information (in two to four sentences) on how your skills and experiences are a match for the position—think of it as your "elevator pitch."

  - *Why do you want this job?* For this type of question, you need to demonstrate a genuine desire and excitement for the job. While recruiters and hiring managers may be sympathetic about needing a job to pay the bills, that's not the answer that they want to hear. They want to hear about why you are their ideal candidate and what about their company and/or the position compelled you to put yourself through the application process.

  - *What are your strengths and weaknesses?* The answers to these questions require a delicate balance. You do not want to come off particularly arrogant, but you don't want to demonstrate weaknesses in a way that might lower your chances of advancing in the interview process.

For the weakness question, avoid saying that you have a "weakness" that is secretly a strength. Many employers can see through this, possibly get frustrated, and press you to mention an actual weakness.

- *Rehearse, record, and review your answers to interview questions.* No question, this can be super awkward. I personally do not enjoy hearing my voice or seeing videos of myself. But reviewing yourself—your voice, your body language, your responses—can also be helpful in improving your interviewing technique. If this is difficult to do on your own, call in a friend to help with your review and offer constructive feedback.

- *Research the company and the position to which you are applying.* This can be time-consuming, but adequately and thoroughly researching the company and the potential position can help you stand out among other candidates.

Aside from a company's website and the job listing, other potential places for information can include the following:

- Financial statements and SEC filings (for publicly traded companies)

- Social media platforms, including Facebook, LinkedIn, Twitter, and Reddit

- News sites

- Industry-specific news sites (e.g., TechCrunch and Engadget)

- Employer ratings and reviews (found on sites like Glassdoor or Fairy Godboss)

Summary

- Resume may come in a variety of formats—chronological, functional, and a combination, to name a few—but the important thing is to demonstrate the value you can bring to an organization.

- Applicant tracking systems decrease the likelihood of your resume being seen by human eyes, and recruiters do not spend a lot of time reviewing resume. Ensure that your resume is in perfect order before applying.

- LinkedIn allows you to be more creative in setting yourself apart as a professional. Consider using its robust features.

- There are other ways to show what you know. From writing to public speaking to online platforms, pursue other channels to help you stand out above the crowd.

- Practice interviewing whenever possible.

CHAPTER 8

Job Offers and Negotiating Compensation

You've made it through all the job applications, interviews, and background checks and have received a job offer! Congratulations! Now comes the other, important part of the equation—making sure that your compensation package is fair and competitive. This chapter will cover the components that make up compensation, how to assess if an offer is a good one, and how to approach the negotiation process.

A Cautionary Tale (or, Don't Do This!)

My first professional job was as a receptionist for a start-up software-development consulting firm. I was so excited to have my first real office job with pay and benefits, and I finally felt like a grown-up!

I was offered the following:

- $35,255.39 (salary adjusted for inflation to 2019 dollars)
- Approximately 20 vacation and sick days
- Health insurance, paying roughly 20 percent of the monthly premium costs

- A share of the company's yearly profit, which they would determine based on my performance

The salary was low, but I rationalized the offer by remembering I had no other professional experience and everything else (people, location and other benefits) were good. I said yes to the offer almost immediately and started working shortly thereafter. Many years, and jobs, later, I realized that there were things I could've done differently.

First, I assumed that the employer was giving me a salary that was in line with what the job market said was fair. I incorrectly assumed that since these people really seemed to love me and wanted me to start, they would pay me what I was worth. I also didn't think I should or could ask for more—I was just grateful to have a job, so why rock the boat?

Second, I did not conduct any research on whether this was a fair job offer. Had I done some homework, I would have discovered that the median pay for a receptionist in the New York City area was approximately $48,897.69 in today's dollars. While not an ideal salary, especially for an expensive area like NYC, it was still nearly 39 percent better than what I was offered. I also would've figured out that since the company was open all year, holidays that I assumed were automatic time off (Christmas, New Year's Day, etc.) would be coming out of my total vacation time available. And while it was great to be included in a profit-sharing plan, this was not guaranteed money and was entirely dependent on how the manager *felt* I was contributing to the company's success and *if* the company made money that year. As it was a start-up, that was anyone's guess.

Third, and perhaps the worst part of it, I repeated this pattern for just about every job offer I received up until the last few years. In my head, I was just grateful to have a job and thought asking for more might make me seem greedy or have them take away my offer. Who was I to ask for more?

I didn't realize that not only was my approach and reasoning very faulty, but by not asking, I was hurting myself financially in the long run. By not negotiating (or asking for raises), I had less money overall —less money to pay bills, to invest in savings and my retirement, and to spend toward things that made me happy.

It's no secret that women—and specifically, women of color—are underpaid in about every industry, not just tech. While it is on companies to fix their approaches to compensation, it is our right and duty to demand fair compensation for our work.

I realize that there are some situations in life that dictate that you take the first job you can get. There are times when we do not have the luxury to wait for the right job to come along; we've got to take the job that's in front of us now. For entry-level jobs, there may not be much wiggle room for you to ask for more. All that said, I encourage you to negotiate your compensation as often as you can and early in your career.

Understanding Compensation and Salary

There are many reasons why negotiation should be considered when receiving a job offer. Before jumping in, we should define some key terms and concepts.

Compensation

Compensation is the total cash and noncash benefits that an employer pays to you or on your behalf in exchange for your service. The total compensation a company pays will vary by company but generally includes the following:

- **Salary:** This is a fixed amount of cash that your employer pays you directly for your work by the hour, day, week, etc.
- **Benefits:** This can include vacation and sick time, medical insurance, and retirement pay.
- **Taxes:** These are government-required fees that employers must pay on behalf of their employees, like Social Security and Medicare.

Depending on the organization, employers may be paying on average 25–46 percent in benefits and taxes in addition to salary for one employee. So, when a company advertises a position that pays a salary of $90,000 a year, that should not be read as the company is paying only $90,000 overall for that employee. Factoring in benefits and taxes, the true cost to the employer for that employee is closer to $112,500–$131,400.

Given these costs, it partially explains why a job offer may be on the low end. Employers want to hire amazing people but are trying to do so at the lowest cost possible. Brianne Wilson, a product manager for compensation management software, offers some insight: "Every company is different, and it depends on their compensation philosophy, if they have one. Some companies do not think of compensation beyond budgets and salary survey data. Some companies have experts who understand competitive salaries and the obvious line between employee engagement and the money you pay them. But, if they're only thinking of the bottom line, then obviously it is in a company's best interest to offer you the lowest they can."

Salary

When you accept a job offer, employers agree to pay your salary in a fixed time period, be it weekly, every other week, or sometimes even on a monthly basis. This is your *gross salary*, or the salary you make before any money is taken out.

When they pay you, they are legally required to a certain sum of money from your paycheck right off the top for:

- Social Security and Medicare (sometimes referred as FICA)
- Federal, state, and local taxes (depending on where you live)

What is left over after all the required taxes are taken out is called your *disposable income*. This can also be referred to as your *net income* or *take-home pay*. It varies by where you live and your family status (e.g., being single or married), but generally, people can expect to see 25 percent of their pay deducted for taxes, Social Security, and Medicare. For a person making $90,000 a year, they may receive $67,500 in cash, while $22,500 is withheld to pay taxes.

We're still not quite done yet. We haven't factored in your essentials or necessities, like the following:

- Rent or housing payments
- Food
- Clothing
- Utilities
- Other necessary goods and services

Once these are factored in, you now have your total *discretionary income*—the remaining amount of money you have for savings, going out, or other types of spending.

How much you have left as discretionary income will vary. People who live in expensive areas, like San Francisco or New York, may receive higher salaries, but it is to offset their cost of living expenses, which can be significantly higher than other parts of the United States.

I bring this up to stress the importance of asking for what you are worth. Your initial salary offer may be sound great (and it very well may be), but when you factor in taxes and necessary expenses, it may not leave you a ton of money for leisure, paying down debt, furthering your education, or other pursuits.

Table 8.1 shows what a household with a $90,000 gross salary (now $67,500 after taxes) spends, on average, on certain items.

Table 8.1: Average US Household Costs

	AVERAGE PERCENTAGE OF INCOME (ANNUAL)	AVERAGE COST BASED ON $90,000 GROSS SALARY (ANNUAL)*
Housing	32.8%	$22,140
Transportation	15.9%	$10,736
Utilities	11%	$7,425
Food	12.9%	$8,708
Healthcare	8.1%	$5,468
Clothes	3%	$2,025
Personal Care	1%	$675

Source: Consumer Expenditures Survey—2018, United States Bureau of Labor Statistics

* Assumes 25 percent is deducted from a $90,000 gross salary for mandatory taxes, leaving $67,500 in disposable (net) income.

Using the figures from Table 8.1, that leaves $10,328 for you to use at your discretion, or about $861 per month. Your personal budget figures will vary (some expenses may be higher or lower; you may also have other obligations to include like debt obligations), and having some extra money is better than none.

But imagine how much more you'd be able to put toward your goals with more money. For example, assuming your household costs and taxes remain more or less the same, if you brought in a $95,000 gross salary (almost a modest 5.6 percent increase), you would have $14,078 a year left over. An additional $3,750 in the bank sounds pretty good to me.

The Job Offer Process

Every organization has its own unique process for calculating what to offer potential candidates and onboarding new employees. Most, however, follow these steps:

1. The company reaches out to you to let you know they've picked you for the job. This can occur by email but usually is done over the phone by a recruiter, an HR representative, or the hiring manager.

2. During the call, they will do the following:

   1. Confirm the title and position you are being offered

   2. Tell you the salary that you will be paid, usually quoted per year

   3. Tell you who you will be reporting to

   4. Tell you the location you'll be working in

   5. Give you your start date

   6. Offer a time frame for you think about the offer and when you'll need to respond

   7. Let you know how you should respond to the offer (via email; phone call, etc.)

   8. Inform you of any critical pieces of information they believe you need to make an informed decision

   9. Tell you additional information they need from you to complete background and/or reference checks

3. After the call, they'll likely send you a formal offer letter, recapping what was discussed and outlining some additional details. This can include:

   1. The frequency in which you are paid (weekly, biweekly, etc.).

   2. Time frame when you'd be eligible for company benefits, like medical and dental.

   3. The amount of vacation or sick time you are eligible for.

   4. The conditions of your offer. This is a statement that says you are being offered this job because of the information you presented about yourself in your job application and interview process. If it's found out at any point—at the start of your job or during it—that the information you presented is false, they can either take away your offer or have you dismissed without notice.

Evaluating a Job Offer

You're super excited to have a job offer, but it is important to take a moment and step back to ensure that the offer is a good one. How do you know if one is? Let's look at some things to consider before saying yes.

Do You Like the Job and This Company?

These may sound like weird questions to ask. You might be thinking, "Why on Earth would I apply for and take a job that I don't like?" You'd be surprised how many times people will take jobs they really aren't interested in or will work for companies they don't like. Maybe it's because of the overall prestige of the company, the money that's being offered, because they need the experience, or their life/financial situation demands that they take the job. I've been there, done that, and I get it. Sometimes having *a job* is better than *no job*.

I'm not suggesting outright to *not* take a job for the reasons mentioned. Yet, I would ask you to consider that the longer you stay at a place or career that doesn't fulfill your needs, you'll make less progress and have less time to devote to the career path you want. Career paths are not linear—you may likely end up having multiple careers during your life—but you don't want to spend too much time at a place where you're spinning your wheels and getting nowhere fast. Also, going to a place where you're excited to work and you feel like your work has purpose leads to better job engagement and overall career happiness.

If a job or company gives you bad feelings, *run, don't walk*, away from these offers. I believe in trusting your gut; sometimes you just know something is off, but it's hard to pinpoint what exactly. There are some tangible signs you can pay attention to that this may not be the right job.

■ **The employer asks inappropriate questions during the interview process.** Employers are not allowed to ask questions about your age, race, ethnicity, gender, sex, disability, marital status, or whether you are or plan to be pregnant. Although inexperienced interviewers may not know this, to me that is not a valid excuse. It's the employer's job to ensure that all interviewers know what questions they may or may not ask candidates, and proper interviewing etiquette. Employers who don't enforce this may be likely to let other discriminatory practices creep into the workplace.

■ **You're being pressured to give an answer to the employer's offer immediately and to start working . . . now.** This is usually a sign that they are experiencing unexpected turnover (employees leaving the company). They are just looking for someone, anyone, to fill the position and don't care about your needs or long-term career growth.

■ **The job details are vague.** You have no idea what you'll actually be doing in the job because they've written the job description in a very ambiguous, head-scratching way. With the job description being so vague and open ended, you may end up doing tasks you don't want to do.

- **The employer won't put the job details in writing.** A verbal job offer is legally binding, but having a written job offer is best to avoid situations where it would be your word against theirs, as well as to prevent confusion about what your salary and benefits should be. An employer's reluctance or refusal to put this in writing is a huge red flag.

- **The employer won't let you speak to other coworkers.** I had this happen in a previous job, and I sincerely regretted not exploring this further. If I had talked to my soon-to-be coworkers, I would've figured out sooner how toxic the culture was and that there were no advancement opportunities. It was truly a dead-end job. If they won't let you talk to someone who isn't a manager or part of the recruiting department, it may be that they are trying to keep something from you.

- **The employer has negative reviews on anonymous company review sites like Glassdoor.com.** In general, take online anonymous salary reviews with a grain of salt. Not every review written can be taken at face value, and there isn't a way to verify if what is being presented is true. An ex-employee might have been asked to leave for poor performance and may be choosing to lash out in an anonymous, no serious repercussions way. However, I am a believer of the phrase "where there's smoke, there's fire." If there are several different reviews that highlight the same themes, like a toxic work environment, then there's probably truth there.

- **The employer gives you a job offer, even though you didn't apply or interview for a position with them.** Without any effort or outreach on your part, an employer you've never heard of says you're hired to work for them, and wants you to send them money and/or provide your personal details to proceed with the application process. These are straight-up scams; stay clear as they're trying to steal your money, or your identity.

Are Your "Must Haves" Addressed?

Know what your "must haves" are very early into your job-hunting process, preferably before you even start interviewing. What are the things that you absolutely, positively must have to even take an offer seriously?

While your desired salary range is a large (and important) factor, there are other things you will want to take into account, like the following:

- Vacation and sick time
- Benefits such as medical insurance, retirement plan options, tuition reimbursement, etc.
- How close the job will be to your home (your commute time)
- Other types of pay available, such as bonuses, commission, or equity in the company
- Ability to be considered for promotions and raises
- Opportunities to travel or work from home
- Paid relocation expenses (should you need to move for the job)

For example, suppose you receive a job offer with an incredibly awesome salary but discover that the employer does not offer health insurance. If having health insurance is important to you, are you comfortable shouldering the costs of the health insurance premiums, which are incredibly expensive, on your own? Are they willing to offer a stipend to you to offset the costs?

"It's just like dating," Wilson says. "You first have to ask yourself what is it you need, set those boundaries, and make sure those needs are met. Know your worth. And know that your compensation is only one piece of knowing it's the right fit, but a *big* piece!"

Some benefits may be more important to you than others, but the point is that you want to know what these are before getting an offer so that you know where there's room to negotiate.

Is the Salary Offered Fair?

You'll need to do a bit of research to assess if the salary being offered is fair. There are a few places you can go to find information.

The salary that you are offered depends on several factors. The main ones are as follows:

- **Experience:** The more years of professional experience you have, the more money you can command. While some employers recognize internship, co-op, and similar experiences, others may only consider the number of years of relevant full-time employment.
- **Education:** The more formal education you have, the likelier you are to be paid more. Where you obtained your degree and what you studied can also influence what's offered.

- **Professional certifications:** Widely recognized business and technical certifications can influence what's offered.

- **Location:** Cities like San Francisco and New York City pay higher wages because they have higher costs of living than other parts of the country.

- **Sector:** Private employers may be able to offer more in terms of salary in comparison to nonprofit, government, or academic jobs.

With that in mind, a good place to research salary ranges is the Occupational Outlook Handbook (OOH) (www.bls.gov/ooh), maintained by the United States Department of Labor Bureau of Labor Statistics. OOH allows you to review national median pay, growth, and educational requirements for select professions.

Another is Career OneStop, sponsored by the US Department of Labor. In addition to career information and education requirement information, Career OneStop (www.careeronestop.org) allows you to review median salary information at local and state levels.

Tech staffing agencies, like Robert Half (www.roberthalf.com/salary-guide) and Randstad (www.randstadusa.com/salary), annually publish salary guides to give employers and prospective employees an idea of what certain tech jobs pay annually. These guides also contain information on what skills employers are having a hard time filling (which can translate into an opportunity for you), as well as what technical and socioeconomic developments will impact what the industry looks like in years to come.

In addition to allowing current and former employees to leave reviews on companies, Glassdoor and similar websites (PayScale (www.payscale.com), FairyGodboss (www.fairygodboss.com), and others) allow users to submit salary information by company and title. Again, the accuracy of this information will depend on how honest the people doing the reporting are, and if enough people wrote reviews for the position you are interested in, but these sites can still give you a good sense of what a reasonable salary range looks like.

Also, don't forget to reach out to your network for information. Your mentors, coaches, classmates and colleagues may be willing to share their information or at least point you in the direction of where you can find more tailored and concrete information.

Why Negotiate Your Job Offer?

As you can see, preparing to negotiate a job offer and negotiating the actual offer can take a fair bit of work. Is it really worth the effort? Absolutely. Let's discuss a few reasons why.

More of What You Want, Now

The most immediate benefit is having what you want now versus having to wait, and potentially work harder for it, later. Getting a higher salary now means more money in your bank account immediately.

Solidify Your Negotiation Skills

As mentioned earlier in this chapter, you will find the need for negotiation skills throughout your life. The more you use and practice these skills, the more adept you will become in using them. This will become important when you find yourself in complex negotiation situations.

Show Employers You Know Your Value

Negotiating your salary with a future employer exudes confidence and that you know what you are worth. A friend recalled that when she asked the recruiter if her job offer could be negotiated, the first thing that the recruiter said was that she was happy that she asked. The recruiter was happy that she took the initiative and did good research, and commented that so few of the women she spoke with even asked the question!

There Are Few Downsides to Asking

As my wonderful colleague Sam Demezieux would say, "The closed mouth does not get fed." You won't get what you want if you don't ask for it. Some of the fear attached to asking is that the consequences can range from being thought of as "pushy," "aggressive," or "greedy," to the employer deciding to take back an offer. You also can't assume that things will automatically be given to you because you're a smart and nice person.

While I have said in the past that the worst an employer can say is no, it would be naïve of me to think, and to say to you, that there won't be consequences. It's a real and valid concern. Women, not just those of color and certainly not just in the tech industry, have reported experiencing negative effects for asking for more.

First, few employers take away offers because someone asked for more. The employer may turn around and give you a hard no. But if they completely take away an offer, it is usually because of a failed background check or an internal matter within the organization (i.e., the company is downsizing)

Second, if an employer does threaten to take an offer away or attempt to make you feel bad or guilty for asking, you may need to take a moment, and ask yourself if this you really want to work for this company. I'm a believer that how you are treated during a company's interview and hiring process can be a good indicator of the type of treatment you can expect once you start.

Lastly, they want you. It takes employers a great deal of time and money to find phenomenal talent (like you). They don't send out job offers with the mind-set of "Let's hope for the best." They send them out because they believe in your ability to add value. If that means they have to pay a little bit more to get you, they'll do it (provided they have the wiggle room to do it).

You May Not Get as Much Later

Although you may be eligible for raises and salary reviews once you are in the company, you may not be able to get much more money. Per the Bureau of Labor Statistics, the average salary raise in 2018 was 3 percent, although workers in the tech industry may see yearly raises closer to 5 percent. Also, even if your manager loves you and wants to give you a raise, he or she may not be able to because of budget cuts or freezes within the organization. Finally, if you were already being paid well under what the market says you should be making, you may need a significant raise just to be at market level—a normal raise may not cut it.

In contrast, when you receive a job offer, you may be able to negotiate for far more money, anywhere from 1 percent to 20 percent.

You'll Hurt Your Finances in the Long Run

Not asking for more money can lead to real-world consequences. In my opening story, by not attempting to negotiate, I potentially lost out on making more than $13,000, and it only required a minor output of effort on my part. I repeated this pattern again and again, causing me to work much harder than perhaps needed. You may be walking away from a sizeable amount of money over the course of your career.

Preparing to Negotiate

Negotiation is the process in which two or more people or parties reach an agreement that is beneficial to everyone. Good negotiation practices are when all parties come away from the process feeling positive about what they'll receive from the agreement, rather than feeling like they've lost or received nothing.

You may think this is the first time you've had to negotiate, but I'm certain that you have negotiated many times before during the course of your life. If you've ever had to figure out where to go for lunch or dinner with a group of friends, you have negotiated. If you've ever asked a parent or loved one for something for you, or permission to do something, in exchange for something that you will do for them, then you've negotiated. I remember asking my dad if I could have a sleepover at our house if I got a B or better on a science test in junior high school (and I did). This may be the first time you have had to negotiate something a bit more high stakes. In any case, you already possess the basic skills necessary to have successful negotiations.

There are many different approaches and strategies that you can use, but I think that these are the basic things you need and should do before walking into any negotiation situation:

- **Do your research.** Walking into a salary negotiation with unrealistic expectations, or no expectations, is almost guaranteed not to end well.

- **Know your minimum requirements.** Establish what is the lowest possible salary you will take for the position. Take care not to undercut yourself—if there is a minimum amount of money you need to keep your household functioning, then accepting a figure below this amount may hurt you. Additionally, you may grow to resent that employer as you'll feel that they took advantage of you. Stick with this figure.

- **Establish a salary range.** Use the lowest number you'll possibly accept; then from your research, establish what is the most that you can ask for. You can start from the top of the range, and if necessary, go further down your range to what will be a mutually acceptable number.

- **Know what your "nice to haves" are.** If the employer is unable to meet the salary range (and not your minimum requirement), they may have some additional options that can help sweeten the deal. Do you want to have more vacation time? Would you like to work from home or another location? Are you able to get equity (or partial ownership) in the company? Keep other benefits in mind; you might be surprised what you're able to negotiate.

- **Practice, practice, practice.** Go through a mock negotiation exercise with a trusted friend, mentor, coach, or colleague. Explain the situation and ask them to provide critical feedback on what went well and what could be improved.

- **Understand compensation strategy, terminology, and concepts.** Knowing how employers generally approach setting salary and overall compensation is beneficial. For example, many employers use what's called a *compa-ratio* when determining pay. A compa-ratio calculates where your salary for your position lands in relation to what the market typically pays. As Wilson explains, "If your job has a salary range of, say, $50,000–$80,000 [per year] and you have a salary of $65,000 [per year], you have a compa-ratio of 1." Employers use this and several other metrics to evaluate how competitive salaries are. You don't need to be a compensation expert, but having this knowledge can be beneficial to you come negotiation time.

Negotiation Dos and Don'ts

It's the moment of truth—time to get down to business and negotiate your salary. Now that you've done your homework and have an offer in hand, here's what to do and what to avoid during the negotiations process.

Do:

- **Be confident.** If you've done your homework, asking for what you're worth shouldn't be too difficult, as you'll have the info to back up your request. You want to make good eye contact and exude confident body language. If the negotiation is being conducted over the phone, keep your tone positive; if you're conducting the negotiation by email, use positive and unambiguous language.

- **Always maintain a positive and respectful attitude.** While there are some who really enjoy the negotiation process, others might find this to be an anxiety-riddled, frustrating exercise. It can certainly play on your emotions and tax your nerves. But it is important to keep your cool, no matter what. Avoid yelling, threatening, or engaging in unprofessional behavior at any point during the negotiation process.

- **Be flexible and open-minded about the offer.** There are times when employers just can't offer you more at the time of the offer. If the offer doesn't contain any of your deal breakers, there may be other things that they can offer you. Also, consider asking if you can have a formal salary review a few months after your hire date.

- **Take your time.** You may not get a ton of time to decide, but you can usually take a few days to think about the offer before giving an answer. This is the perfect time to do more research, talk to others to get their advice, or compare this offer to others you're considering. Take all the time you're able to take so that you'll feel comfortable with the choice you've made.

- **Re-emphasize the value you bring.** As Wilson states, "Don't be afraid to highlight projects you did in bootcamps, list any relevant skills, make note of specific classes you took, provide links to an online portfolio or GitHub account. Even if you wrote only one program in Java, list it as a skill! The key is to not sell yourself short."

- **Document everything.** If the terms of the offer change, make sure that these changes are noted somewhere in paper or electronic form, just in case.

Don't:

- **Make it personal.** You are wonderful and incredibly talented, and at the end of the day, the decision to offer you more will be based on your skills, what you bring to the table and, largely, what the employer has the capacity to offer you. It not a reflection of how they feel about you as a person, but more of a quantitative, business decision.

- **Try to threaten or coerce the other side into giving you a higher salary.** This includes saying you have another offer from another company or inflating your past salary history.

> **NOTE**   Although there are many states that outlaw the practice of asking for salary history because it has historically put women at a disadvantage (women are offered a lower salary because they were already making a low salary from previous employers), it is not a widespread practice or nationwide law, and some employers can ask for a paystub or W2 to verify any past salary claims you are making

- **Make unilateral concessions.** A unilateral concession is where you agree to give up something without expectation of the employer giving you anything in return. This is what's called negotiating "against" yourself. Avoid being your own worst enemy.

  For example, if you say to an employer that your salary expectation is $90,000 per year but you'd be willing to accept $80,000, and they are not going to give you anything for the $10,000 you're sacrificing, you've given the employer a concession and got nothing else to show for the $10K you're now out of.

- **Try to negotiate after you've accepted the offer.** If you realize later that your salary requirements are higher than you thought *after* you already said yes or you forgot to negotiate at all, that's unfortunately on you, not them. Again, and I can't stress this enough, do your homework.

- **Present irrelevant facts and information when presenting your case for more money.** When presenting your case for more money, you should focus on compelling reasons why you are worth the added expense to the employer. It's not enough to say that you were top of your class or are a hard worker. These are great accolades and traits, but employers want skills and achievements that have the potential to translate into real value for them.

- **Press employers further if that's their "best" or "final" offer.** Despite best efforts, employers may not be able to offer you any more than what they've given. At this point, you need to decide if you are okay with the offer or if you want to hold out and evaluate other ones.

- **Beat yourself up if things don't go well.** "If you stumble in your first few attempts when starting, don't beat yourself up" says Wilson. "It definitely takes practice, just like building confidence takes practice."

You Didn't Negotiate! Is It Too Late?

For a variety of reasons, you may not have been able to negotiate your salary when you got the offer. Perhaps the employer said that the offer you got was the best they could do, or you just couldn't negotiate at that time. You may have to wait to have this conversation, but asking for more isn't a one-and-done event.

Perhaps as part of your annual performance evaluation process, there may be an opportunity for you to receive a raise. During this time, you'll want to highlight your accomplishments for the year and how they translated into value for the organization.

Of course, you can always ask your manager for time to discuss a raise at any time. You may want to wait, at least three to six months, before asking; this way, you give your organization time to see the value you bring. Volunteer and get involved in "stretch" projects—projects that are just a little beyond your current skill set but won't completely overwhelm you and are critical to business functions. Make suggestions of where the company can improve their performance and then volunteer to take them on. The point is, show your boss and others that you are committed and vested in helping the company be successful.

When the time comes, again, be prepared. Wilson advises, "Come in prepared with your contributions to the company. Make a list throughout the year if that works best for you. Check those salary surveys. And don't be afraid to ask your peers if they're willing to share their salaries with you."

Additional Resources

Here are some additional resources:

American Association of University Women: AAUW is a professional organization that seeks to advance women in academics and the workplace through education, training, and economic support. In partnership with LUNA Bars (the nutritional bar aimed at women), it hosts a free salary negotiation workshop for women of color, which can be taken online or in person at a city near you.

Online salary negotiation workshop: `salary.aauw.org`

In-person salary negotiation workshops: `salary.aauw.org/attend`

Ladies Get Paid: Perhaps one of the most comprehensive women's career development organizations I've seen, Ladies Get Paid offers a wealth of classes, webinars, and events dedicated to getting you the salary you des.erve. It also hosts a Slack channel, where you can find job opportunities and connect with other professionals for practical advice.

www.ladiesgetpaid.com

Getting to Yes: Negotiating Agreement Without Giving In (Penguin Books, 2011): I had to read this book three times—twice for two classes at Northwestern and once for work—and I understand why. This great book by Roger Fisher and William Ury provides an easy-to-understand framework to approach negotiations, whether it's at work, school, or other areas of your life.

www.williamury.com/books/getting-to-yes

Final Thoughts—It's Okay to Want (and Ask for) Money

Despite many strides in women's pay equity and parity, it still feels as if women from all walks of life and backgrounds are hesitant to express their want for more money. Emotions and rationalizations for not asking can go from "I'm just grateful to have a job" to "I care only about the work, not the money."

"It's like we have this dose of being overly realistic when it comes to jobs and money," Wilson says. "We know we need to get our foot in the door, so we'll put up with less than we deserve. White women make on average $0.80 for every $1.00 men make, [for] Black women it's $0.61, and [for] Latina women it's even less at $0.53. If you're offered the equivalent of, say, $0.85 for every $1.00, are you being greedy to ask for $0.15 more when you're so fortunate to be above the average?"[1]

I love working in tech. It is my hope and desire to build a legacy as a respected technical professional. I love helping others succeed, and I love being able to work with the latest and greatest in technology. These are all incredibly important things to me. But I also love—and need—to provide for myself and my family. I love being able to donate to causes that I believe in. I love being able to indulge in my hobbies when I can, and ideally, fingers crossed, take a vacation soon! In order to do all of that, I need money.

---

[1]LeanIn.org, "The Gender Pay Gap by the Numbers," https://leanin.org/equal-pay-data-about-the-gender-pay-gapv.

It is not wrong to want money. It is not wrong to ask for money. There is nothing wrong with talking about your salary and compensation expectations to employers and receiving what you are worth. It becomes a problem only when the pursuit of money is your only focus and you lose sight of other things that are important to you.

Approach these conversations with confidence, knowing that it is your right to be paid what you are worth. Do not worry about the opinions of others; their opinions aren't going to pay your bills and put a roof over your head.

Summary

- Compensation includes the total amount of cash you receive from an employer (salary), as well as any benefits that an employer provides to you.

- Negotiation is where two or more people or parties reach an agreement that is beneficial to everyone.

- A good negotiation is where all parties in the process come away feeling like they've won.

- You can, and should, negotiate job offers as early and often in your career. Prepare for negotiations early in the interviewing process.

- Although you can negotiate your salary during annual reviews or other points of time with an employer, you are likelier to receive more money during the job offer process.

- When considering a job offer, think about whether the job/company helps you to fulfill your career goals, if your "must haves" are being met, and if the salary you are being offered is fair.

- You deserve to be paid what you are worth, and it is okay to want and ask for more money from prospective employers.

When Times Get Tough

*"You may shoot me with your words
You may cut me with your eyes
You may kill me with your hatefulness
But still, like air, I rise"*

—"Still I Rise," Maya Angelou

I feel it is important to openly address issues that may make your journey more challenging. It is not my intention to suggest that every woman of color's personal story is filled with hardships and strife or that the issues raised in this chapter are ones you will face. In fact, I would be incredibly happy if none of these issues comes up for you ever—it is my hope that you're in supportive, nurturing environments with people who want you to succeed.

Unfortunately, women of color are more likely to be dealing with several unique situations at home, school, and work than any other group. In this chapter, I will attempt to outline strategies to help you through.

The Need for Grit

It's no secret that women of color have a lot on their shoulders. In addition to dealing with common, everyday issues, we're often contending with more demands on our time and energy, with few resources and support.

Many of the people interviewed for this book did not have a mentorship or someone to give them guidance on how to start and navigate their career.

Many juggled the demands of work, school, and family to complete or advance their education. Angela Dogan is pursuing her doctorate degree in information technology, assurance, and cybersecurity while working full-time. In her path to working for a Fortune 100 company, Titilayo Robinson had to take several part-time jobs and unpaid internships to get the money and skills she needed to advance in her career.

For some, life events also tested their resolve. Earlier in her career, Juliet Okafor of Habitu8 discovered that she was pregnant after losing her job in a mass layoff a month prior. Unable to go to job interviews, she had to go on public assistance to care for her and her child. She found a position several months later, but it was 2 hours away and paid her 50 percent of her previous job. She persisted, though, and ended up replacing her own boss 4 months into the job—she found herself leading sales teams in the Philippines, India, and other countries.

My mother had been diagnosed with a brain tumor when I was very young. This initial tumor led to more health issues for her over the years, including a decline into dementia, a loss of some of her short-term memory, and impacted mobility. The latter half of her life was spent in and out of hospitals, having numerous operations and medical incidents. My father was left to care for me and my sister, while also supporting several other family members in one house. Between work and caring for my mom, he couldn't be around much, and fortunately, some nearby relatives and family friends helped to raise and care for us. As there was only one income (already too high to qualify for most public assistance programs) and my mother needed many medications, there were times where a choice had to be made between eating, having phone service, making critical house repairs, or having the lights stay on.

This went on for nearly two decades, up until my mother's death. It wasn't until well into my adult life that I realized I was living in "survival mode" and just trying to exist. I was spending most of my time trying to find happiness in my life; having a meaningful and engaging career was not an immediate goal or one I thought was achievable for me.

These stories are not offered for sympathy. Rather, I offer them for a few reasons. First, while I believe 110 percent in celebrating success, big or small, I do think there is not enough acknowledgment in popular culture to highlight the "blood, sweat, and tears" it takes to be successful. Even with hard work, success is not guaranteed, easy to attain, or a permanent state.

The iceberg analogy, while somewhat overused in popular culture, is my favorite. I feel it accurately portrays the path to success.

When we look at icebergs, we see them only from the surface of the water. According to *National Geographic*, we may see only 1/8th of an iceberg from where we are standing. The iceberg's true size, though, can be quite massive, with some being almost 9,000 square miles and weighing more than 200,000 metric tons. One iceberg can take anywhere from 2,000 to 4,000 years to form.

The same can be said about how we may see a person's success, without understanding the true depth of what it took for them to get there. We'll see a friend or colleague getting a promotion at work, but we do not see or know what it took for them to get said accolades. We do not see the countless hours of networking, preparation, negotiation, and late nights it took to get said promotion. We also don't know how long it took—it may have taken months or maybe even years to be recognized. We may not know any or all the professional and personal setbacks the person faced along the way. All we see is this surface-level moment of success, not the effort that made this moment possible.

Second, these stories are to illustrate that success is possible, even through the hardest of circumstances. The unifying theme of these stories is grit. Grit is defined as "having courage and resolve." It means doing and facing things that can be hard and challenging in order to achieve success.

Grit does not mean that you need to be a skilled expert or working yourself like crazy. But it does mean putting in steady effort to attain your goals and addressing challenges. No matter what career path you take, you need grit.

The Problem with "Twice as Good"

Many women of color have been told that in order to be successful in their careers, they need to be "twice as good," meaning they need to have the same, if not more, skills than their white counterparts and strive for perfection at every part of their academic or professional career. I have been told this many, many times in different ways throughout my life by well-meaning family, friends, teachers, and mentors.

I have mixed feelings about the "twice as good" mantra. I don't want to suggest that there aren't workplaces where a woman of color isn't criticized, judged, or penalized more harshly for similar actions taken by her white colleagues. It's been studied extensively by many universities and research organizations, the results of which point to this claim having validity.

However, I believe the mantra is harmful, as I feel it unnecessarily burdens women of color with an unattainable and unsustainable standard of perfection. This causes us to overwork ourselves to the point of burnout and exhaustion. It suppresses us, as we feel like we are not allowed to speak freely, to challenge people, or to make mistakes. And when we ultimately do fail at something, we cloak ourselves in shame and judge ourselves harshly.

While we need to put in the work to be successful, it should never be at the sacrifice of our well-being or to satisfy how others believe we should navigate our lives. We may not have full power or agency to address this issue on our own, but it is within our control to work smarter toward our goals, not harder.

- **Don't multitask.** Numerous studies have proven time and again that when you try to do two or more tasks at the same time, the output quality will be poor and may ultimately lead to you needing to redo both tasks eventually. Concentrate on one task at work or school at a time so that you can do it well and move on to the next.

- **Prioritize what matters to you right now.** You can't do it all at once. Nor should you. If finishing up a degree or certificate is your priority, then you can decide that all activities and tasks related to that effort will take priority over other activities that are nonessential.

- **Strive for improvement, not perfection.** Not only can the pursuit for perfection take a negative emotional toll on you, but it can rob you of appreciating the learning process. By making perfection the focus of your learning experiences versus taking the time to learn from trial and error, you may hinder your overall skill development.

- **Make the most of unexpected free time.** If you find yourself suddenly given the gift of free time—maybe a class or meeting was cancelled—why not use that to finish another assignment or use it toward study time toward skill building?

- **Rest.** It may sound counterproductive, but the more uninterrupted, quality rest you get or the more breaks you take, the better your focus will be, translating to better work output and productivity.

Failure

A failed exam. A rejection letter for a job you really wanted. A project you were working so long and hard on ended up imploding. These and many more are examples of the other "F-word"—failure.

Failure sucks; there's no getting around it. I have failed many, *many* times throughout the course of my life, personally and professionally. Some of these failures were minor and had no lasting effect; others were incredibly big, and their effects were felt for a long time. Some made me angry, others reduced me to tears, but all of them hurt my pride and were hard to admit to myself, let alone to other people. Even in my current job, there are some projects that I led or was on where I absolutely killed it, and others ended up being a straight-up mess.

To me, it's one of the most uncomfortable feelings on Earth. As much as I hate the feeling, I don't avoid situations where my chances of success are low or unknown. My successes make me feel good, but my failures have been far more valuable in terms of lessons learned and becoming more confident in my abilities. It also helped me to become humbler, more empathetic, and more compassionate toward others, as I've now had an opportunity to walk in their shoes.

When we only seek out situations where we know our likelihood of success is high or guaranteed, we are short-changing ourselves. We're missing out on opportunities that will help us to learn and grow and to understand others. Perhaps you will lose some time, you will lose some money, or your pride will take a hit. But most failures that we encounter are recoverable and not the end of the world.

That's not to say that I do activities that I know will fail in the end or repeat failed activities without thinking about how to do things differently—as my husband likes to say, "Doing something the same way and expecting a different result is the very definition of insanity."

To learn from failure so that it can be minimized or avoided in the future, try to do the following when it happens:

- **Feel your feelings about the failure and work through them.** It is okay and natural to be upset when things go wrong. Pretending that it didn't happen, bottling up your feelings, or trying to rush through your pain will only make the work of learning from your mistakes harder. There's nothing wrong with taking a moment and stepping back; just don't stay in that moment for too long.

- **Examine what went wrong.** As best as you can, review the situation and where the failure(s) happened. This can be difficult to do, especially if the failure was one where you were deeply emotionally invested. If you are having trouble seeing things clearly on your own, you may want to seek a trusted friend or adviser to help talk you through it.

- **Ask why.** Get at the heart of why the failure occurred. A technique used by many analysts and consultants is the "five whys." With this technique, you ask the question "Why?" five times to uncover the true cause, or multiple causes, of why a problem happened.

Let's work through something that happened to me personally, where I failed a major exam for a database design course that I was taking.

Issue: I failed a recent database management exam.

Why?

I did not study the material that was covered on the exam.

Why?

I did not know that the material covered would be on the exam. I assumed that other material would be covered.

Why?

I missed class.

Why?

I was sick that day.

Why?

I had a really bad cold!

Although I had been sick, I didn't understand what would be on the exam because I wasn't in class when that information had been discussed. From here, you can now think about how to respond.

- **Accept your role in the failure.** If you discover that your actions, or lack of action, was part of the reason the failure happened, accept and own it. Avoid blaming or taking your frustrations out on others.

  In the previous example, although I was sick, I didn't reach out to my professor or my classmates. If I had made that contact, would it have made a difference in passing the exam? Maybe, maybe not. But because I didn't take that opportunity, I'll never know.

  Accepting your role does not mean beating yourself up about it! We're all human, and things happen. It means accepting responsibility without blame or judgment on yourself and toward others.

- **Identify areas for improvement.** Now that you know what went wrong, think about ways you'll handle the situation differently if it comes up again or how you'll avoid the situation in the future.

  Looking at the previous example, I could've asked my professor about what was going to be covered on the exam, or if I had explained the situation (that I had been sick), the professor might have granted me an extension so that I could take the exam when I was feeling well. Alternatively, I could've reached out to a classmate and asked for the class notes.

- **Seek help and guidance.** If you feel that you are struggling with a problem, reach out to peers, mentors, family, or others who can help. They may be able to offer a different perspective on how to approach a problem or suggest resources that you may not have been aware were available.

I emphasize that academic or professional failures do not, in turn, make you a "failure." There's a tendency in our society to equate our career and academic achievements as a complete measure of our self-worth and value in the world. Subsequently, when we face failures and setbacks, we use these unfortunate events to reinforce in our heads that we're failures. Over time, this mindset negatively impacts how we approach our work and interact with others. Your mistakes and failures do not define you. Ideally, they make you better in the long run.

Impostor Syndrome

Impostor syndrome happens when, despite your (proven) skills and success, deep inside you have this overwhelming feeling of self-doubt about your abilities. The self-doubt is so severe that you secretly believe you are an "impostor," or someone who goes out of their way to deceive others for their personal benefit. Your anxiety goes through the roof because you constantly think that you don't belong or someone will find out "the truth"—that you are a fraud.

There's a big difference between being nervous about beginning a new role or being recognized for great work versus having impostor syndrome. While you can suffer from bouts of insecurity and anxiety, these feelings pass, and there is still a fundamental belief that you can accomplish the task before you. With impostor syndrome, the insecurity and anxiety are persistent, almost deafening, and you attribute your success to pure luck, a mistake, or something other than your own efforts and hard work. High-achieving women of color, suffer from impostor syndrome at least once in their careers.

In Valerie Young's book, *The Secret Thoughts of Successful Women* (Currency, 2011), she highlighted five types of impostor syndrome:

- **The perfectionist:** This person places incredibly high expectations on herself. When she doesn't succeed at something, she assumes complete blame and develops negative thinking about her abilities. When things go right, it's because of luck or someone else's efforts.

- **The superwoman:** When this person feels that she doesn't quite measure up to the skill sets of her peers, this person works herself extremely hard to be at her perceived skill level. She has difficulty knowing how to relax and let go.

- **The natural genius:** If she doesn't get something right the first time or is struggling to grasp material in her first few tries, this person thinks that there is something wrong with her. She tends to avoid situations where she may fail and, in her eyes, look like a fool.

- **The soloist:** Asking for help is a serious no-no for this person. She wants to be perceived as being self-sufficient and struggles to ask anyone for help, even if she clearly needs it.

- **The expert:** People who suffer from this hate to be referred to as an expert on a subject because they don't feel they have enough knowledge to be labeled as one. They worry that if presented a question that they don't know the answer to, they'll be labeled as a fraud.

I have had, and still struggle with, impostor syndrome. A lot. I've had just about every variation of impostor syndrome listed here! I sometimes joke that the application tracking system software had made a mistake in letting my job application go through for my current job. While I'm joking, I realize the joke masks a deep fear that my colleagues would get to know me and realize that I had nothing to offer—which I know in my heart is not true. Just during the writing of this book, I can't tell you the number of times I thought, "Good Lord, why are they asking *me*, of all people, to write this book?"

Here are my key tips for addressing impostor syndrome when it rears its ugly head:

- **Examine your feelings.** Spend some time thinking about and understanding what may be driving these feelings. Is it that you don't know a certain skill as well as you think you should, or do you feel that you need external validation (e.g., constant praise from peers/managers and/or accolades)? By examining your emotions and fears, you can understand where the feelings are stemming from and the best means of addressing them.

- **Ask for help.** Asking for help is a sign of strength, not weakness. It really is okay not to know how to do something or how something works. Pretending like you do ends up getting you in more trouble than it's worth. By acknowledging this and seeking help, you can get better.

- **Talk it out.** Talk with someone you trust—a friend, mentor, teacher, etc.—and explain what you are feeling. Talk honestly about why you feel that you are not good enough for a specific role or honor. They can help you to examine if there is any merit to your feelings.

- **Avoid comparisons and set realistic expectations for yourself.** When I first started my current job, I felt enormous *personal* pressure to perform at the same level as my more senior colleagues. This was not realistic—my colleagues have been doing their jobs and have been in the industry for several years, whereas I was just really beginning mine. They had many experiences over the years to refine their skill. It's not to say that I don't aspire to be as great as they are at their jobs, but I also recognize the need to hold myself to realistic expectations of what I can learn and accomplish in a given time frame.

- **Acknowledge your power and accomplishments.** You have worked incredibly long and hard to get where you are—you deserve recognition and success. Don't minimize that by attributing your success to others alone or chalking it up to luck.

To quote author Marianne Williamson:

"Our deepest fear is not that we are inadequate. Our deepest fear is that we are powerful beyond measure. It is our light, not our darkness, that most frightens us. We ask ourselves: Who am I to be brilliant, gorgeous, talented, fabulous? Actually, who are you not to be?"

Bias

You have likely faced instances of bias already in your life. To recap from Chapter 1, "The Current State of Women of Color in Tech", bias is when a person or group expresses prejudice against another person or group. Bias can be either explicit, where a person is very clear and direct about their feelings and attitudes, or implicit, where a person's actions are unconsciously influenced by prejudiced behaviors and beliefs.

Bias is an incredibly hard and tricky issue to both pinpoint and address. On one side, when you are on the receiving end of a biased comment or behavior, it makes you feel small, weak, and angry. If the behavior is obvious enough—for instance, someone uses a racial slur—this clearly crosses a line, and the offender is usually dealt with quickly (although, sadly, I know this is not always true in every workplace or academic environment).

But bias can also be subtle. Take *microaggressions,* or "everyday verbal, nonverbal, and environmental slights, snubs, or insults, whether intentional or unintentional, which communicate hostile, derogatory, or negative messages to target persons based solely upon their marginalized group membership."[1]

Dr. Derald Sing Sue, a professor of counseling psychology at Columbia University, defined microaggressions as taking one of three forms:

- **Microassaults:** Someone will say an offensive comment but attempt to deflect harm by saying "I was just kidding" or "I was just joking."

- **Microinsults:** A person will make a comment or engage in behavior that they believe is complimentary or helpful but not fully understand that their actions can be looked at as discriminatory from the perspective of the other person. An example of this would be where a person says to a person of color that they are "very articulate," not realizing that comment might convey that you thought they wouldn't be because they are inferior.

- **Microinvalidations:** This is where a person will seek to minimize or deny the hardship a marginalized group may face. An example would be someone telling a woman of color that they are being "too sensitive" when calling out discriminatory behavior.

When people make biased comments, they can stop you cold, with several conflicting emotions roiling through your head and your heart.

How do I respond? Should I call them out for what they just said? Is the comment being made from complete ignorance (they honestly didn't know better), or is this a sign that they harbor truly racist or sexist tendencies? What are the consequences if I do respond? What if I don't? Could I be overreacting, or are my feelings valid?

There are no hard answers or guidance for these questions.

---

[1] *Microaggressions in Everyday Life: Race, Gender, and Sexual Orientation,* 2010

Although it can be a difficult or tense conversation, I recommend directly addressing biased comments or actions as they happen. Whether the comment was made from ignorance or malice, it's often the best way to stop the behavior from happening again.

- **Ask them.** If you are unsure of the intent of their message, ask the offenders, "Can you tell me what you meant when you said [comment]?" Give them the opportunity to walk through what they were attempting to convey. In some cases, they have chosen a truly poor choice of words to get their message across.

- **Tell them.** Explain to the offender that their comment offended you and why it bothered you. Having them understand why the comment hurt you or made you angry can make them realize how careless they are being. They may welcome the feedback so that they don't offend others in the future. You may also need to be prepared for the offender to react negatively or dismiss what you are saying—in this case, having a discussion with your manager or someone in a position of authority may be needed.

- **Avoid labeling.** Hold back on from calling someone a "racist" or "sexist" or other similar labels when talking to the offender. Even if the labels fully apply, these words have very heavy implications; offenders may decide to dig in their heels further rather than be open to having a dialog on adjusting their behavior.

At a previous job, a manager, frustrated with the operations staff's negative view of how the office was being run, angrily said during an all-staff meeting that the employees should just liken their plight to those in *Roots*.

After the meeting, I spoke with my manager and explained that while I in some ways understood his frustration (he took it personally that people didn't think it was the best place to work), I was offended by the comment because he compared trivial office politics to a horrible time in our history. Making light of slavery is in no way acceptable to me.

In addition, being the only Black person in the office, seeing my colleagues immediately swivel in their chairs toward my direction to see my reaction after the comment had made me more aware of my "otherness." The manager understood why I found this upsetting and apologized the following day for what happened.

Having that conversation was not easy, and it took some time for me to feel comfortable working there, but it was a conversation that needed to be had.

Tokenism and Being "The Only"

While there are schools and companies that are legitimately doing their best to make their environments more diverse and inclusive, there are some organizations that, unfortunately, hire or recruit women of color only to serve as a false symbol of diversity or to "check off a box." This is *tokenism*.

Being "the only" or "the few" (meaning the only person or the few people of your race or gender in a given environment) is different than being the "token." While you may be the only or few in a given setting, your teammates are actively engaging with you. You are holding leadership positions with real authority and resources to do your job. You are consulted on issues surrounding making an environment more diverse and inclusive. You are a fully functioning and respected member of your team.

With tokenism, almost none of these things is true. You are brought in to give the appearance of having a diverse population but not an inclusive one. You are not likely to be in a position of authority, and if you are, your power and resources may be limited or nonexistent. You are likely the start and stop of an organization's diversity efforts, meaning that the organization doesn't see the need to diversify any further—they've got you, so there you go!

While being the only woman of color can at times be lonesome, being tokenized feels worse. It can be demoralizing to realize that an organization is using as you as a prop rather than valuing everything you bring to the table. Over time, you begin to doubt your own abilities and skills and may grow suspicious of every opportunity you're being considered for—"Are they considering me because they believe I'm one of the best candidates, or are they considering me only for the fact that I'm a woman of color?"

Addressing tokenism, much like addressing bias, unfortunately is not something that you alone can address. It is also not our responsibility to address this. It is up to organizations and their leaders to correct and address tokenism so that women of color are fully engaged.

That said, you can (and should!) push back or outright refuse to participate in activities or projects that you believe are simply vehicles to show off hollow diversity and inclusion efforts.

If you are the only woman of color in your group or organization, or one of the few, reach out and communicate with professional organizations or affinity groups within your organization (affinity groups are formed around a shared interest or common goal). This will help minimize the feelings of loneliness and give you an opportunity to speak with others who may share the same feelings.

Also, take the time to find the things you and your colleagues do have in common. You'll be surprised by how many interests you and your colleagues share by taking the time to get to know one another.

Bullying

Bullying is abusive behavior that seeks to harm and intimidate others. Bullying can be physical, but it can also take the form of verbal abuse and threats, sabotaging others' work, or subjecting someone to public humiliation.

Bullying doesn't happen only in school and between students; it can happen between students and teachers, as well as in the workplace. According the Workplace Bullying Institute's June 2017 workplace bullying survey, of the 1,008 respondents, 19 percent reported being direct targets of workplace bullying. Out of those, 65 percent were women, and 21 percent and 25 percent of the respondents were Black and Hispanic, respectively.

Actions that are more obvious of a bully include yelling at you, using offensive language when talking to you, finding opportunities to humiliate you publicly, messing up your work, or physically assaulting you. Yet, there are other, quieter and more subtle signs that someone may be bullying you too:

- Leaving you out of important work or group communications often

- Avoiding or ignoring you on purpose

- Dismissing your concerns surrounding work or school issues

- Finding ways to diminish or downplay your work and contributions

- Taking credit for your work

- Changing your job role and responsibilities without notice or discussing it with you

- Consistently grading your assignments and exercises low without adequate information or explanation

Here's how to deal with the bullying where you are:

- **Document every time you were bullied.** Write down and keep a record of all incidents of bullying that you have encountered with someone. Include the day and time that the incident happened, what occurred, and if there were any other witnesses around who can speak to what happened.

- **When they go low, go high.** To paraphrase Michelle Obama, don't match a bully's bad actions with your own bad actions. Engaging in bad behavior of your own may only lead to you being disciplined.

  Keep your cool while calmly confronting their behavior and letting them know that you have limits to what you will take from them. This can be hard, but it is necessary to stop a bully in their tracks.

- **Speak up.** You do not have to suffer in silence. Reach out to those in authority to help you, be it a manager, a Human Resources representative, or a school dean. It's their job to protect you and to foster spaces where you feel safe and welcome. Most schools and workplaces have handbooks that cover how acts of bullying are addressed.

Lack of Support and Help

One of the hardest things to deal with when doing something new is when you feel, or know, that you don't have support from the people who are closest to you. Going in uncharted territory can be difficult, but to do it alone can make things feel even more difficult.

Teneika Askew's mom was less than thrilled when she made the decision early in her life to pursue a career in tech versus one in nursing. "She just kept thinking I was being bad or defiant because I keep getting on the computer after she told me not to. She took the computer cord away. I'd find another one at a local recycle bin site and use that and she'd ask, 'how do you keep getting these computer cords?'"

Hereford Johnson, the only person in his family to have a master's degree, also recalled feeling like he didn't have support through his journey. "When you are the only person in your family pursuing something, whether by ignorance, or they know you're doing it but don't support it, sometimes you don't get the support you need from your 'built-in infrastructure.'"

Unhelpful people mean well and want you to succeed but can't, or don't, provide help other than surface-level encouragement or platitudes (phrases that are meant to inspire you but may come off as empty and meaningless). They'll say things like, "You're smart, you'll figure it out," but have no actionable advice to give you, or at least provide direction if they can't help you. They may give advice that is completely off-base or unrealistic, or they'll share a personal story that they believe is helpful or inspiring, only to realize that they wanted to take that opportunity to talk about themselves.

People who fall under this category I believe mean well, and general encouragement statements are important to hear—they have their place and time. But I'm very weary of the people who only offer clichés and overused phrases when someone comes to them for help.

I classify unsupportive people as those who are aware of your goals and what you want to accomplish, but who show their disapproval of your goals through their words and actions. They may express disappointment in your choices or tell you that you will fail in your endeavors. In some cases, with parents or guardians, they may try to withhold financial support for school if they don't like the academic program or school that their child attends.

There are many reasons why people are not helpful or supportive, but I believe that much of it stems from them not understanding what you're doing and why you are doing it. Also, some people have strong opinions on what career path you should take, and ultimately the life you ought to live, and become very upset when you choose another path.

After volunteering at a daylong STEM career conference for high school students in the Chicago suburbs, one of the volunteers I was working with was complaining about her son. He was 20 and had decided to take time off from school to work full-time and figure out his next move. He had been studying chemical engineering but did not enjoy it and left the program. The mother was upset, as she believed that having an engineering degree was the best possible, and only, way to ensure a secure future for himself, especially being a Black man in America.

The woman herself was an engineer, her husband was an engineer, and her other two sons were also engineers. To her, all of them make a good living and seem to be happy—why would he not want that for himself? The career fields her son was leaning toward, communications and marketing, were not something she saw as worthwhile. She was contemplating giving him a six-month timetable to move out of their home if he decided to take that path. She just felt like she couldn't support a path that was not engineering, as she didn't see his desired career paths as a good way to support himself.

I listened as she talked. I felt a lot sympathy for her because I could clearly tell that she loves her son to care so much and wants what she believes is best for him. But I felt much more sympathy for her son. If the conversation was any indication, the son probably didn't have his mother's support as he was going through what can be a challenging time in a young person's life—trying to create and navigate one's own path in the world, amid a sea of uncertainty. Holding on to this unchangeable idea in her mind of what her son's life should be may be the very thing that pushes him out of her life.

Here is how to cope with lack of support and help from those closest to you:

- **Set realistic expectations of others.** Many of the people in your life may be weathering challenges of their own or their own ways of thinking about the world. We really don't know what everyone is going through. They may be happy for you, but they may not have the time or resources to be as supportive or helpful as you'd like them to be.

- **Understand the support you need and ask for it.** Make it clear to those around you where and how you need help as you embark on a new career path. Do you need their moral support? Do you need their financial support? Do you need their help with caregiving or other housekeeping responsibilities? What do you need? Try not to assume that people will automatically know—tell them.

- **Seek to understand them and help them understand you.** Many times, unhelpful or unsupportive people are acting out of lack of knowledge. Helping them to understand the path you are taking, and why you are taking it, can go a long way.

If they respond with a mixed or negative opinion about what you're doing, ask them why they feel that way. You may uncover that their negativity is rooted in sincere worry for you—worrying about your chances of success, being able to support yourself, or just seeing you in stress or pain. Sometimes negativity isn't rooted out of pure jealously or mean-spiritedness; sometimes it's just because they don't want to see you hurt. Assure them that you have thought through all the challenges and, even so, going down this path is what you believe is best for you.

- **Limit your time with them.** Of course, there are some people in your circle that can be spiteful and envious; where the negativity is just because they are . . . unpleasant. It's an unfortunate reality of life. Being around those who don't have your best interests at heart or can't be happy for you not only drains your time, it drains on your energy and spirit too. Keep the time that you spend with and around them to a minimum so that you are not drained by their negativity.

- **Rely on your network.** Your network of trusted friends, mentors, advisers, and the like can help in the areas where support may be lacking.

The Importance of Mental Health

> **"Caring for myself is not self-indulgent, it is self- preservation, that is an act of political warfare."**
>
> *"A Burst of Light and Other Essays," Audre Lorde*

Given what women of color are tasked to do and deal with on a regular basis, it's not surprising that they experience more feelings of psychological distress—depression, anxiety, hopelessness, and worthlessness—than their white counterparts.

Although having access to mental health resources is a challenge, regardless of race or gender, Black women also grapple with attempting to live up to the "strong Black woman" complex, and the negative stigma of seeking a therapist or mental health within their community.

At any given time, Black women are taking on the roles of caregiver, employee, and student, sometimes all at once, while internalizing stressors, traumas, and fears to give off the appearance of self-reliance. We don't outwardly express the pain that we are feeling or our vulnerability because we don't want to be perceived as weak or incapable by anyone.

We put our needs last for the good of others and downplay the pain we may be experiencing. The Office of Minority Health (part of the US Department of Health and Human Services) claims that African Americans are 20 percent more likely to have or experience mental health problems than the rest of the population but are the least likely to seek help.

I have struggled with major clinical depression and generalized anxiety for many years now. I've had the good fortune of being able to seek professional therapy, especially during the more difficult moments of my life. Some days are more challenging than others, but I have been able to live a great and fulfilling life. I know that having depression and anxiety are nothing to be ashamed of, and I know that seeking therapy was the best and most important thing I could do for myself.

Still, I'm reluctant to share that with many people because there is still a stigma attached to it. When I have shared that information, some reactions were incredibly supportive, but some have either minimized my feelings to a passing case of "the blues" or expressed disapproval of attending therapy. One person very close to me suggested that I was "choosing" to be depressed and unhappy and that all I had to do was "choose" to be happy. If it were that easy, believe me, I'd be making that choice every day.

The tech industry, sadly, also has a bad track record when it comes to mental health. The messaging app Blind reported that 57 percent of its 11,000 tech sector respondents felt "stressed" and "burned out." This statistic isn't even factoring in the intersectional dimensions of gender and race.

Your mental health is an important part of your overall health. If you feel like you are struggling and need help, please don't suffer in silence. Talk to a loved one you can trust or reach out to a trained mental health professional. You may be able to access free or discounted mental health resources through your school or insurance.

If you don't have access to insurance or have a limited budget, the mental health providers OpenPath Psychotherapy Collective (openpathcollective .org) see patients on a reduced scale of $30–$60 per session.

Here are some other resources:

Dear Black Women (DBW) Project: DBW (dearblackwomenproject .com) is an online community containing information on mental health and mind/body wellness resources, as well as an app offering daily positive affirmations.

Open Sourcing Mental Illness (OSMI): OSMI (osmihelp.org) is a nonprofit organization dedicated to improving mental wellness in the tech community. It publishes a guide for employees, employers, and others on how to promote wellness in their organizations, and it hosts public online forums where tech workers can discuss their issues with professionals.

Online Therapy Platforms: If you'd strongly prefer talking to someone through chat instead, and potentially at a more affordable price point, there are many online platforms like TalkSpace (`talkspace.com`), 7 Cups (`7cups.com`), and Ginger.io (`ginger.io`) available for quick mental health access.

Allies and When They Fall Short

Allies are people who belong to a dominant socioeconomic group and seek to make work and other environments more open, inclusive, and welcoming for underrepresented or marginalized groups.

Being an ally is not a "one-and-done" event, nor is it a passive effort. Good allyship requires assertive, consistent, and meaningful efforts to enact change. Allies use their privilege(s), status, and resources to challenge how things are currently being done in their respective organizations. They listen to marginalized groups without dismissing them, and while they can't completely grasp or understand everything that an underrepresented/marginalized person or group may be going through, they do their best to advocate on their behalf and without the expectation of recognition.

The Need for Allyship

One of the important things that I have learned is that even if you have a solid and compelling case to take a certain action, your intended audience may not listen to your message. The failure of a message to reach its intended audience isn't always because the audience doesn't like us or they don't agree with what we're saying. Rather, they are likelier to listen to someone else because of their shared background, experiences, etc. Sometimes the messenger matters more than the message itself.

For example, when a parent or loved one gives us advice that we'd be wise to take but don't, it isn't because we don't love them or value them. It could be that they are delivering the advice in a tone or using a method that we don't like, or at a time that isn't convenient for us. Yet, when a good friend that you admire gives you the same advice, you listen and act on it.

It's no different in organizations, which is why having allies is important. When it feels like your message isn't connecting with people or not compelling people to act, allies can amplify your message and increase the chances that your message will be heard.

Allies may also have access to more people and professional spaces than a woman of color may have. While it is unfair that there are still academic and professional spaces we have yet to inhabit, an ally who already has a seat at the table can advocate on our behalf.

Finally, we will not be able to address the complex and systemic issues that keep women of color out of professional spaces and positions of authority. Solutions to problems this systemic cannot be made in isolation and require hard work and conversations by everyone.

Allies Are Human

The wonderful, and frustrating, thing about allies is that they are human, like us. They have great capacity for good and empathy and are doing what they can to make environments more inclusive and welcoming for everyone.

But like all humans, they mess up. Sometimes a lot. They may say or do things that run counter to the message they are trying to convey—this can confuse, anger, or hurt us. It make us wonder, "Is this person really on my side?" or do they have a hidden agenda?

How do you cope when your ally or allies disappoint you?

- **Ask them, and then tell them.** Much like encountering bias, clarify what your ally intended to do or say. It really could be one of those situations where they intended to say one thing, but something else came out. If they caused offense, say so and explain the reason why it hurt or offended you. Allies genuinely want to know when their words and actions fall short so that they don't repeat the mistake.

- **Know and accept that they will mess up.** I'm not suggesting giving free license for someone to say ignorant and hurtful things all the time. But I do accept that my allies may not have experienced life through my unique lens as a woman of color. It would be almost impossible, and unrealistic, for me to expect them to fully grasp why a comment or action they took may be offensive. To me, it's almost a certainty that this ally will eventually say something disappointing.

  For example, during a discussion with a white female ally, she expressed happiness, but some dismay, about women in technology groups centered around race (i.e., Black women in technology, Latinx women in technology, etc.) At the time, she commented that we're all women facing the same issues and that it's better for us to stand united together rather than focus on our differences.

I humbly, and strongly, disagreed with her. While yes, we face common struggles, we experience these issues more sharply, particularly around career advancement and pay. I also stressed that the reason women of color should have these groups is to be able to talk freely about what we are feeling and experiencing, without feeling like we need to defend our feelings, and to not feel as if we're being minimized. Her suggestion of banding together, which I know was well intentioned, came off as trying to minimize what we were uniquely facing.

It was a difficult conversation, but it is one that I'm glad that we had, as she has a better understanding of my perspective and I hers. But ultimately, she felt that it helped her to become a better ally as she better understood our perspective.

- **Forgive.** If the ally, up until this point, has demonstrated themselves to be genuine and sincere in their efforts, I'd say to give them the benefit of the doubt that this infraction was a rare misstep, especially if they show genuine remorse for what's happened. If it becomes indicative of a troubling pattern, it may be time to reevaluate the relationship.

Summary

- Grit, or having courage and resolve to see something through despite life's challenges, can be a key determinant in being successful.
- Striving for perfection and trying to be "twice as good" can be harmful to you and undermine your success. Avoid these unattainable standards at all costs.
- Failure may not be pleasant, but it is an unavoidable and necessary part of growth.
- Bias and microaggressions should be called out as soon as they occur to prevent them from happening again.
- There's a difference in being the "only" and being the "token." Push back on any work or assignments that are not true showcases of your skills and talents.

- Bullying can happen at school and at work and can be perpetrated by those in a position of authority (teachers, professors, managers, etc.). Confronting bullies directly is the best way to cut a bully down to size.

- Unhelpful and unsupportive people can distract you from pursuing your goals. While you can seek to educate them on why what you're doing matters, limit your overall time with them should they continue to be a drain.

- Getting adequate mental health is important to your self-care routine. Talk to a loved one or trained professional if you are experiencing distress (anxiety, stress, burnout, etc.).

- Seek allies to amplify and carry your message and change the status quo whenever possible.

The Importance and Joy of Giving Back

As you progress through your career, consider devoting time to community service. Your act of kindness, no matter the size, will yield more benefits to you and others than you can imagine.

Why Give Back

Devoting yourself to volunteerism and community service can be one of the most rewarding experiences that you can have. The benefits are plentiful, and honestly, I can think of almost no downsides when doing so.

You Make a Difference

While many nonprofit and charitable organizations exist to bring more women of color into tech, they are often doing so with very minimal resources. Many are dependent on grants and donations, meaning that they must be very careful about how they spend funds. Even if these organizations have hired some staff members, the employees may be working part-time and doing the jobs of two or three people. Simply put, these organizations need extra hands and minds to help fulfill their mission (see Figure 10.1).

Figure 10.1: Leading students through a resume workshop

Helping Others See and Know What's Possible

One of the things I enjoyed about living in Chicago was its lively and growing tech sector. There was no shortage of free or low-cost tech conferences to attend. The limitation was mostly just having the time to attend.

Women in tech-specific conferences were plentiful there too, which was awesome. I enjoyed going because it was great to meet other amazing women, learn from them, and build my network.

After time, however, something began to wear on me. While there were plenty of women, I began to notice there were not many women of color attending. More concerning was that conferences made for younger women (high school and college aged) also seemed to have a low number or lack of women of color. Adding insult to injury, few women of color—specifically Black women—were participating as speakers.

I remember thinking, *this can't be right*. In a city that's so big and diverse, I could not believe—or accept—that women of color were not interested in pursuing tech jobs.

I don't want to single out any one city or tech conference. I think it is a far more pervasive problem across the United States and with industry conferences. The distance and costs involved to attend tech conferences can be burdensome, and without sponsorship or financial assistance, attending them can be difficult for anyone. I recently went to a major open-source tech conference that boasted more than 12,000 people in attendance in California. The number of women who attended was roughly around 11 percent, so roughly 1,320 women. The number of women of color was . . . well, low. To say that I stood out among the crowd would be an understatement.

It wasn't until I started working in tech myself that I realized there was more that was contributing to our continued absence in these spaces: the lack of role models for girls of color to identify with—women who look like them, who have some understanding of what they are going through, and who are serving as leaders within the tech community. If girls of color are not seeing or learning about successful women of color in these roles, particularly those in technical leadership, why would they think that certain career paths are meant for them?

It may be difficult for a young woman of color to picture herself as a software developer, a designer, or a product manager if she isn't exposed to people doing those jobs and with whom she can personally identify. In two recent Indiana University studies, girls of color who had accessible role models that were closely aligned with their own identities felt a better sense of belonging in school and, specifically, that a STEM career was right for them. I think about my own academic career and wonder whether I would have ended up in tech earlier in life if I had developed relationships with accessible role models.

For this reason, I try my best to devote volunteer time to organizations that serve young women and people of color, like Black Girls Code. By sharing about my work and how I got to be here, I believe it gives future tech leaders more option in terms of what their potential career could look like. Helping them to understand that while it does require hard work and perseverance to grow your career, a path in tech is attainable, rewarding, and fun.

Great Rewards

During one of the workshop events where I was volunteering, I met a young man named Arshan. Arshan was working the security desk in the building where the volunteering event was being held. We randomly struck up a conversation, where I discovered that he was going to both school and work, and he was looking to get into tech but wasn't sure how. I gave him my business card and told him I'd be more than happy to help him, as I remember all too well what it was like to be in his position. From there, we set up an informal mentoring relationship; we met as our schedules permitted and built a great relationship.

Fast-forward, I was having a somewhat difficult patch in late spring of 2019—I was adjusting to my newish role at work and writing this book, and for some reason, I decided to schedule not one but two of my very first public speaking events (one was the mentoring speech in Portland I mentioned in Chapter 7, "Demonstrating Your Skills," and the other was a live webinar on cloud computing for Systers, an online community that is part of AnitaB.org for those working in technical computing fields). I was doing a lot of studying and practicing on top of dealing with the trials of everyday life. It was a lot, and I could feel the weight of all these (good) things on my shoulders.

The week prior to the speaking engagements, Arshan shot me an update text telling me what had been going on in his world, and then asked how things were going for me as I was preparing for Portland. Figure 10.2 shows part of our exchange.

Figure 10.2: Words of encouragement from my mentee

I cannot tell you how touched I was by Arshan's words. It meant the world to me to have that surprise encouragement from someone I was trying to help succeed. I won't lie, I teared up, and that exchange helped get me through the challenges of the week with renewed positivity. It was the reminder that I needed of why I do this, and I look at this exchange all the time.

At the end of the mentoring speech, a young woman of color in the audience, Alina, asked me if I would be willing to serve as a mentor. Again, I was touched, and it was all I could do to hold back my emotions. Seeing both Arshan and Alina succeed in their respective paths, and that they reached out to me to help them, has meant more to me than you know.

Having the willingness to put yourself out there and offer to help can yield so many positive feelings and boost your confidence.

Building Relationships

Much like networking, volunteering puts you in contact with other great people within your industry and community. This can help broaden your network and give you access to amazing mentors, industry contacts, and others who are in similar career trajectories to yours. And don't forget the potential of making great friends!

Also, if you're like me in that you struggle with what to say or do in situations where you need to interact with strangers, volunteering can take off some of the pressure of getting to know people. Unlike a networking event where you're randomly brought together with others, a volunteering event brings together people who have similar interests and mind-sets and is centered around a group activity for everyone to focus on. This is preferred over nervously sipping your drink and peering off into space trying to figure out what to say!

Coping with a Bad Day

If you're having a tremendously, hideously bad day, taking part in a volunteer activity may not be a good idea. Rather, you may need to call it a day and get a good night's rest to start tomorrow renewed, refreshed, and with your head straight. The last thing you want to do is bring a bad energy and attitude into an activity that can rub off on others.

Barring bad situations, though, volunteering can help improve your mood, find some perspective on the challenges you are facing, and who knows, even have a bit of fun.

This past fall, I signed up to be a resume reviewer for an evening event for the Women in Technology and Entrepreneurship in New York (WiTNY). It was a very long workday, and to add insult to injury, it was raining heavily outside. I was already running 30 minutes late, and because I got the address mixed up, I ended up having to walk outside for a considerable amount of time to get to the event location.

When I got to the event, my pants and sneakers were completely soaked. My umbrella was virtually no help in keeping me dry. I was grumpy, and honestly, I would have loved to have gone home, gotten into some dry, comfy clothes, and watched something on Netflix until I fell asleep.

But I knew that the young women there also had long days, if not longer, than mine—most of the students were commuter students enrolled in a City University of New York school and were balancing the demands of schoolwork, family, and jobs. They probably had "craptastic" days themselves. If they could make the time, then I could too.

After taking several paper towels to my pants and shoes and getting settled, I helped a few of the young women in the room with their unique resume challenges. It didn't help my pants get any drier, but even in the soggy clothes, I felt much happier. I enjoyed talking with them and learning about their goals and dreams. By the end of the event, I completely forgot about all the unpleasantness I had to deal with before getting there.

There may also be some scientific evidence that volunteer work keeps you healthy too. In a 2013 study by Carnegie Mellon University, researchers found a positive correlation between study participants who had performed 200 or more hours of volunteering per year and lower blood pressure; lower blood pressure decreases the likelihood of having a stroke, heart attack, and other negative cardiovascular events.

You've Been in Their Shoes

You may be at, or near, a place where you have amassed a wonderful network, a great career, and other resources, which is amazing! Remember that right now, there is someone who is starting their own journey, and may be having the same feelings, concerns, and doubts that you had at that point. They need your help.

Being an expert or having amassed a wealth of experiences is not necessary to help. You already possess enough knowledge and skills that can prove to be invaluable to those beginning academic or professional tracks similar to yours. All you need is empathy and a genuine desire to help others. You have more to offer to others than you may realize.

It is never lost on me how fortunate and privileged I am to be where I am now. I remember the struggles and how hard it was just to get here, and I know that I was afforded opportunities that my peers were not. If I can spare other young women even the slightest bit of strife along their path, or make things easier to help them achieve their dreams, I'm not only happy to, but I believe it is my duty to do so.

How to Give Back

The great thing about giving back is that you can totally decide how and when to share your gifts with the rest of the world. Your contribution doesn't need to cost a lot of money, or any money, or require you to make any grand gestures; it can just be simple, deliberate actions you can take through the course of your day. There is no right or wrong way to give back; you just need a sincere willingness to do so without any expectations or anything in return.

One way that Angela Dogan gives back is by going into public schools and colleges and talking about the different careers that exist in cybersecurity. "I speak at public schools to bring awareness of cybersecurity to women and minorities. It's something I hold very near and dear to my heart. . . . There [are] still difficulties in trying to get into the field and challenges [women of color] are facing, so just helping people along the way is very important."

In addition to her day-to-day duties, Teneika Askew also started her own nonprofit, Ribbons of Beauty, dedicated to helping young women prepare for careers and college. "I mentored and gave back my own money and time as well—260 hours a year helping young women get into college." Teneika helps them understand what colleges and employers are looking for: "How do you get into college? "Why does your ACT/ SAT score matter? How you write your resume? How do you create an elevator pitch? What's your personal brand? How do you build a personal branding statement? How do you leverage that time during your college experience? I help students because I know what it's like."

I engage primarily in mentoring. I formally engage in mentoring programs at work, but I maintain several informal mentoring relationships as well. When meeting with my mentees, we talk a lot about career development—doing resume reviews and talking about potential career options or salary negotiations. Although my preferred method of contact is in person, I realize that schedules and distance may make that difficult, so we'll also talk over the phone or video conference. Much like Teneika, I empathize with them because I was in their place not too long ago. If I can help make the path a little easier for someone else, I'll gladly help in any way I can.

Perhaps the best ways to give back are to find interests that you are passionate about and find out how you can contribute. Sites like VolunteerMatch offer no shortage of opportunities that help different communities and allow you to utilize a variety of skills.

You're not limited only to opportunities that are presented on volunteer portals or those being advertised by your local nonprofits. If you recognize a need in your community that you don't think is being adequately fulfilled, you can take the initiative and make something happen.

For example, let's say you are in a school where there is a severe lack of computing resources (for example, there's no dedicated computer lab for students to use, or if there are, the computers are *really* old and barely functioning). Working with the school administration, you can help organize a fundraiser and/or apply for grants to help in those efforts. Or, perhaps you are working at a company where women or minority support groups currently do not exist. You can work with other colleagues to get a group up and running. Neither of these things requires explicit permission for you to get started—you can start the work toward these efforts right now! You're limited only by your time and your creativity.

I completely understand about the lack of time. Some days there's barely time to eat and get a good night's rest, let alone time to volunteer. But as I previously mentioned, volunteering doesn't need to be a grand gesture or require you devote large periods of time.

Giving back can take as little as 5 minutes and doesn't require you to leave your computer or take out your wallet. While making a direct money donation may be the easiest and quickest way if you have the resources to do that, it's not the only way. Here are some examples:

- Share information on jobs, free classes, and professional events with your network.

- Help a friend with their resume, with interviewing, or with another project they're working on.

- Donate old tablets, smartphones, and other electronics you no longer use to charity.

- Use sites like Amazon Smile (`smile.amazon.com`) and SurveyMonkey Contribute (`contribute.surveymonkey.com`). Amazon gives a portion of your order proceeds to an approved charity of your choice, while SurveyMonkey Contribute sends money to a charity of your choice in exchange for completing surveys.

Also remember that volunteerism and giving opportunities need not be tech-focused. For example, a problem facing a number of US-based schools is school lunch debt, where students and families struggle to pay for the food served during the course of the school day. An organization

I like to fundraise for is School Lunch Fairy, which raises money to set up emergency lunch funds at public schools so kids will be able to eat. School kids need proper nutrition (in addition to having a warm, safe home and adequate rest) to be successful. If they are hungry or wondering where their next meal is coming from, their studying and cognitive function will suffer.

Summary

- Giving back is a great way to bring more women of color into the tech industry; it also offers benefits for you personally and professionally.

- Giving back can take many different forms. When figuring out how to give back, think about your interests and how you want to make a difference in the lives of others.

- Although we're all crunched for time, there are many easy ways that you can help without expending a lot of time, energy, and money. Every little bit helps!

Index